D1373911

Critical Essays on
DANTE GABRIEL ROSSETTI

CRITICAL ESSAYS
ON
BRITISH LITERATURE

Zack Bowen, General Editor
University of Miami

Critical Essays on

DANTE GABRIEL ROSSETTI

edited by

DAVID G. RIEDE

G. K. Hall & Co. / New York
Maxwell Macmillan Canada / Toronto
Maxwell Macmillan International / New York Oxford Singapore Sydney

Allen County Public Library
900 Webster Street
PO Box 2270
Fort Wayne, IN 46801-2270

Copyright © 1992 by David G. Riede

All rights reserved. No part of this book may be reproduced or transmitted
in any form or by any means, electronic or mechanical, including
photocopying, recording, or by any information storage and retrieval
system, without permission in writing from the Publisher.

Twayne Publishers
Macmillan Publishing Company
866 Third Avenue
New York, New York 10022

Maxwell Macmillan Canada, Inc.
1200 Eglinton Avenue East
Suite 200
Don Mills, Ontario M3C 3N1

Macmillan Publishing Company is part of the Maxwell Communication
Group of Companies.

Library of Congress Cataloging-in-Publication Data

Critical essays on Dante Gabriel Rossetti / edited by David G. Riede.
    p.   cm.—(Critical essays on British literature)
    Includes bibliographical references and index.
    ISBN 0-8161-8863-7 (alk. paper) :
    1. Rossetti, Dante Gabriel, 1828–1882.—Criticism and
interpretation.   I. Series.
PR5247.C7   1992
821'.8—dc20   92–228
                                                        CIP

The paper used in this publication meets the minimum requirements of
American National Standard for Information Sciences—Permanence of
Paper for Printed Library Materials. ANSI Z3948-1984.∞™

10 9 8 7 6 5 4 3 2 1

Printed in the United States of America

Contents

♦

General Editor's Note

◆

The Critical Essays on British Literature series provides a variety of approaches to both classical and contemporary writers of Britain and Ireland. The formats of the volumes in the series vary with the thematic designs of individual editors, and with the amount and nature of existing reviews and criticism, augmented, where appropriate, by original essays by recognized authorities. It is hoped that each volume will be unique in developing a new overall perspective on its particular subject.

David Riede surveys a century-long cycle of criticism beginning with the enthusiasm of Rossetti's friends and contemporaries through the denigration of critics whose moral sensibilities were equally offended by Rossetti's personal life and his explicitly erotic poetry. In Riede's view, for nearly 100 years Rossetti criticism, infused with biographical interpretation, became as much a discussion of moral standards as an appreciation of the poet's art. Riede's introduction and selection of essays then turns toward the revitalization of Rossetti criticism in the 1960s and thereafter, concluding with a variety of contemporary critical commentary including a feminist approach.

ZACK BOWEN
University of Miami

Publisher's Note

◆

Producing a volume that contains both newly commissioned and reprinted material presents the publisher with the challenge of balancing the desire to achieve stylistic consistency with the need to preserve the integrity of works first published elsewhere. In the Critical Essays series, essays commissioned especially for a particular volume are edited to be consistent with G. K. Hall's house style; reprinted essays appear in the style in which they were first published, with only typographical errors corrected. Consequently, shifts in style from one essay to another are the result of our efforts to be faithful to each text as it was originally published.

Introduction

DAVID G. RIEDE

Dante Gabriel Rossetti is generally remembered today as the colorful leader of the Pre-Raphaelite movement in painting and as a significant though somewhat minor poet of the Victorian period, but current estimates of his achievement do not even approach the extraordinary admiration bestowed upon him by many of his most illustrious contemporaries. He was extravagantly praised, for example, by such figures as William Morris, Algernon Swinburne, Edward Burne-Jones, and George Meredith. John Ruskin, at least in certain moods, regarded him as the greatest genius of the age, and Walter Pater, equally emphatic, reportedly remarked that "of the six men then living who were destined to be famous—Tennyson, Browning, Ruskin, Matthew Arnold, Swinburne, and Rossetti—Rossetti was 'the most significant as well as the most fascinating.' "[1] As the reputed leader of the Pre-Raphaelite Brotherhood from 1848 into the early 1850s, and as the acknowledged center of an artistic coterie including Morris, Swinburne, Meredith, Burne-Jones, and numerous lesser figures, Rossetti seemed the leader of the arts in general. At the very least, he seemed to his contemporaries to be the leading spirit behind two of the most important movements in modern culture—both lumped together under the term "Pre-Raphaelite." And the importance of these movements can hardly be overestimated: in both the pictorial arts and literature Rossetti himself and the circles of artists revolving around him contributed mightily to changing the cultural climate of Victorian England and clearing the way for the aesthetic movement in the closing decades of the century. To many of the writers of the next generation, said Arthur Symons, he provided "a kind of leadership in art."[2] William Butler Yeats said of the young poets of the 1890s that "we were all Pre-Raphaelites then," and described Rossetti's influence on his generation as "subconscious" but "perhaps the most powerful of all."[3] According to John Masefield, his "poems and paintings, his intelligence in all matters of art, the beauty and

1

fire of his faith, made him by much the most kindling influence among the young men of my time."[4]

But subsequent generations have not been so kind, and the critical tradition has tended to discount earlier praises of Rossetti's achievement as hyperbolic reactions to his magnetic personality. After all, more often than not his contemporaries praised him as an extraordinary leader, not as a great poet or painter. As the blind poet Philip Bourke Marston put it, "What a supreme man is Rossetti! Why is he not some great exiled king, that we might give our lives in trying to restore him to his kingdom?"[5] Even the usually caustic James McNeill Whistler is said to have rebuked a gossiping bystander from his deathbed with the words, "You must not say anything against Rossetti. Rossetti was a king!"[6] Later critics, regarding Rossetti's reputation and influence as far in excess of his actual achievement, have suggested that he imposed on others through sheer force of personality, that his works do not merit the acclaim they once received, and even that his undoubtedly great influence in the arts was pernicious insofar as it led to a sterile aestheticism and literary decadence. Writing in 1911, Ford Madox Hueffer (later known as Ford Madox Ford) went so far as to say that "the art of writing in English received the numbing blow of a sandbag when Rossetti wrote at the age of eighteen *The Blessed Damozel*. From that time forward and until to-day . . . the idea has been inherent in the mind of the English writer that writing was a matter of digging for obsolete words with which to express ideas forever dead and gone."[7]

By this reading, indeed, Rossetti becomes, in Evelyn Waugh's phrase, little more than "a melancholy old fraud"[8] leading younger artists astray. Of course Hueffer and Waugh were writing for effect, and in reaction not only against Rossetti, but against what they saw as the posturings of lesser figures, the aesthetes and decadents of the late nineteenth century. Nevertheless, their comments help to indicate the contours of Rossetti's posthumous reputation—among the writers of the late nineteenth century he held an extremely high place, but his influence and apparent importance seemed to have worn themselves out in the decadence of the 1890s, and he subsequently came to seem important primarily as a historical figure, as a dominating personality rather than as a major painter and poet. Only in the past quarter of a century has something like a consensus been reached on a reasonably balanced assessment of his achievement and influence.

Though the belief that Rossetti was in some way a greater personality than an artist has contributed to injustice in appraisals of his poetry and painting and to an excessive biographical slant in approaches to his work, it was a view first promoted by his friends. A comment by Theodore Watts-Dunton was characteristic of this tendency: "wonderful as was Rossetti as an artist and poet, he was still more wonderful, I think, as a man."[9] The unusual force of Rossetti's personality and the rather melodramatic circumstances of his life made him a particularly inviting subject for biographical speculation.

His Italian heritage, his part in the Pre-Raphaelite Brotherhood, his love affairs, the mysterious death of his wife in 1861, his emotional decision to bury his poems in her coffin, his later decision to exhume her coffin to reclaim his poems, his strangely bohemian life with a variety of friends and a menagerie of animals at Cheyne Walk, his drug addiction, his nervous breakdown in 1872, and his seclusion from then until his death in 1882— all seemed to beg for commentary. Indeed, the combination of his leadership in the arts and his mysterious seclusion made him something of a legend in his own lifetime. And in the years immediately following his death it seemed as though nearly everyone who knew him rushed into print with memoirs and testimonials. But just as inevitably, the rather melodramatic circumstances of Rossetti's life invited censorious, sensationalized, often lurid accounts.

The biographical tradition, which began with Hall Caine's sympathetic but somewhat sensational account of Rossetti's reclusive and paranoid last years, has continued well into this century, and has consisted of attacks on Rossetti's moral character, defenses, and counterattacks. Much of the biographical tradition has consisted of outright novelization, presenting Rossetti sometimes under a transparent nom de guerre (most notably as "Walter Hamlin" in Vernon Lee's *Miss Brown: A Novel* [1884] and "D'Arcy" in Watts-Dunton's *Aylwin: A Novel* [1898]) and sometimes under his own name, as in Nerina Shute's oxymoronically subtitled *Victorian Love Story: A Study of the Victorian Romantics Based on the Life of Dante Gabriel Rossetti: A Novel* (1954), John Hale's *The Love School* (1975), Elizabeth Savage's *Willowwood: A Novel* (1978), and others. The novelistic treatments of Rossetti would not merit attention here if they could be readily separated from the serious critical tradition, but unfortunately much fiction has passed itself off as sober scholarship, most notably in Violet Hunt's abusive treatment of Rossetti in *The Wife of Rossetti: Her Life and Death* (1932), and Frances Winwar's *Poor Splendid Wings: The Rossettis and Their Circle* (1933). The problem is not only that the biographical tradition in Rossetti studies has been plagued by sensationalism and inaccuracy, but also that it has too often taken the place of serious discussions of Rossetti's work. Even the best biography of Rossetti to date, Oswald Doughty's *A Victorian Romantic: Dante Gabriel Rossetti* (1957), treats Rossetti's poetry mainly as cryptic documentary evidence concerning his love affairs, particularly his love for Jane Morris. Perhaps more seriously, studies claiming to be primarily critical, such as David Sonstroem's *Rossetti and the Fair Lady* (1970), have too often read the poems primarily as manifestations of the poet's peculiar psyche. As William E. Fredeman has argued, Rossetti far more than most poets "has been victimized by critics who have relied mainly on biographical data to explicate the poetry and by biographers who have poached on the poetry for 'evidence' to document their biographical assumptions."[10]

No doubt considerable biographical emphasis in criticism of Rossetti was inevitable—association of the moral quality of the work with that of the poet was characteristic of Victorian critical practice. John Ruskin and Robert Browning, for example, typically read back from the moral qualities of the work of art to those of the artist's soul, and Rossetti himself advanced an aesthetic of personal expression, and seemed, in much of his work at least, to be transcribing his own passions. His early prose tale, "Hand and Soul," which has often been taken as a kind of artistic manifesto, was only one of many works to suggest that the artist's highest function was to paint or transcribe his own soul. In fact, the best and the most favorable early critical discussions of Rossetti's work took for granted that, as Walter Pater put it, the poetry was the "wholly natural expression of certain wonderful things he really felt and saw" and that his language was the wholly sincere expression of the poet's own "peculiar phase of soul which he alone knew, precisely as he knew it."[11] Even when avoiding intrusive biographical speculation, F.W.H. Myers speculated that biographical facts lay behind the poetry: "Without intruding into the private story of a life which has not yet been authoritatively recounted to us, we may recognise that on Rossetti the shock of severance, of bereavement, must have fallen with desolating force." Given the assumption that the ultimate "meaning" veiled by the poetry is to be found in "the private story" of the life, and given the curiosity provoked by gossip about Rossetti, the subsequent biographical and pseudobiographical traditions are hardly surprising.

Further, considering the breaches of Victorian moral decorum that characterized Rossetti's life and the explicitly erotic subject matter of much of his poetry, it is certainly not surprising that much of the early criticism was morally censorious. And if the early criticism often took a deeply personal tone, Rossetti himself was in large part to blame. The critical tradition, indeed, begins with Rossetti's fears of criticism: preparing to publish his first volume of original poetry in 1870, he made sure of a positive reception by packing the critical jury. He arranged for so many personal friends to praise his poems in influential journals that at least one of them could not even find an organ through which to puff him. Swinburne, Morris, and others lavished praise on the volume and on Rossetti himself, but Meredith, unable to find an outlet, wrote to Rossetti that Swinburne "threw flowers on you in the *Fortnightly*: not one was undeserved. After first finishing this book my voice would have been as unrestrained, less eloquent."[12] Swinburne's review was nothing if not florid—he saluted Rossetti as the leading poet of the age, a poet to be spoken of in the same breath with Aeschylus, with Dante, with Shakespeare, and he praised him as a magisterial post-Christian poet, and a masterful poet of "fleshly form and intellectual fire." But such excess of praise from within the coterie, and the nature of the praise in a still emphatically Christian society, inevitably provoked a reaction. It took the egregious, but nevertheless effective, form of Robert Buchanan's 1871 attack in the *Contemporary Review*, "The Fleshly School of Poetry: Mr. D. G. Rossetti." To modern readers, Buchanan's review, published pseudonymously under the name Thomas Maitland, seems simply silly in its censure of the "nasty" eroticism of Rossetti's poetry, in its claims that Rossetti and other "fleshly gentlemen have bound themselves by solemn league and covenant to extol fleshliness as the distinct and supreme end of poetic and pictorial art; to aver that poetic expression is greater than poetic thought, and by inference that the body is greater than the soul, and sound superior to sense; and that the poet, properly to develop his poetic faculty, must be an intellectual hermaphrodite, to whom the very facts of day and night are lost in a whirl of aesthetic terminology." Even Rossetti thought this laughable at first, and responded to it rationally and effectively with "The Stealthy School of Criticism." Nevertheless, though Buchanan's attack took an apparently absurd form, it had immense significance in the history of Rossetti criticism if only because when he reissued it in an enlarged and even more preposterous form in 1872, it led directly to Rossetti's nervous breakdown and increased the sense of paranoia that plagued him for the remainder of his life. Rossetti was, in a sense, right to take the criticism personally, since the critical discussion centered as much on his moral character, his manliness, and his sincerity, as on the poetry. For Buchanan, indeed, the man and the work were one and the same, since "Mr. Rossetti is never dramatic, never impersonal—always attitudinizing, posturing, and describing his own exquisite emotions."

Though Buchanan was effectively rebutted by Rossetti, Swinburne, and others, and though he eventually recanted, his essay did, to a very great extent, set the terms for subsequent discussion of Rossetti's poetry. At the center of critical debate were its moral value, its "manliness" (or lack of it), its "fleshliness," its sincerity, and its "aestheticism" (characterized as remoteness from "real" life and excessive artificiality). In fact, Buchanan had been speaking for a great many others who had regarded, and continued to regard, Rossetti's verse as effeminate, offensively erotic, and excessively artificial. Even Robert Browning, in a private letter, remarked that Rossetti's verse was "scented with poetry, as it were—like trifles of various sorts you take out of a cedar or sandalwood box: you know I hate the effeminacy of his school."[13] The suggestion that Rossetti's poetry was somehow effeminate, or at least effete, became a staple in critical discussions. A characteristic early review maintained that his "aesthetic" poetry appealed to "the perfumed taste of overeducated coteries,"[14] and even generally sympathetic critics could concede that the verse suffered from a "perfumed air."[15] The implication that the poetry was unmanly, even that it was un-British, could also be given a positive slant, as in the remark by F. S. Boas that "He lived and wrote in an atmosphere heavy with scent and sound and beauty, essentially un-English; but for that very reason his work is of special value, and he holds a unique position among English poets." But even Boas expressed a degree of ambivalence. Rossetti was, she thought, somewhat too unreserved and hypersensitive, but it must not "be forgotten that from only one grandparent—his mother's mother—could he have hoped to inherit that commodity so useful in times of intolerable strain—British pluck."[16]

As Boas's comment indicates, Rossetti's foreign heritage was often used to explain what was perceived to be his most important attribute as an artist: his originality. In one of the earliest critiques of his work, H. Buxton Forman affirmed that "the transfusion of Italian blood into a newly-opened vein of English verse is not the least among the notable accomplishments of this poet."[17] Lafcadio Hearn, similarly, declared that Rossetti was unique among the great English poets by virtue of his Italian "blood, religion, and feeling."[18] The emphasis on Rossetti's foreign "blood," on his "exotic" nature, was primarily a way to account for what Pater called "his characteristic, his really revealing work . . . the adding to poetry of fresh poetic material, of a new order of phenomena, in the creation of a new ideal." The new ideal was, at least in part, a Dantean spirituality introduced into poetry of modern love, a worship of female beauty. To Buchanan and others, of course, this was merely an insincere pretense for "unmanly," "nasty" eroticism, but for Rossetti's admirers it was the sincere, virile expression of a spiritual vision. As F.W.H. Myers argued, Rossetti was a kind of modern, though lesser, Dante, a "Dante still in the *selva oscura*; . . . He is not a prophet but an artist; yet an artist who, both by the very intensity of his artistic vision, and by some inborn bent towards symbol and mysticism, stands on the side of those who see in material things a spiritual significance, and utters words of universal meaning from the fulness of his own heart." Not a prophet but an artist, Rossetti could still, as Myers argued, be among the founders of the great modern movement, the "aesthetic movement," and its establishment of a "Religion of Art," a "Worship of Beauty."

For Myers, as for other admirers of Rossetti's work and influence, his great achievement was a kind of aesthetic spiritualism that contributed to "the reaction of Art against Materialism, which becomes more marked as the dominant tone of science grows more soulless and severe." Rossetti seemed the very embodiment of the aesthetic withdrawal from philistine society, the leading spirit in establishing the autonomy, the social and moral independence, of art and the artistic spirit. His foreignness was, finally, less a matter of his Italian blood than of his remoteness, for good or ill, from the workaday Victorian world and way of life. Hearn's most important point about Rossetti, finally, was that though Rossetti "was one of our very greatest English poets, he takes a place apart, for he does not reflect the century at all" (Hearn, 37). The most widespread view in the late nineteenth century was that expressed by Edward Dowden: "Not a little of the special attention of his work lies in its remoteness from all contemporary influences which make up a great part of the environment of each of us. We enter the dreamer's magic shallop with its prow of carven moonstone and are wafted to the strand of an enchanted island; all around us is exact and definite as if we saw it with a painter's eye, yet all is steeped in magic and mystery."[19] Rossetti's art created a world apart, as Arthur Rickett argued, "a world of wonder and delight, full of sweet sights and sounds, and out of earshot of the roar and clamour of every-day life."[20]

While Rossetti's poetry was said to have created a world apart, an autonomous, dreamlike world of beauty, his alienation from Victorian society, a kind of voluntary exile from the life of his times, made him seem a martyr in the cult of art. At times this was expressed in terms of his foreign blood, as in Ruskin's comment that he was "really not an Englishman, but a great Italian tormented in the Inferno of London."[21] More often, however, it was simply his devotion to beauty that was said to have doomed him: "He has stimulated the sense of beauty, the desire to extract the very essence of delight from emotion, and form, and colour; he has inculcated devotion to art, and profound intention, and deliberate isolation; but the upshot is that he stands alone, in a fever of sense and spirit, a figure clasping its hands in a poignancy of agitation, and rather overshadowed by the doom of art than crowned with its laurels" (Benson, 202). But once again, the emphasis falls less on Rossetti's achievement than on what Arthur Symons called "the tragical and wonderful life of that man of supreme genius."[22] And indeed much of Rossetti's influence on the aesthetes of the coming generation re-sulted from the perception of what seemed his exemplary, if painful, devotion to an ideal of beauty, his exemplary role as a new type of the artist. Lionel Stevenson has made the point that Rossetti "was the first English poet who entirely fulfilled the public image of the *poète maudit*—manic-depressive in temperament, alienated from the mores of his time, sensually self-indulgent, and disintegrating under the influences of sex, alcohol, and drugs."[23]

Rossetti himself would deplore such representations of his life, and was in fact always anxious to dissociate himself from the coming generation of aesthetic young men. As his self-defense in "The Stealthy School of Criticism" makes clear, he certainly did not regard himself as an "aesthetic poet"—he utterly rejected the claim that he believed beauty of form more important than thematic and moral purpose. Nevertheless, even though some admiring critics could justifiably assert that "the vapid emotionalism of the Aesthetic School received no encouragement from their master, Rossetti" (Rickett, 116), he was inescapably associated with a poetry of aesthetic escape, and his critical reputation has risen and fallen with current estimates of "aesthetic poetry" in general. Rossetti was, after all, associated even by Swinburne with the doctrine of "art for art's sake,"[24] and nearly all readers have agreed that he "differed from the other great Victorians not merely in his foreign origin but in his uncompromising doctrine of what poetry ought to be. For them the poet had duties to society and must not only delight but instruct and improve; but as William Michael Rossetti said, 'in all poetic literature anything of a didactic, hortatory, or expressly ethical quality was alien from my brother's liking.' "[25] But many of those who have praised Rossetti's devotion to a cult of beauty and his creation of a world apart, have also expressed reservations about it. Myers, for example, tried to demonstrate that the "aesthetic side" represented by Rossetti need not be at odds with the "ethical side" represented by his censorious critics, but he was manifestly uneasy with the idea that a "Religion of Art" might supplant a more rigorous ethical system, and he acknowledged that such poetry as Rossetti's could not reach the lofty moral heights attained by poets like Wordsworth. Dowden, similarly, claimed that Rossetti's creation of a magical world apart was not an achievement of the same order as Wordsworth's magical transformation of the actual world, and Rickett admitted that in "broad human interest" Rossetti's "work no doubt suffers from comparison with the work of poets like Tennyson and Browning" (Rickett, 138–39).

Not surprisingly, when in the twentieth century the study of English literature became increasingly institutionalized as, among other things, a kind of ethical training, Rossetti's work fell increasingly into disrepute and neglect. Despite the occasional critical encomia offered by Paull Franklin Baum and a few others, Rossetti's poetry was generally either ignored or abused from the 1920s through the 1950s, most often on the grounds that it is divorced from the actualities of human experience, that it is too self-consciously aesthetic, too literary. In a still influential study, Graham Hough wrote that though great poetry may "create a world of its own," Rossetti's poetry merely takes us "into some literary suburb": "His dream world is built up out of easily recognisable properties, most of which have been used before, and its hushed stillness is due not so much to a real remoteness from this vale of tears as to an extremely efficient sound-proofing system."[26]

Hough had some positive things to say about Rossetti as well, but other, more generally influential critics, had nothing but contempt. F. R. Leavis, in comments fairly representative of the New Critical disdain for Victorian poetry in general, disparaged "Rossetti's shamelessly cheap evocation of a romantic and bogus Platonism—an evocation in which 'significance' is vagueness and profundity an uninhibited proffer of large drafts on a merely nominal account . . .—exemplifies in a gross form the consequences of that separation of feeling . . . from thinking which the Victorian tradition, in its 'poetical' use of language, carries with it." For Leavis, Rossetti's poetry is characterized by "a complete nullity of thought—nullity made aggressively vulgar by a wordy pretentiousness."[27] For Douglas Bush, similarly, Rossetti's poetry was too ostentatiously literary: "while we feel the power of great lines, in the end we are stifled and thirst for reality."[28] As Stevenson has noted, much twentieth-century criticism seems merely to recapitulate the moral indignation of Buchanan.[29] John Heath-Stubbs, for example, has argued that the poetry is "cheaply sentimental and muddled to the point of absurdity"—after all, "an undisciplined, rootless man like Rossetti was incapable of attaining the crystalline clarity and perfect balance of his models."[30]

With a few notable exceptions, such as the work of Baum, George Ford, and C. M. Bowra,[31] critical discussions of Rossetti throughout the first six decades of this century have added few valuable insights into his work. But thanks to a general revaluation of the Victorian poets, to new anthologies of Pre-Raphaelite poetry edited by Cecil Y. Lang and Jerome H. Buckley,[32] and to critical revaluations by W. E. Fredeman, Jerome McGann, and others, a renewal of interest and appreciation of Rossetti's work has occurred since the midsixties. For that reason the essays collected in this volume consist entirely of very early responses and then, skipping over more than half a century of neglect, of work done in the past 25 years. These essays by no means exhaust the often excellent critical work done on Rossetti in recent years, but I have attempted to represent something of the diversity of approaches and evaluations.

The traditional objections to Rossetti's work have still not entirely lost their force, and many of them are recapitulated in a particularly cogent form in Harold L. Weatherby's "Problems of Form and Content in the Poetry of Dante Gabriel Rossetti." According to Weatherby (as according to many others from Buchanan through Leavis), the problem with Rossetti's poetry is a disparity between overwrought form and a lack of significant "content" or meaning. Weatherby, to be sure, does not write in the hostile mode of Rossetti's earlier critics, but rather finds the poetry an especially interesting manifestation of what he sees as the general "difficulty that beset the Victorian art for art's sake movement—the failure of content, the failure of meaning, the failure of traditional symbols to function properly when they were cut loose from the belief in spiritual realities." His criticism may be seen as a more sophisticated version of Buchanan's attack on Rossetti's sincerity: "Rossetti, one feels, tried to make poetic use of the supernatural without ever believing in it." The result of this "lack of faith in the reality of his material," for Weatherby as for Buchanan, is a poetry that is both "exceedingly ornate" and "unhealthily sensuous."

The essay immediately following Weatherby's offers a strong rebuttal to the traditional objections. Jerome J. McGann's seminal essay, "Rossetti's Significant Details," a direct response to the critiques of Weatherby and others, makes the case that Rossetti was well aware of the emptiness of his spiritual symbolism, that his poetry is in important ways precisely about that emptiness. Rossetti, consequently, insists upon the primacy of the physical world, and his poetry insists upon the integrity of the image rather than seeing it as the manifestation or symbol of some hidden spiritual meaning. McGann's readings of the often abused "My Sister's Sleep" and of "The Woodspurge" convincingly demonstrate that Rossetti's "form" and "content" are far more integrally and subtly unified than previous critics had recognized. Though in a highly positive sense, by McGann's account Rossetti remains very much on what Myers called the "aesthetic side" rather than the "ethical side": "A sensibility more committed to moral absolutes than to artistic ones will likely not think much of Rossetti's poetry. Rossetti will seem an aesthete because he places a higher value on images than on concepts."

Other recent critics, however, have continued to stress Rossetti's aspiration for higher meanings than the material world readily affords. Stephen J. Spector's "Love, Unity, and Desire in the Poetry of Dante Gabriel Rossetti" shows more thoroughly than previous studies how Rossetti's poetry explores fundamental epistemological problems bequeathed by the earlier romantic poets. As Spector convincingly shows, Rossetti's poetry reflects the dangerous proximity of creative subjectivity to the self-isolation of solipsism. Unlike McGann, Spector argues that Rossetti sought some source of transcendent meaning, and that the imagery and themes of his love poetry, especially, express not merely physical desire, but rather a metaphysical desire—"the lover's desire for unity with his beloved is best understood as a manifestation of man's overarching desire to be united with something outside of himself, especially God." John P. McGowan presents a view directly at odds with McGann's, arguing that Rossetti did, in fact, believe that the created world "contains within it certain universal meanings" and that it is "the artist's task to uncover those meanings." In some ways McGowan repeats the traditional charge that Rossetti's poetry fails to express the reality it seeks, but rather than simply blaming Rossetti for "insincere" use of traditional symbolism, he sees the interest and poignancy of the poetry in its honest and anguished search for ultimate meanings. My own essay, "Aestheticism to Experience: Revisions for *Poems* (1870)," attempts to explore shifts in Rossetti's uses of traditional Christian symbolism by examining his careful secularization of his symbolism in the extensive revisions of his early poetry before its publication in 1870.

The three remaining essays in this volume represent something of a new wave in Rossetti criticism, a movement consistent with the general shift in critical approaches to literature over the past several years toward more ideologically detached commentary. Robin Sheets's "Pornography and Art: The Case of 'Jenny' " is one of several excellent discussions of that poem to appear in recent years, and is also among the first feminist essays on Rossetti's poetry. Since Rossetti's poetry and painting were obsessively concerned with female beauty and the supposed "mysteries" of womanhood, the feminist critiques now beginning to appear will continue to increase our understanding of Rossetti and his age. With Jerome J. McGann's "Dante Gabriel Rossetti and the Betrayal of Truth" I have taken the somewhat unusual step of including a second essay by a single critic both because of its intrinsic interest and because, like his earlier work, it promises to be a stimulating influence on subsequent studies. McGann's "new historicist" reading of Rossetti's works provides a new perspective by stepping outside of the romantic ideology in which both Rossetti and his critics operated. For McGann, in fact, Rossetti's work is of tremendous interest precisely because in its aspirations and disillusionments it so clearly exposes the central illusion of romanticism, the belief that art and imagination are "transcendental forms standing free of the sublunary orders of human things." As McGann shows, the crucial and insuperable problem of Rossetti's career was the conflict between his faith in the transcendent power of art and the actualities of the material conditions of art in his age. Antony H. Harrison's "Dante Rossetti: Parody and Ideology" argues that Rossetti's early poetry is characterized by a deliberate, programmatic intertextuality. In what Harrison defines as a mode of parody, "The Blessed Damozel," "The Burden of Nineveh," and "The Portrait" are shown to invoke the works of earlier poets both to appropriate their authority and to subvert their ideological positions. Harrison makes the new historicist point that the result is a specifically literary or "aesthetic" emphasis in Rossetti's work, and that the displacement of social or political implications by aesthetic strategies contributes to a new ideology of aestheticism. Taken all together, the essays in this volume, I hope, will both reflect the traditional assessments of Rossetti's career, and indicate the directions that criticism of Rossetti is likely to take in the coming years.

Notes

1. Thomas Wright, *The Life of Walter Pater*, 2 vols. (New York: Putnam, 1907), 2:23.
2. Arthur Symons, *Figures of Several Centuries* (London: Constable, 1916), 201.
3. William Butler Yeats, *The Autobiography of William Butler Yeats* (New York: Macmillan, 1938), 147, 257.
4. John Masefield, *Thanks before Going: Notes on Some of the Original Poems of Dante Gabriel Rossetti* (New York: Macmillan, 1947), 5.
5. Quoted in Arthur C. Benson, *Rossetti* (London: Macmillan, 1926), 207–8. Hereafter cited as Benson.
6. The anecdote is offered on the dubious authority of the ever-unreliable Ford Madox Hueffer, who claimed to have heard it from "one of the watchers at Whistler's bedside." It should be regarded as a part of the legend, not as gospel. See Ford Madox Hueffer, *Ancient Lights and Certain New Reflections* (London: Chapman and Hall, 1911), 30.
7. Ford Madox Hueffer, *Memories and Impressions: A Study in Atmospheres* (New York: Harper and Brothers, 1911), 59.
8. Evelyn Waugh, *Rossetti: His Life and Works* (London: Duckworth, 1928), 223.
9. Theodore Watts-Dunton, *Old Familiar Faces* (New York: E. P. Dutton and Company, 1916), 75.
10. William E. Fredeman, "Impediments and Motives: Biography as Unfair Sport," *Modern Philology* 70 (1972): 149.
11. The quotations from Pater, along with all the other uncited quotations in this introduction, appear in the articles reprinted in this volume.
12. George Meredith, *The Letters of George Meredith*, 3 vols., ed. C. L. Cline (Oxford: Clarendon, 1970), 1:418.
13. Robert Browning, *Dearest Isa: Robert Browning's Letters to Isabella Blagden*, ed. Edward C. McAleer (Austin: University of Texas Press, 1951), 336.

14. J. C. Shairp, "Aesthetic Poetry: Dante Gabriel Rossetti," *Contemporary Review* 42 (1882): 32.

15. Stopford A. Brooke, "Dante Gabriel Rossetti," in *Four Poets: Clough, Arnold, Rossetti, Morris* (London: Duckworth, 1913), 202.

16. Mrs. Frederick S. Boas, *Rossetti and His Poetry* (London: G. G. Harrap, 1918), 148, 131.

17. H. Buxton Forman, *Our Living Poets: An Essay in Criticism* (London: Tinsley Brothers, 1871), 227.

18. Lafcadio Hearn, "Studies in Rossetti," in *Appreciations of Poetry* (London: William Heinemann, 1919), 37. The essay is reconstituted from notes taken at lectures given by Hearn, apparently in 1899. Hereafter cited as Hearn.

19. Edward Dowden, *Transcripts and Studies*, 2d. ed. (London: Kegan Paul, Trench, Trübner and Co., 1896), 227.

20. Arthur Rickett, *Personal Forces in Modern Literature* (London: J. M. Dent, 1906), 138. Hereafter cited as Rickett.

21. John Ruskin, *Praeiterita*, in *The Works of John Ruskin*, 39 vols., ed. E. T. Cook and Alexander Wedderburn (London: George Allen, 1908), 35: 486.

22. Arthur Symons, *Dramatis Personae* (Indianapolis: Bobbs-Merrill, 1923), 118.

23. Lionel Stevenson, *The Pre-Raphaelite Poets* (New York: W. W. Norton, 1974), 77.

24. Algernon Charles Swinburne, *The Swinburne Letters*, 6 vols., ed. Cecil Y. Lang (New Haven: Yale University Press, 1959–62), 1:195–96.

25. Quoted in C. M. Bowra, *The Romantic Imagination* (Cambridge: Harvard University Press, 1949), 200.

26. Graham Hough, *The Last Romantics* (1947; rpt., London: Methuen, 1961), 70.

27. F. R. Leavis, *The Common Pursuit* (London: Chatto and Windus, 1952), 47.

28. Douglas Bush, *Mythology and the Romantic Tradition in English Poetry* (1937; reissued with a new preface, Cambridge: Harvard University Press, 1969), 410.

29. See Stevenson, 57–58.

30. John Heath-Stubbs, *The Darkling Plain: A Study of the Later Fortunes of Romanticism in English Poetry from George Darley to W. B. Yeats* (London: Eyre and Spottiswoode, 1950), 57.

31. For Baum, see particularly the introduction to his edition of *The House of Life: A Sonnet-Sequence* (Cambridge: Harvard University Press, 1928). For Ford, see "Rossetti," in *Keats and the Victorians* (New Haven: Yale University Press, 1944), 91–145. For Bowra, see *"The House of Life"* in *The Romantic Imagination* (Cambridge: Harvard University Press, 1949), 197–220.

32. Cecil Y. Lang, ed., *The Pre-Raphaelites and Their Circle* (Boston: Houghton Mifflin, 1968); Jerome H. Buckley, ed., *The Pre-Raphaelites* (New York: Modern Library, 1968).

EARLY RESPONSES

◆

The Poetry of Dante Gabriel Rossetti

Algernon Charles Swinburne

In every generation that takes any heed of the art, the phrase of "greatest living poet," or (with a difference of reservation) "first of his age and country," is flung about freely and foolishly enough: but if more than mere caprice— be it caprice of culture or caprice of ignorance—is to go to the making up of the definition, we must decide what qualities are of first necessity for the best poet, and proceed to try how far the claimant can be surely said to possess them. Variety is a rare and high quality, but poets of the first order have had little or none of it; witness Keats and Coleridge; men otherwise greater than these have had much, and yet have fallen far short of the final place among poets held by these; witness Byron and Scott. But in all great poets there must be an ardent harmony, a heat of spiritual life, guiding without constraining the bodily grace of motion, which shall give charm and power to their least work; sweetness that cannot be weak and force that will not be rough. There must be an instinct and a resolution of excellence which will allow no shortcoming or malformation of thought or word: there must also be so natural a sense of right as to make any such deformity or defect impossible, and leave upon the work done no trace of any effort to avoid or to achieve. It must be serious, simple, perfect; and it must be thus by evident and native impulse. The mark of painstaking as surely lowers the level of style as any sign of negligence; in the best work there must be no trace of a laborious or a languid hand.

In all these points the style of Mr. Rossetti excels that of any English poet of our day. It has the fullest fervour and fluency of impulse, and the impulse is always towards harmony and perfection. It has the inimitable note of instinct, and the instinct is always high and right. It carries weight enough to overbear the style of a weaker man, but no weight of thought can break it, no subtlety of emotion attenuate, no ardour of passion deface. It can breathe unvexed in the finest air and pass unsinged through the keenest fire; it has all the grace of perfect force and all the force of perfect grace. It is sinuous as water or as light; flexible and penetrative, delicate and rapid; it works on its way without halt or jar or collapse. And in plain strength and weight of sense and sound these faultless verses exceed those of faultier

Excerpted and reprinted from *Fortnightly Review* n.s. 7 (1870): 551–79.

workmen who cover their effects by their defects; who attain at times and by fits to some memorable impression of thought upon speech, and speech upon memory, at the cost generally of inharmonious and insufficient work. No such coarse or cheap stuff is here used as a ground to set off the rich surprises of casual ornament and intermittent embroidery. The woof of each poem is perfect, and the flowers that flash out from it seem not so much interwoven with the thread of it or set in the soil, as grown and sprung by mere nature from the ground, under the inevitable rains and sunbeams of the atmosphere which bred them.

It is said sometimes that a man may have a strong and perfect style who has nothing to convey worth conveyance under cover of it. This is indeed a favourite saying of men who have no words in which to convey the thoughts which they have not; of men born dumb, who express by grunts and chokes the inexpressible eloquence which is not in them, and would fain seem to labour in miscarriage of ideas which they have never conceived. But it remains for them to prove as well as assert that beauty and power of expression can accord with emptiness or sterility of matter, or that impotence of articulation must imply depth and wealth of thought. This flattering unction the very foolishest of malignants will hardly in this case be able to lay upon the corrosive sore which he calls his soul: the ulcer of ill-will must rot unrelieved by the rancid ointment of such fiction. Hardly could a fool here or a knave there fail to see or hope to deny the fullness of living thought and subtle strength of nature underlying this veil of radiant and harmonious words.

It is on the other side that attack might be looked for from the more ingenious enemies of good work: and of these there was never any lack. Much of Mr. Rossetti's work is so intense in aim, so delicate and deep in significance, so exuberant in offshoot and undergrowth of sentiment and thought, that even the sweet lucidity and steady current of his style may not suffice to save it from the charges of darkness and difficulty. He is too great a master of speech to incur the blame of hard or tortuous expression; and his thought is too sound and pure to be otherwise dark than as a deep well-spring at noon may be, even where the sun is strongest and the water brightest. In its furthest depth there is nothing of weed or of mud; whatever of haze may seem to quiver there is a weft of the sun's spinning, a web not of woven darkness but of molten light. But such work as this can be neither unwoven nor recast by any process of analysis. The infinite depth and wealth of life which breathes and plays among these songs and sonnets cannot be parcelled and portioned out for praise or comment. This "House of Life" has in it so many mansions, so many halls of state and bowers of music, chapels for worship and chambers for festival, that no guest can declare on a first entrance the secret of its scheme. Spirit and sense together, eyesight and hearing and thought, are absorbed in splendour of sounds and glory of colours distinguishable only by delight. But the scheme is solid and harmonious; there is no waste in this luxury of genius: the whole is lovelier than its loveliest part. Again and again may one turn the leaves in search of some one poem or some two which may be chosen for sample and thanksgiving; but there is no choice to be made. Sonnet is poured upon sonnet, and song hands on the torch to song; and each in turn (as another poet has said of the lark's note falling from the height of dawn) "Rings like a golden jewel down a golden stair." There are no poems of the class in English—I doubt if there be any even in Dante's Italian—so rich at once and pure. Their golden affluence of images and jewel-coloured words never once disguises the firm outline, the justice and chastity of form. No nakedness could be more harmonious, more consummate in its fleshly sculpture, than the imperial array and ornament of this august poetry. Mailed in gold as of the morning and girdled with gems of strange water, the beautiful body as of a carven goddess gleams through them tangible and taintless, without spot or default. There is not a jewel here but it fits, not a beauty but it subserves an end. There seems no story in this sequence of sonnets, yet they hold in them all the action and passion of a spiritual history with tragic stages and elegiac pauses and lyric motions of the living soul. Their earnest subtleties and exquisite ardours recall to mind the sonnets of Shakespeare; poems in their way unapproachable, and here in no wise imitated. Shakespeare's have at times a far more passionate and instant force, a sharper note of delight or agony or mystery, fear or desire or remorse—a keener truth and more pungent simpleness of sudden phrase, with touches of sound and flashes of light beyond all reach; Mr. Rossetti's have a nobler fullness of form, a more stately and shapely beauty of build: they are of a purer and less turbid water than the others are at times, and not less fervent when more serene than they; the subject-matter of them is sweet throughout, natural always and clear, how-ever intense and fine in remote and delicate intricacy of spiritual stuff. There is nothing here which may not be felt by any student who can grasp the subtle sense of it in full, as a just thing and admirable, fit for the fellowship of men's feelings; if men, indeed, have in them enough of noble fervour and loving delicacy, enough of truth and warmth in the blood and breath of their souls, enough of brain and heart for such fellow-feeling. For something of these they must have to bring with them who would follow the radiant track of this verse through brakes of flowers and solitudes of sunlight, past fountains hidden under green bloom of leaves, beneath roof-work of moving boughs where song and silence are one music. All passion and regret and strenuous hope and fiery contemplation, all beauty and glory of thought and vision, are built into this golden house where the life that reigns is love; the very face of sorrow is not cold or withered, but has the breath of heaven between its fresh live lips and the light of pure sweet blood in its cheeks; there is a glow of summer on the red leaves of its regrets and the starry frost-flakes of its tears. Resignation and fruition, forethought and afterthought, have one voice to sing with in many keys of spirit. A more bitter sweetness of sincerity was never pressed into verse than beats and burns here under the veil and girdle of glorious words; there are no poems anywhere of more passionate meditation or vision more intense than those on "Lost Days," "Vain Virtues," "The Sun's Shame"; none of more godlike grace and sovereign charm than those headed "Newborn Death," "A Superscription," "A Dark Day," "Known in Vain," "The One Hope"; and of all splendid and profound love-poetry, what is there more luminous or more deep in sense and spirit than the marvellous opening cycle of twenty-six sonnets, which embrace and express all sorrow and all joy of passion in union, of outer love and inner, triumphant or dejected or piteous or at peace? No one, till he has read these, knows all of majesty and melody, all of energy and emotion, all of supple and significant loveliness, all of tender cunning and exquisite strength, which our language can show at need in proof of its powers and uses. The birth of love, his eucharistic presence, his supreme vision, his utter union in flesh and spirit, the secret of the sanctuary of his heart, his louder music and his lower, his graver and his lighter seasons; all work of love and all play, all dreams and devices of his memory and his belief, all fuller and emptier hours from the first which longs for him to the last which loses, all change of lights from his mid-day to his moonrise, all his foreknowledge of evil things and good, all glad and sad hours of his night-watches, all the fear and ardour which feels and fights against the advent of his difference and dawn of his division, all agonies and consolations that embitter and allay the wounds of his mortal hour; the pains of breach and death, the songs and visions of the wilderness of his penance, the wood of desolation made beautiful and bitter by the same remembrance, haunted by shadows of the same hours for sorrow and for solace, and, beyond all, the light of the unaccomplished hour which missed its chance in one life to meet it in another, where the sundered spirits revive into reunion; all these things are here done into words and sung into hearing of men as they never were till now. With a most noble and tender power all forms and colours of the world without are touched and drawn into service of the spirit; and this with no ingenious abuse of imagery or misuse of figures, but with such gracious force of imagination that they seem to offer voluntary service. . . .

In all the glorious poem built up of all these poems there is no great quality more notable than the sweet and sovereign unity of perfect spirit and sense, of fleshly form and intellectual fire. This Muse is as the woman praised in the divine words of the poet himself, "Whose speech Truth knows not from her thought,/ Nor Love her body from her soul." And if not love, how then should judgment? for love and judgment must be one in those who would look into such high and lovely things. No scrutiny can distinguish nor sentence divorce the solid spiritual truth from the bodily beauty of the poem, the very and visible soul from the dazzling veil and vesture of fair limbs and features. There has been no work of the same pitch attempted since Dante sealed up his youth in the sacred leaves of the "Vita Nuova";

and this poem of his namechild and translator is a more various and mature work of kindred genius and spirit. . . .

A certain section of Mr. Rossetti's work as poet and as painter may be classed under the head of sacred art: and this section comprises much of his most exquisite and especial work. Its religious quality is singular and personal in kind; we cannot properly bracket it with any other workman's. The fire of feeling and imagination which feeds it is essentially Christian, and is therefore formally and spiritually Catholic. It has nothing of rebellious Protestant personality, nothing of the popular compromise of sentiment which, in the hybrid jargon of a school of hybrids, we may call liberalized Christianism. The influence which plainly has passed over the writer's mind, attracting it as by charm of sound or vision, by spell of colour or of dream, towards the Christian forms and images, is in the main an influence from the mythologic side of the creed. It is from the sandbanks of tradition and poetry that the sacred sirens have sung to this seafarer. This divides him at once from the passionate evangelists of positive belief and from the artists upon whom no such influence has fallen in any comparable degree. There are two living and leading writers of high and diverse genius whom any student of their work—utterly apart as their ways of work lie—may and must, without prejudice or presumption, assume to hold fast, with a force of personal passion, the radical tenet of Christian faith. It is as difficult for a reasonable reader to doubt the actual and positive adherence to Christian doctrine of the Protestant thinker as of the Catholic priest; to doubt that faith in Christ as God—a tough, hard, vital faith which can bear at need hard stress of weather and hard thought—dictated "A Death in the Desert" or "Christmas Eve and Easter Day," as to doubt that it dictated the "Apologia" or "Dream of Gerontius": though neither in the personal creed set forth by Mr. Browning, nor in the clerical creed delivered by Dr. Newman, do we find apparent or flagrant—however they may lurk, tacit and latent, in the last logical expression of either man's theories—the viler forms and more hideous outcomes of Christianity, its more brutal aspects and deadlier consequences; a happy default due rather to nobility of instinct than to ingenuity of evasion. Now the sacred art of Mr. Rossetti, for all its Christian colouring, has actually no more in common with the spirit of either than it has with the semi-Christianity of "In Memoriam" or the demi-semi-Christianity of "Dipsychus." It has no trace, on the other hand, of the fretful and fruitless prurience of soul which would fain grasp and embrace and enjoy a creed beyond its power of possession; no letch after Gods dead or unborn, such as vexes the weaker nerves of barren brains, and makes pathetic the vocal lips of sorrowing scepticism and "doubt that deserves to believe." As little can it be likened to another form of bastard belief, another cross-breed between faith and unfaith, which has been fostered in ages of doubt; a ghost raised rather by fear than love; by fear of a dead God as judge, than by love of a dead God as comforter. The hankering and restless habit of half fearful retrospect towards the unburied corpses of old creeds which, as we need not Shelley's evidence to know, infected the spiritual life and disturbed the intellectual force of Byron, is a mirage without attraction for this traveller; that spiritual calenture of Christianity is a sickness unknown to his soul; nor has he ever suffered from the distemper of minds fretted and worried by gnatstings and fleabites of belief and unbelief till the whole lifeblood of the intellect is enfeebled and inflamed. In a later poet, whose name as yet is far enough from inscription on the canonical roll of converts, there was some trace of a seeming recrudescence of faith not unlike yet not like Byron's. The intermittent Christian reaction apparently perceptible in Baudelaire was more than half of it mere repulsion from the philanthropic optimism of sciolists in whose eyes the whole aim or mission of things is to make the human spirit finally comfortable. Contempt of such facile free-thinking, still more easy than free, took in him at times the form of apparent reversion to cast creeds; as though the spirit should seek a fiery refuge in the good old hell of the faithful from the watery new paradise of liberal theosophy and ultimate amiability of all things. Alone among the higher artists of his age, Mr. Rossetti has felt and given the mere physical charm of Christianity, with no admixture of doctrine or of doubt. Here as in other things he belongs, if to any school at all, to that of the great Venetians. He takes the matter in hand with the thorough comprehension of Tintoretto or Veronese, with their thorough subjection of creed and history to the primary purpose of art and proper bearing of a picture. He works after the manner of Titian painting his Assumption with an equal hand whether the girl exalted into goddess be Mary or Ariadne: but his instinct is too masterly for any confusion or discord of colours; and hence comes the spiritual charm and satisfaction of his sacred art. In this class of his poems the first place and the fairest palm belong to the "Blessed Damozel." This paradisal poem, "sweeter than honey or the honeycomb," has found a somewhat further echo than any of its early fellows, and is perhaps known where little else is known of its author's. The sweet intense impression of it must rest for life upon all spirits that ever once received it into their depths, and hold it yet as a thing too dear and fair for praise or price. Itself the flower of a splendid youth, it has the special charm for youth of fresh first work and opening love; "the dew of its birth is of the womb of the morning"; it has the odour and colour of cloudless air, the splendour of an hour without spot. The divine admixtures of earth which humanize its heavenly passion have the flavour and bloom upon them of a maiden beauty, the fine force of a pure first sunrise. No poem shows more plainly the strength and wealth of the workman's lavish yet studious hand. . . .

Among the lesser poems of this volume "The Portrait" holds a place of honour in right of its earnest beauty of thought and rich simplicity of noble images. Above them all in reach and scope of power stands the poem of

"Jenny," great among the few greatest works of the artist. Its plain truth and masculine tenderness are invested with a natural array of thought and imagination which doubles their worth and force. Without a taint on it of anything coarse or trivial, without shadow or suspicion of any facile or vulgar aim at pathetic effect of a tragical or moral kind, it cleaves to absolute fact and reality closer than any common preacher or realist could come; no side of the study is thrown out or thrown back into false light or furtive shadow; but the purity and nobility of its high and ardent pathos are qualities of a moral weight and beauty beyond reach of any rivalry. A divine pity fills it, or a pity something better than divine; the more just and deeper compassion of human fellowship and fleshly brotherhood. Here is nothing of sickly fiction or theatrical violence of tone. No spiritual station of command is assumed, no vantage-ground of outlook from hills of holiness, or heights of moral indifference, or barriers of hard contempt; no unction of facile tears is poured out upon this fallen golden head of a common woman; no loose-tongued effusion of slippery sympathy, to wash out shame with sentiment. And therefore is "the pity of it" a noble pity, and worth the paying; a genuine sin-offering for intercession, pleading with fate for mercy without thought or purpose of pleading. The man whose thought is thus gloriously done into words is as other men are, only with a better brain and heart than the common, with more of mind and compassion, with better eye to see and quicker pulse to beat, with a more generous intellect and a finer taste of things; and his chance companion of a night is no ruined angel or self-immolated sacrifice, but a girl who plies her trade like any other trade, without show or sense of reluctance or repulsion; there is no hint that she was first made to fit better into a smoother groove of life, to run more easily on a higher line of being; that anything seen in prospect or retrospect rebukes or recalls her fancy into any fairer field than she may reach by her present road. All the open sources of pathetic effusion to which a common shepherd of souls would have led the flock of his readers to drink and weep and be refreshed, and leave the medicinal well-spring of sentiment warmer and fuller from their easy tears, are here dried up. This poor hireling of the streets and casinos is professionally pitiable; the world's contempt of her fellow tradeswomen is not in itself groundless or unrighteous; there is no need to raise any mirage about her as of a fallen star, a glorious wreck; but not in that bitterest cry of Othello's own agony—"a sufferance panging as soul and body's severing"—was there a more divine heat of burning compassion than the high heart of a man may naturally lavish, as in this poem, upon such an one as she is. Iago indeed could not share it, nor Roderigo; the naked understanding cannot feel this, nor the mere fool of flesh apprehend it; but only in one or the other of these can all sense be dead of "the pity of it.". . .

The whole work is worthy to fill its place for ever as one of the most perfect and memorable poems of an age or generation. It deals with deep and common things; with the present hour, and with all time; with that

which is of the instant among us, and that which has a message for all souls
of men; with the outward and immediate matter of the day, and with the
inner and immutable ground of human nature. Its plainness of speech and
subject gives it power to touch the heights and sound the depths of tragic
thought without losing the force of its hold and grasp upon the palpable
truths which men often seek and cry out for in poetry, without knowing
that these are only good when greatly treated, and that to artists who can
treat them greatly all times and all truths are equal, and the present, though
assuredly no worse, yet assuredly no better topic than the past. All the
ineffably foolish jargon and jangle of criticasters about classic subjects and
romantic, remote or immediate interests, duties of the poet to face and
handle this thing instead of that or his own age instead of another, can only
serve to darken counsel by words without knowledge: a poet of the first order
raises all subjects to the first rank, and puts the life-blood of an equal interest
into Hebrew forms or Greek, mediæval or modern, yesterday or yesterage.
Thus there is here just the same life-blood and breath of poetic interest in
this episode of a London street and lodging as in the song of "Troy Town"
and the song of "Eden Bower"; just as much, and no jot more. These two
songs are the masterpieces of Mr. Rossetti's magnificent lyric faculty. Full
of fire and music and movement, delicate as moonlight and passionate as
sunlight, fresh as dawn and fine as air, sonorous as the motion of deep waters,
the infallible verse bears up the spirit safe and joyous on its wide clear way.
There is a strength and breadth of style about these poems also which ennobles
their sweetness and brightness, giving them a perfume that savours of no
hotbed, but of hill-flowers that face the sea and the sunrise; a colour that
grows in no greenhouse, but such as comes with morning upon the moun-
tains. They are good certainly, but they are also great; great as no other
man's work of the same age and country. . . .

Among English-speaking poets of his age I know of none who can
reasonably be said to have given higher proof of the highest qualities than
Mr. Rossetti—if the qualities we rate highest in poetry be imagination,
passion, thought, harmony and variety of singing power. Each man who has
anything has his own circle of work and realm of rule, his own field to till
and to reign in; no rival can overmatch, for firm completion of lyric line, for
pathos made perfect, and careful melody of high or of intimate emotion,
"New-Year's Eve" or "The Grandmother," "Œnone" or "Boadicea," the
majestic hymn or the rich lament for love won and lost in "Maud"; none can
emulate the fiery subtlety and sinuous ardour of spirit which penetrates and
lights up all secret gulfs and glimmering heights of human evil and good in
"The Ring and the Book," making the work done live because "the soul of
man is precious to man": none can "blow in power" again through the
notched reed of Pan by the river, to detain the sun on the hills with music;
none can outrun that smooth speed of gracious strength which touched its
Grecian goal in "Thyrsis" and the "Harp-player;" none can light as with fires

or lull as with flutes of magic the reaches of so full a stream of story as flows round the "Earthly Paradise" with ships of heroes afloat on it. But for height and range and depth, for diversity and perfection of powers, Mr. Rossetti is abreast of elder poets not less surely than of younger. Again I take to witness four singled poems; "The Burden of Nineveh," "Sister Helen," "Jenny," and "Eden Bower." Though there were not others as great as these to cite at need, we might be content to pass judgment on the strength of these only; but others as great there are. If he have not the full effluence of romance, or the keen passion of human science, that give power on this hand to Morris and on that to Browning, his work has form and voice, shapeliness and sweetness, unknown to the great analyst; it has weight and heat, gravity and intensity, wanting to the less serious and ardent work of the latest master of romance. Neither by any defect of form, nor by any default of force, does he ever fall short of either mark, or fight with either hand "as one that beateth the air." In sureness of choice and scope of interest, in solidity of subject and sublimity of object, the general worth of his work excels the rate of other men's; he wastes no breath and mistakes no distance, sets his genius to no tasks unfit for it, and spends his strength in the culture of no fruitless fields. What he would do is always what a poet should, and what he would do is always done. Born a light-bearer and leader of men, he has always fulfilled his office with readiness and done his work with might. Help and strength and delight and fresh life have long been gifts of his giving, and freely given as only great gifts can be. And now that at length we receive from hands yet young and strong this treasure of many years, the gathered flower of youth and ripe firstlings of manhood, a fruit of the topmost branch "more golden than gold," all men may witness and assure themselves what manner of harvest the life of this man was to bear; all may see that although, in the perfect phrase of his own sonnet, the last birth of life be death, as her three first-born were love and art and song, yet two of these which she has borne to him, art, namely, and song, cannot now be made subject to that last; that life and love with it may pass away, but very surely no death that ever may be born shall have power upon these for ever.

The Fleshly School of Poetry: Mr. D. G. Rossetti

[ROBERT BUCHANAN]

If, on the occasion of any public performance of Shakspere's great tragedy, the actors who perform the parts of Rosencranz and Guildenstern were, by a preconcerted arrangement and by means of what is technically known as "gagging," to make themselves fully as prominent as the leading character, and to indulge in soliloquies and business strictly belonging to Hamlet himself, the result would be, to say the least of it, astonishing; yet a very similar effect is produced on the unprejudiced mind when the "walking gentlemen" of the fleshly school of poetry, who bear precisely the same relation to Mr. Tennyson as Rosencranz and Guildenstern do to the Prince of Denmark in the play, obtrude their lesser identities and parade their smaller idiosyncrasies in the front rank of leading performers. In their own place, the gentlemen are interesting and useful. Pursuing still the theatrical analogy, the present drama of poetry might be cast as follows: Mr. Tennyson supporting the part of Hamlet, Mr. Matthew Arnold that of Horatio, Mr. Bailey that of Voltimand, Mr. Buchanan that of Cornelius, Messrs. Swinburne and Morris the parts of Rosencranz and Guildenstern, Mr. Rossetti that of Osric, and Mr. Robert Lytton that of "A Gentleman." It will be seen that we have left no place for Mr. Browning, who may be said, however, to play the leading character in his own peculiar fashion on alternate nights.

This may seem a frivolous and inadequate way of opening our remarks on a school of verse-writers which some people regard as possessing great merits; but in good truth, it is scarcely possible to discuss with any seriousness the pretensions with which foolish friends and small critics have surrounded the fleshly school, which, in spite of its spasmodic ramifications in the erotic direction, is merely one of the many sub-Tennysonian schools expanded to supernatural dimensions, and endeavouring by affectations all its own to overshadow its connection with the great original. In the sweep of one single poem, the weird and doubtful "Vivien," Mr. Tennyson has concentrated all the epicene force which, wearisomely expanded, constitutes the characteristic of the writers at present under consideration; and if in "Vivien" he has

Reprinted from Thomas Maitland [pseudonym of Robert Buchanan], "The Fleshly School of Poetry: Mr. D. G. Rossetti," *Contemporary Review* 18 (1871): 334–50.

indicated for them the bounds of sensualism in art, he has in "Maud," in the dramatic person of the hero, afforded distinct precedent for the hysteric tone and overloaded style which is now so familiar to readers of Mr. Swinburne. The fleshliness of "Vivien" may indeed be described as the distinct quality held in common by all the members of the last sub-Tennysonian school, and it is a quality which becomes unwholesome when there is no moral or intellectual quality to temper and control it. Fully conscious of this themselves, the fleshly gentlemen have bound themselves by solemn league and covenant to extol fleshliness as the distinct and supreme end of poetic and pictorial art; to aver that poetic expression is greater than poetic thought, and by inference that the body is greater than the soul, and sound superior to sense; and that the poet, properly to develop his poetic faculty, must be an intellectual hermaphrodite, to whom the very facts of day and night are lost in a whirl of æsthetic terminology. After Mr. Tennyson has probed the depths of modern speculation in a series of commanding moods, all right and interesting in him as the reigning personage, the walking gentlemen, knowing that something of the sort is expected from all leading performers, bare their roseate bosoms and aver that *they* are creedless; the only possible question here being, if any disinterested person cares twopence whether Rosencranz, Guildenstern, and Osric are creedless or not—their self-revelation on that score being so perfectly gratuitous? But having gone so far, it was and is too late to retreat. Rosencranz, Guildenstern, and Osric, finding it impossible to risk an individual bid for the leading business, have arranged all to play leading business together, and mutually to praise, extol, and imitate each other; and although by these measures they have fairly earned for themselves the title of the Mutual Admiration School, they have in a great measure succeeded in their object—to the general stupefaction of a British audience. It is time, therefore, to ascertain whether any of these gentlemen has actually in himself the making of a leading performer. When the *Athenæum*—once more cautious in such matters—advertised nearly every week some interesting particular about Mr. Swinburne's health, Mr. Morris's holiday-making, or Mr. Rossetti's genealogy, varied with such startling statements as "We are informed that Mr. Swinburne dashed off his noble ode *at a sitting*," or "Mr. Swinburne's songs have already reached a second edition," or "Good poetry seems to be in demand; the first edition of Mr. O'Shaughnessy's poems is exhausted"; when the *Academy* informed us that "During the past year or two Mr. Swinburne has written several novels" (!), and that some review or other is to be praised for giving Mr. Rossetti's poems "the attentive study which they demand"—when we read these things we might or might not know pretty well how and where they originated; but to a provincial eye, perhaps, the whole thing really looked like leading business. It would be scarcely worth while, however, to inquire into the pretensions of the writers on merely literary grounds, because sooner or later all literature finds its own level, whatever criticism may say or do in the matter; but it unfortunately happens in the present case that the fleshly school of verse-writers are, so to speak, public offenders, because they are diligently spreading the seeds of disease broadcast wherever they are read and understood. Their complaint too is catching, and carries off many young persons. What the complaint is, and how it works, may be seen on a very slight examination of the works of Mr. Dante Gabriel Rossetti, to whom we shall confine our attention in the present article.

Mr. Rossetti has been known for many years as a painter of exceptional powers, who, for reasons best known to himself, has shrunk from publicly exhibiting his pictures, and from allowing anything like a popular estimate to be formed of their qualities. He belongs, or is said to belong, to the so-called Pre-Raphaelite school, a school which is generally considered to exhibit much genius for colour, and great indifference to perspective. It would be unfair to judge the painter by the glimpses we have had of his works, or by the photographs which are sold of the principal paintings. Judged by the photographs, he is an artist who conceives unpleasantly, and draws ill. Like Mr. Simeon Solomon, however, with whom he seems to have many points in common, he is distinctively a colourist, and of his capabilities in colour we cannot speak, though we should guess that they are great; for if there is any good quality by which his poems are specially marked, it is a great sensitiveness to hues and tints as conveyed in poetic epithet. These qualities, which impress the casual spectator of the photographs from his pictures, are to be found abundantly among his verses. There is the same thinness and transparence of design, the same combination of the simple and the grotesque, the same morbid deviation from healthy forms of life, the same sense of weary, wasting, yet exquisite sensuality; nothing virile, nothing tender, nothing completely sane; a superfluity of extreme sensibility, of delight in beautiful forms, hues, and tints, and a deep-seated indifference to all agitating forces and agencies, all tumultuous griefs and sorrows, all the thunderous stress of life, and all the straining storm of speculation. Mr. Morris is often pure, fresh, and wholesome as his own great model; Mr. Swinburne startles us more than once by some fine flash of insight; but the mind of Mr. Rossetti is like a glassy mere, broken only by the dive of some water-bird or the hum of winged insects, and brooded over by an atmosphere of insufferable closeness, with a light blue sky above it, sultry depths mirrored within it, and a surface so thickly sown with water-lilies that it retains its glassy smoothness even in the strongest wind. Judged relatively to his poetic associates, Mr. Rossetti must be pronounced inferior to either. He cannot tell a pleasant story like Mr. Morris, nor forge alliterative thunderbolts like Mr. Swinburne. It must be conceded, nevertheless, that he is neither so glibly imitative as the one, nor so transcendently superficial as the other.

Although he has been known for many years as a poet as well as a painter—as a painter and poet idolized by his own family and personal associates—and although he has once or twice appeared in print as a contributor to magazines, Mr. Rossetti did not formally appeal to the public until rather more than a year ago, when he published a copious volume of poems, with the announcement that the book, although it contained pieces composed at intervals during a period of many years, "included nothing which the author believes to be immature." This work was inscribed to his brother, Mr. William Rossetti, who, having written much both in poetry and criticism, will perhaps be known to bibliographers as the editor of the worst edition of Shelley which has yet seen the light. No sooner had the work appeared than the chorus of eulogy began. "The book is satisfactory from end to end," wrote Mr. Morris in the *Academy*; "I think these lyrics, with all their other merits, the most complete of their time; nor do I know what lyrics of any time are to be called *great*, if we are to deny the title to these." On the same subject Mr. Swinburne went into a hysteria of admiration: "golden affluence," "jewel-coloured words," "chastity of form," "harmonious nakedness," "consummate fleshly sculpture," and so on in Mr. Swinburne's well-known manner when reviewing his friends. Other critics, with a singular similarity of phrase, followed suit. Strange to say, moreover, no one accused Mr. Rossetti of naughtiness. What had been heinous in Mr. Swinburne was majestic exquisiteness in Mr. Rossetti. Yet we question if there is anything in the unfortunate "Poems and Ballads" quite so questionable on the score of thorough nastiness as many pieces in Mr. Rossetti's collection. Mr. Swinburne was wilder, more outrageous, more blasphemous, and his subjects were more atrocious in themselves; yet the hysterical tone slew the animalism, the furiousness of epithet lowered the sensation; and the first feeling of disgust at such themes as "Laus Veneris" and "Anactoria," faded away into comic amazement. It was only a little mad boy letting off squibs; not a great strong man, who might be really dangerous to society. "I *will* be naughty!" screamed the little boy; but, after all, what did it matter? It is quite different, however, when a grown man, with the self-control and easy audacity of actual experience, comes forward to chronicle his amorous sensations, and, first proclaiming in a loud voice his literary maturity, and consequent responsibility, shamelessly prints and publishes such a piece of writing as this sonnet on "Nuptial Sleep":—

> At length their long kiss severed, with sweet smart:
>   And as the last slow sudden drops are shed
>   From sparkling eaves when all the storm has fled,
> So singly flagged the pulses of each heart.
> Their bosoms sundered, with the opening start
>   Of married flowers to either side outspread
>   From the knit stem; yet still their mouths, burnt red,
> Fawned on each other where they lay apart.
>
> Sleep sank them lower than the tide of dreams,
>   And their dreams watched them sink, and slid away.

> Slowly their souls swam up again, through gleams
> Of watered light and dull drowned waifs of day;
> Till from some wonder of new woods and streams
> He woke, and wondered more: for there she lay.

This, then, is "the golden affluence of words, the firm outline, the justice and chastity of form." Here is a full-grown man, presumably intelligent and cultivated, putting on record for other full-grown men to read, the most secret mysteries of sexual connection, and that with so sickening a desire to reproduce the sensual mood, so careful a choice of epithet to convey mere animal sensations, that we merely shudder at the shameless nakedness. We are no purists in such matters. We hold the sensual part of our nature to be as holy as the spiritual or intellectual part, and we believe that such things must find their equivalent in all; but it is neither poetic, nor manly, nor even human, to obtrude such things as the themes of whole poems. It is simply nasty. Nasty as it is, we are very mistaken if many readers do not think it nice. English society of one kind purchases the *Day's Doings*. English society of another kind goes into ecstasy over Mr. Solomon's pictures—pretty pieces of morality, such as "Love dying by the breath of Lust." There is not much to choose between the two objects of admiration, except that painters like Mr. Solomon lend actual genius to worthless subjects, and thereby produce veritable monsters—like the lovely devils that danced round Saint Anthony. Mr. Rossetti owes his so-called success to the same causes. In poems like "Nuptial Sleep," the man who is too sensitive to exhibit his pictures, and so modest that it takes him years to make up his mind to publish his poems, parades his private sensations before a coarse public, and is gratified by their applause.

It must not be supposed that all Mr. Rossetti's poems are made up of trash like this. Some of them are as noteworthy for delicacy of touch as others are for shamelessness of exposition. They contain some exquisite pictures of nature, occasional passages of real meaning, much beautiful phraseology, lines of peculiar sweetness, and epithets chosen with true literary cunning. But the fleshly feeling is everywhere. Sometimes, as in "The Stream's Secret," it is deliciously modulated, and adds greatly to our emotion of pleasure at perusing a finely-wrought poem; at other times, as in the "Last Confession," it is fiercely held in check by the exigencies of a powerful situation and the strength of a dramatic speaker; but it is generally in the foreground, flushing the whole poem with unhealthy rose-colour, stifling the senses with overpowering sickliness, as of too much civet. Mr. Rossetti is never dramatic, never impersonal—always attitudinizing, posturing, and describing his own exquisite emotions. He is the "Blessed Damozel," leaning over the "gold bar of heaven," and seeing "Time like a pulse shake fierce/ Thro' all the worlds"; he is "heaven-born Helen, Sparta's queen," whose "each twin breast is an apple sweet"; he is Lilith the first wife of Adam; he is the rosy Virgin of the poem called "Ave," and the Queen in the "Staff and Scrip"; he is "Sister Helen" melting her waxen man; he is all these, just as surely as he is Mr. Rossetti soliloquizing over Jenny in her London lodging, or the very nuptial person writing erotic sonnets to his wife. In petticoats or pantaloons, in modern times or in the middle ages, he is just Mr. Rossetti, a fleshly person, with nothing particular to tell us or teach us, with extreme self-control, a strong sense of colour, and a careful choice of diction. Amid all his "affluence of jewel-coloured words," he has not given us one rounded and noteworthy piece of art, though his verses are all art; not one poem which is memorable for its own sake, and quite separable from the displeasing identity of the composer. The nearest approach to a perfect whole is the "Blessed Damozel," a peculiar poem, placed first in the book, perhaps by accident, perhaps because it is a key to the poems which follow. This poem appeared in a rough shape many years ago in the *Germ*, an unwholesome periodical started by the Pre-Raphaelites, and suffered, after gasping through a few feeble numbers, to die the death of all such publications. In spite of its affected title, and of numberless affectations throughout the text, the "Blessed Damozel" has great merits of its own, and a few lines of real genius. We have heard it described as the record of actual grief and love, or, in simple words, the apotheosis of one actually lost by the writer; but, without having any private knowledge of the circumstance of its composition, we feel that such an account of the poem is inadmissible. It does not contain one single note of sorrow. It is a "composition," and a clever one. Read the opening stanzas:—

> "The blessed damozel leaned out
>   From the gold bar of Heaven;
> Her eyes were deeper than the depth
>   Of water stilled at even;
> She had three lilies in her hand,
>   And the stars in her hair were seven.
>
> "Her robe, ungirt from clasp to hem,
>   No wrought flowers did adorn,
> But a white rose of Mary's gift,
>   For service meetly worn;
> Her hair that lay along her back
>   Was yellow like ripe corn."

This is a careful sketch for a picture, which, worked into actual colour by a master, might have been worth seeing. The steadiness of hand lessens as the poem proceeds, and although there are several passages of considerable power,—such as that where, far down the void, "this earth/ Spins like a fretful midge," or that other, describing how

> "the curled moon
>   Was like a little feather
>   Fluttering far down the
>   gulf,"—

the general effect is that of a queer old painting in a missal, very affected and very odd. What moved the British critic to ecstasy in this poem seems to us very sad nonsense indeed, or, if not sad nonsense, very meretricious affectation. Thus, we have seen the following verses quoted with enthusiasm, as italicised—

> "And still she bowed herself and stooped
>   Out of the circling charm;
> *Until her bosom must have made*
> *The bar she leaned on warm,*
> And the lilies lay as if asleep
>   Along her bended arm.

> "From the fixed place of Heaven she saw
> *Time like a pulse shake fierce*
> *Thro' all the worlds.* Her gaze still strove
>   Within the gulf to pierce
> Its path; and now she spoke as when
>   The stars sang in their spheres."

It seems to us that all these lines are very bad, with the exception of the two admirable lines ending the first verse, and that the italicised portions are quite without merit, and almost without meaning. On the whole, one feels disheartened and amazed at the poet who, in the nineteenth century, talks about "damozels," "citherns," and "citoles," and addresses the mother of Christ as the "Lady Mary,"—

> "With her five handmaidens, whose names
>   Are five sweet symphonies,
> Cecily, Gertrude, Magdalen,
>   Margaret and Rosalys."

A suspicion is awakened that the writer is laughing at us. We hover uncertainly between picturesqueness and namby-pamby, and the effect, as Artemus Ward would express it, is "weakening to the intellect." The thing would have been almost too much in the shape of a picture, though the workmanship might have made amends. The truth is that literature, and more particularly poetry, is in a very bad way when one art gets hold of another, and imposes upon it its conditions and limitations. In the first few verses of the "Damozel" we have the subject, or part of the subject, of a picture, and the inventor should either have painted it or left it alone altogether; and, had he done the latter, the world would have lost nothing. Poetry is something more than painting; and an idea will not become a poem because it is too smudgy for a picture.

In a short notice from a well-known pen, giving the best estimate we have seen of Mr. Rossetti's powers as a poet, the *North American Review* offers a certain explanation for affectation such as that of Mr. Rossetti. The writer suggests that "it may probably be the expression of genuine moods of mind in natures too little comprehensive." We would rather believe that Mr. Rossetti lacks comprehension than that he is deficient in sincerity; yet really, to paraphrase the words which Johnson applied to Thomas Sheridan, Mr. Rossetti is affected, naturally affected, but it must have taken him a great deal of trouble to become what we now see him—such an excess of affectation is not in nature. There is very little writing in the volume spontaneous in the sense that some of Swinburne's verses are spontaneous; the poems all look as if they had taken a great deal of trouble. The grotesque mediævalism of "Stratton Water" and "Sister Helen," the mediæval classicism of "Troy Town," the false and shallow mysticism of "Eden Bower," are one and all essentially imitative, and must have cost the writer much pains. It is time, indeed, to point out that Mr. Rossetti is a poet possessing great powers of assimilation and some faculty for concealing the nutriment on which he feeds. Setting aside the "Vita Nuova" and the early Italian poems, which are familiar to many readers by his own excellent translations, Mr. Rossetti may be described as a writer who has yielded to an unusual extent to the complex influences of the literature surrounding him at the present moment. He has the painter's imitative power developed in proportion to his lack of the poet's conceiving imagination. He reproduces to a nicety the manner of an old ballad, a trick in which Mr. Swinburne is also an adept. Cultivated readers, moreover, will recognise in every one of these poems the tone of Mr. Tennyson broken up by the style of Mr. and Mrs. Browning, and disguised here and there by the eccentricities of the Pre-Raphaelites. The "Burden of Nineveh" is a philosophical edition of "Recollections of the Arabian Nights"; "A Last Confession" and "Dante at Verona" are, in the minutest trick and form of thought, suggestive of Mr. Browning; and that the sonnets have been largely moulded and inspired by Mrs. Browning can be ascertained by any critic who will compare them with the "Sonnets from the Portuguese." Much remains, nevertheless, that is Mr. Rossetti's own. We at once recognise as his own property such passages as this:—

> "I looked up
> And saw where a brown-shouldered harlot leaned
> Half through a tavern window thick with vine.
> Some man had come behind her in the room
> And caught her by her arms, and she had turned

> With that coarse empty laugh on him, as now
> He *munched her neck with kisses, while the vine*
> *Crawled in her back.*

Or this:—

> "As I stooped, her own lips rising there
> *Bubbled with brimming kisses* at my mouth."

Or this:—

> "Have seen your lifted silken skirt
> Advertise dainties through the dirt!"

Or this:—

> "What more prize than love to impel thee,
> *Grip* and *lip* my limbs as I tell thee!"

Passages like these are the common stock of the walking gentlemen of the fleshly school. We cannot forbear expressing our wonder, by the way, at the kind of women whom it seems the unhappy lot of these gentlemen to encounter. We have lived as long in the world as they have, but never yet came across persons of the other sex who conduct themselves in the manner described. Females who bite, scratch, scream, bubble, munch, sweat, writhe, twist, wriggle, foam, and in a general way slaver over their lovers, must surely possess some extraordinary qualities to counteract their otherwise most offensive mode of conducting themselves. It appears, however, on examination, that their poet-lovers conduct themselves in a similar manner. They, too, bite, scratch, scream, bubble, munch, sweat, writhe, twist, wriggle, foam, and slaver, in a style frightful to hear of. Let us hope that it is only their fun, and that they don't mean half they say. At times, in reading such books as this, one cannot help wishing that things had remained for ever in the asexual state described in Mr. Darwin's great chapter on Palingenesis. We get very weary of this protracted hankering after a person of the other sex; it seems meat, drink, thought, sinew, religion for the fleshly school. There is no limit to the fleshliness, and Mr. Rossetti finds in it its own religious justification much in the same way as Holy Willie:—

> "Maybe thou let'st this fleshly thorn
> Perplex thy servant night and morn,
> 'Cause he's so gifted.
> If so, thy hand must e'en be borne,
> Until thou lift it."

Whether he is writing of the holy Damozel, or of the Virgin herself, or of Lilith, or Helen, or of Dante, or of Jenny the street-walker, he is fleshly all over, from the roots of his hair to the tip of his toes; never a true lover merging his identity into that of the beloved one; never spiritual, never tender; always self-conscious and æsthetic. "Nothing," says a modern writer, "in human life is so utterly remorseless—not love, not hate, not ambition, not vanity—as the artistic or æsthetic instinct morbidly developed to the suppression of conscience and feeling"; and at no time do we feel more fully impressed with this truth than after the perusal of "Jenny," in some respects the finest poem in the volume, and in all respects the poem best indicative of the true quality of the writer's humanity. It is a production which bears signs of having been suggested by Mr. Buchanan's quasi-lyrical poems, which it copies in the style of title, and particularly by "Artist and Model"; but certainly Mr. Rossetti cannot be accused, as the Scottish writer has been accused, of maudlin sentiment and affected tenderness. The two first lines are perfect:—"Lazy laughing languid Jenny,/ Fond of a kiss and fond of a guinea"; And the poem is a soliloquy of the poet—who has been spending the evening in dancing at a casino—over his partner, whom he has accompanied home to the usual style of lodgings occupied by such ladies, and who has fallen asleep with her head upon his knee, while he wonders, in a wretched pun—"Whose person or whose purse may be/ The lodestar of your reverie?"

The soliloquy is long, and in some parts beautiful, despite a very constant suspicion that we are listening to an emasculated Mr. Browning, whose whole tone and gesture, so to speak, is occasionally introduced with startling fidelity; and there are here and there glimpses of actual thought and insight, over and above the picturesque touches which belong to the writer's true profession, such as that where, at daybreak—

> "lights creep in
> Past the gauze curtains half drawn-to,
> And *the lamp's doubled shade grows blue.*"

What we object to in this poem is not the subject, which any writer may be fairly left to choose for himself; nor anything particularly vicious in the poetic treatment of it; nor any bad blood bursting through in special passages. But the whole tone, without being more than usually coarse, seems heartless. There is not a drop of piteousness in Mr. Rossetti. He is just to the outcast, even generous; severe to the seducer; sad even at the spectacle of lust in dimity and fine ribbons. Notwithstanding all this, and a certain delicacy and refinement of treatment unusual with this poet, the poem repels and revolts us, and we like Mr. Rossetti least after its perusal. We are angry with the fleshly person at last. The "Blessed Damozel" puzzled us, the "Song of the Bower" amused us, the love-sonnet depressed and sickened us, but

"Jenny," though distinguished by less special viciousness of thought and style than any of these, fairly makes us lose patience. We detect its fleshliness at a glance; we perceive that the scene was fascinating less through its human tenderness than because it, like all the others, possessed an inherent quality of animalism. "The whole work" ("Jenny,") writes Mr. Swinburne, "is worthy to fill its place for ever as one of the most perfect poems of an age or generation. There is just the same life-blood and breath of poetic interest in this episode of a London street and lodging as in the song of 'Troy Town' and the song of 'Eden Bower'; just as much, and no jot more,"—to which last statement we cordially assent; for there is bad blood in all, and breadth of poetic interest in none. "Vengeance of Jenny's case," indeed!—when such a poet as this comes fawning over her, with tender compassion in one eye and æsthetic enjoyment in the other!

It is time that we permitted Mr. Rossetti to speak for himself, which we will do by quoting a fairly representative poem entire:—

Love-Lily.

"Between the hands, between the brows,
　　Between the lips of Love-Lily,
A *spirit is born whose birth endows*
　　My blood with fire to burn through me;
Who breathes upon my gazing eyes,
　　Who laughs and murmurs in mine ear,
At whose least touch my colour flies,
　　And whom my life grows faint to hear.

"Within the voice, within the heart,
　　Within the mind of Love-Lily,
A spirit is born who lifts apart
　　His tremulous wings and looks at me;
Who on my mouth his finger lays,
　　And shows, while whispering lutes confer,
That Eden of Love's watered ways
　　Whose winds and spirits worship her.

"Brows, hands, and lips, heart, mind, and voice,
　　Kisses and words of Love-Lily,—
Oh! bid me with your joy rejoice
　　Till *riotous longing rest in me!*
Ah! let not hope be still distraught,
　　But find in her its gracious goal,
Whose speech Truth knows not from her thought,
　　Nor Love her body from her soul."

With the exception of the usual "riotous longing," which seems to make Mr. Rossetti a burthen to himself, there is nothing to find fault with in the extreme fleshliness of these verses, and to many people who live in the country they may even appear beautiful. Without pausing to criticise a thing so trifling—as well might we dissect a cobweb or anatomize a medusa—let us ask the reader's attention to a peculiarity to which all the students of the fleshly school must sooner or later give their attention—we mean the habit of accenting the last syllable in words which in ordinary speech are accented on the penultimate:—"Between the hands, between the brows,/ Between the lips of Love-Lil*ee*!"—which may be said to give to the speaker's voice a sort of cooing tenderness just bordering on a loving whistle. Still better as an illustration are the lines:—

> "Saturday night is market night
> Everywhere, be it dry or wet,
> And market night in the Haymar-*ket*!"

which the reader may advantageously compare with Mr. Morris's

> "Then said the king
> Thanked be thou; *neither for nothing*
> Shalt thou this good deed do to me;"

or Mr. Swinburne's

> "In either of the twain
> Red roses full of rain;
> She hath for bondwo*men*
> All kinds of flowers."

It is unnecessary to multiply examples of an affectation which disfigures all these writers—Guildenstern, Rosencranz, and Osric; who, in the same spirit which prompts the ambitious nobodies that rent London theatres in the "empty" season to make up for their dullness by fearfully original "new readings," distinguish their attempt at leading business by affecting the construction of their grandfathers and great-grandfathers, and the accentuation of the poets of the court of James I. It is in all respects a sign of remarkable genius, from this point of view, to rhyme "was" with "grass," "death" with "lièth," "love" with "of," "once" with "suns," and so on *ad nauseam*. We are far from disputing the value of bad rhymes used occasionally to break up the monotony of verse, but the case is hard when such blunders become the rule and not the exception, when writers deliberately lay themselves out to be as archaic and affected as possible. Poetry is perfect human speech, and these archaisms are the mere fiddlededeeing of empty heads and hollow hearts. Bad as they are, they are the true indication of false tricks and affectations which lie far deeper. They are trifles, light as air, showing how the wind blows. The soul's speech and the heart's speech are clear, simple, natural, and beautiful, and reject the meretricious tricks to which we have drawn attention.

It is on the score that these tricks and affectations have procured the professors a number of imitators, that the fleshly school deliver their formula that great poets are always to be known because their manner is immediately reproduced by small poets, and that a poet who finds few imitators is probably of inferior rank—by which they mean to infer that they themselves are very great poets indeed. It is quite true that they are imitated. On the stage, twenty provincial "stars" copy Charles Kean, while not one copies his father; there are dozens of actors who reproduce Mr. Charles Dillon, and not one who attempts to reproduce Macready. When we take up the poems of Mr. O'Shaughnessy, we are face to face with a second-hand Mr. Swinburne; when we read Mr. Payne's queer allegories, we remember Mr. Morris's early stage; and every poem of Mr. Marston's reminds us of Mr. Rossetti. But what is really most droll and puzzling in the matter is, that these imitators seem to have no difficulty whatever in writing nearly, if not quite, as well as their masters. It is not bad imitations they offer us, but poems which read just like the originals; the fact being that it is easy to reproduce sound when it has no strict connection with sense, and simple enough to cull phraseology not hopelessly interwoven with thought and spirit. The fact that these gentlemen are so easily imitated is the most damning proof of their inferiority. What merits they have lie with their faults on the surface, and can be caught by any young gentleman as easily as the measles, only they are rather more difficult to get rid of. All young gentlemen have animal faculties, though few have brains; and if animal faculties without brains will make poems, nothing is easier in the world. A great and good poet, however, is great and good irrespective of manner, and often in spite of manner; he is great because he brings great ideas and new light, because his thought is a revelation; and, although it is true that a great manner generally accompanies great matter, the manner of great matter is almost inimitable. The great poet is not Cowley, imitated and idolized and reproduced by every scribbler of his time; nor Pope, whose trick of style was so easily copied that to this day we cannot trace his own hand with any certainty in the *Iliad*; nor Donne, nor Sylvester, nor the Della Cruscans. Shakspere's blank verse is the most difficult and Jonson's the most easy to imitate, of all the Elizabethan stock; and Shakspere's verse is the best verse, because it combines the great qualities of all contemporary verse, with no individual affectations; and so perfectly does this verse, with all its splendour, intersect with the style of contemporaries *at their best*, that we would undertake to select passage after passage which would puzzle a good judge to tell which of the Elizabethans was the author— Marlowe, Beaumont, Dekkar, Marston, Webster, or Shakespere himself. The great poet is Dante, full of the thunder of a great Idea; and Milton, unapproachable in the serene white light of thought and sumptuous wealth of style; and Shakspere, all poets by turns, and all men in succession; and Goethe, always innovating, and ever indifferent to innovation for its own sake; and Wordsworth, clear as crystal and deep as the sea; and Tennyson, with his vivid range, far-piercing sight, and perfect speech; and Browning, great, not by virtue of his eccentricities, but because of his close intellectual grasp. Tell "Paradise Lost," the "Divine Comedy," in naked prose; do the same by *Hamlet, Macbeth*, and *Lear*; read Mr. Hayward's translation of "Faust"; take up the "Excursion," a great poem, though its speech is nearly prose already; turn the "Guinevere" into a mere story; reproduce Pompilia's last dying speech without a line of rhythm. Reduced to bald English, all these poems, and all great poems, lose much; but how much do they not retain? They are poems to the very roots and depths of being, poems born and delivered from the soul, and treat them as cruelly as you may, poems they will remain. So it is with all good and thorough creations, however low in their rank; so it is with the "Ballad in a Wedding" and "Clever Tom Clinch," just as much as with the "Epistle of Karsheesh," or Goethe's torso of "Prometheus"; with Shelley's "Skylark," or Alfred de Musset's "A la Lune," as well as Racine's "Athalie," Victor Hugo's "Parricide," or Hood's "Last Man." A poem is a poem, first as to the soul, next as to the form. The fleshly persons who wish to create form for its own sake are merely pronouncing their own doom. But *such* form! If the Pre-Raphaelite fervour gains ground, we shall soon have popular songs like this:—

> "When winds do roar, and rains do pour,
> Hard is the life of the sail*or*;
> He scarcely as he reels can tell
> The side-lights from the binna*cle*;
> He looketh on the wild wa*ter*," &c.,

and so on, till the English speech seems the speech of raving madmen. Of a piece with other affectations is the device of a burthen, of which the fleshly persons are very fond for its own sake, quite apart from its relevancy. Thus Mr. Rossetti sings:—

> "Why did you melt your waxen man,
>   Sister Helen?
> To-day is the third since you began.
> The time was long, yet the time ran,
>   Little brother.
>   (*O mother, Mary mother,*
> *Three days to-day between Heaven and Hell.*)

This burthen is repeated, with little or no alteration, through thirty-four verses, and might with as much music, and far more point, run as follows:—

> Why did you melt your waxen man,
>   Sister Helen?
> To-day is the third since you began.
> The time was long, yet the time ran,
>   Little brother.
>   (*O Mr. Dante Rossetti,*
> *What stuff is this about Heaven and Hell?*)

About as much to the point is a burthen of Mr. Swinburne's, something to the following effect:—

> "We were three maidens in the green corn,
>   *Hey chickaleerie, the red cock and gray,*
> Fairer maidens were never born,
>   *One o'clock, two o'clock, off and away.*"

We are not quite certain of the words, as we quote from memory, but we are sure our version fairly represents the original, and is quite as expressive. Productions of this sort are "silly sooth" in good earnest, though they delight some newspaper critics of the day, and are copied by young gentlemen with animal faculties morbidly developed by too much tobacco and too little exercise. Such indulgence, however, would ruin the strongest poetical constitution; and it unfortunately happens that neither masters nor pupils were naturally very healthy. In such a poem as "Eden Bower" there is not one scrap of imagination, properly so-called. It is a clever grotesque in the worst manner of Callot, unredeemed by a gleam of true poetry or humour. No good poet would have wrought into a poem the absurd tradition about Lilith; Goethe was content to glance at it merely, with a grim smile, in the great scene in the Brocken. We may remark here that poems of this unnatural and morbid kind are only tolerable when they embody a profound meaning, as do Coleridge's "Ancient Mariner" and "Cristabel." Not that we would insult the memory of Coleridge by comparing his exquisitely conscientious work with this affected rubbish about "Eden Bower" and "Sister Helen," though his influence in their composition is unmistakable. Still more unmistakable is the influence of that most unwholesome poet, Beddoes, who, with all his great powers, treated his subjects in a thoroughly insincere manner, and is now justly forgotten.

The great strong current of English poetry rolls on, ever mirroring in its bosom new prospects of fair and wholesome thought. Morbid deviations are endless and inevitable; there must be marsh and stagnant mere as well as mountain and wood. Glancing backward into the shady places of the obscure, we see the once prosperous nonsense-writers each now consigned to his own little limbo—Skelton and Gower still playing fantastic tricks with the mother-tongue; Gascoigne outlasting the applause of all, and living to see his own works buried before him; Silvester doomed to oblivion by his own fame as a translator; Carew the idol of courts, and Donne the beloved of schoolmen, both buried in the same oblivion; the fantastic Fletchers winning the wonder of collegians, and fading out through sheer poetic impotence; Cowley shaking all England with his pindarics, and perishing with them; Waller, the famous, saved from oblivion by the natural note of one single song—and so on, through league after league of a flat and desolate country which once was prosperous, till we come again to these fantastic figures of the fleshly school, with their droll mediæval garments, their funny archaic speech, and the fatal marks of literary consumption in every pale and delicate visage. Our judgment on Mr. Rossetti, to whom we in the meantime confine our judgment, is substantially that of the *North American Reviewer*, who believes that "we have in him another poetical man, and a man markedly poetical, and of a kind apparently, though not radically, different from any of our secondary writers of poetry, but that we have not in him a new poet of any weight"; and that he is "so affected, sentimental, and painfully self-conscious, that the best to be done in his case is to hope that this book of his, having unpacked his bosom of so much that is unhealthy, may have done him more good than it has given others pleasure." Such, we say, is our opinion, which might very well be wrong, and have to undergo modification, if Mr. Rossetti was younger and less self-possessed. His "maturity" is fatal.

The Stealthy School of Criticism

Dante Gabriel Rossetti

Your paragraph, a fortnight ago, relating to the pseudonymous authorship of an article, violently assailing myself and other writers of poetry, in the *Contemporary Review* for October last, reveals a species of critical masquerade which I have expressed in the heading given to this letter. Since then, Mr. Sidney Colvin's note, qualifying the report that he intends to "answer" that article, has appeared in your pages; and my own view as to the absolute forfeit, under such conditions, of all claim to honourable reply, is precisely the same as Mr. Colvin's. For here a critical organ, professedly adopting the principle of open signature, would seem, in reality, to assert (by silent practice, however, not by enunciation,) that if the anonymous in criticism was—as itself originally inculcated—but an early caterpillar stage, the nominate too is found to be no better than a homely transitional chrysalis, and that the ultimate butterfly form for a critic who likes to sport in sunlight and yet to elude the grasp, is after all the pseudonymous. But, indeed, what I may call the "Siamese" aspect of the entertainment provided by the *Review* will elicit but one verdict. Yet I may, perhaps, as the individual chiefly attacked, be excused for asking your assistance now in giving a specific denial to specific charges which, if unrefuted, may still continue, in spite of their author's strategic *fiasco*, to serve his purpose against me to some extent.

The primary accusation, on which this writer grounds all the rest, seems to be that others and myself "extol fleshliness as the distinct and supreme end of poetic and pictorial art; aver that poetic expression is greater than poetic thought; and, by inference, that the body is greater than the soul, and sound superior to sense."

As my own writings are alone formally dealt with in the article, I shall confine my answer to myself; and this must first take unavoidably the form of a challenge to prove so broad a statement. It is true, some fragmentary pretence at proof is put in here and there throughout the attack, and thus far an opportunity is given of contesting the assertion.

A Sonnet entitled *Nuptial Sleep* is quoted and abused at page 338 of the *Review*, and is there dwelt upon as a "whole poem," describing "merely animal sensations." It is no more a whole poem, in reality, than is any single

Reprinted from *Athenaeum* (December 1871): 792–94.

stanza of any poem throughout the book. The poem, written chiefly in sonnets, and of which this is one sonnet-stanza, is entitled *The House of Life*; and even in my first published instalment of the whole work (as contained in the volume under notice) ample evidence is included that no such passing phase of description as the one headed *Nuptial Sleep* could possibly be put forward by the author of *The House of Life* as his own representative view of the subject of love. In proof of this, I will direct attention (among the love-sonnets of this poem) to Nos. 2, 8, 11, 17, 28, and more especially 13, which, indeed, I had better print here.

Love-Sweetness

"Sweet dimness of her loosened hair's downfall
    About thy face; her sweet hands round thy head
    In gracious fostering union garlanded;
Her tremulous smiles; her glances' sweet recall
Of love; her murmuring sighs memorial;
    Her mouth's culled sweetness by thy kisses shed
    On cheeks and neck and eyelids, and so led
Back to her mouth which answers there for all:—
"What sweeter than these things, except the thing
    In lacking which all these would lose their sweet:—
    The confident heart's still fervour; the swift beat
And soft subsidence of the spirit's wing
Then when it feels, in cloud-girt wayfaring,
    The breath of kindred plumes against its feet?"

Any reader may bring any artistic charge he pleases against the above sonnet; but one charge it would be impossible to maintain against the writer of the series in which it occurs, and that is, the wish on his part to assert that the body is greater than the soul. For here all the passionate and just delights of the body are declared—somewhat figuratively, it is true, but unmistakably—to be as naught if not ennobled by the concurrence of the soul at all times. Moreover, nearly one half of this series of sonnets has nothing to do with love, but treats of quite other life-influences. I would defy any one to couple with fair quotation of Sonnets 29, 30, 31, 39, 40, 41, 43, or others, the slander that their author was not impressed, like all other thinking men, with the responsibilities and higher mysteries of life; while Sonnets 35, 36, and 37, entitled *The Choice*, sum up the general view taken in a manner only to be evaded by conscious insincerity. Thus much for *The House of Life*, of which the sonnet *Nuptial Sleep* is one stanza, embodying, for its small constituent share, a beauty of natural universal function, only to be reprobated in art if dwelt on (as I have shown that it is not here) to the exclusion of those other highest things of which it is the harmonious concomitant.

At page 342, an attempt is made to stigmatize four short quotations as being specially "my own property," that is, (for the context shows the meaning,) as being grossly sensual; though all guiding reference to any precise page or poem in my book is avoided here. The first of these unspecified quotations is from the *Last Confession*; and is the description referring to the harlot's laugh, the hideous character of which, together with its real or imagined resemblance to the laugh heard soon afterwards from the lips of one long cherished as an ideal, is the immediate cause which makes the maddened hero of the poem a murderer. Assailants may say what they please; but no poet or poetic reader will blame me for making the incident recorded in these seven lines as repulsive to the reader as it was to the hearer and beholder. Without this, the chain of motive and result would remain obviously incomplete. Observe also that these are but seven lines in a poem of some five hundred, not one other of which could be classed with them.

A second quotation gives the last two lines *only* of the following sonnet, which is the first of four sonnets in *The House of Life* jointly entitled *Willowwood*:—

> "I sat with Love upon a woodside well,
>   Leaning across the water, I and he;
>   Nor ever did he speak nor looked at me,
> But touched his lute wherein was audible
> The certain secret thing he had to tell:
>   Only our mirrored eyes met silently
>   In the low wave; and that sound seemed to be
> The passionate voice I knew; and my tears fell.
>
> "And at their fall, his eyes beneath grew hers;
>   And with his foot and with his wing-feathers
>   He swept the spring that watered my heart's drouth.
>   Then the dark ripples spread to waving hair,
>   And as I stooped, her own lips rising there
>   Bubbled with brimming kisses at my mouth."

The critic has quoted (as I said) only the last two lines, and he has italicized the second as something unbearable and ridiculous. Of course the inference would be that this was really my own absurd bubble-and-squeak notion of an actual kiss. The reader will perceive at once, from the whole sonnet transcribed above, how untrue such an inference would be. The sonnet describes a dream or trance of divided love momentarily re-united by the longing fancy; and in the imagery of the dream, the face of the beloved rises through deep dark waters to kiss the lover. Thus the phrase, "Bubbled with brimming kisses," etc., bears purely on the special symbolism employed, and from that point of view will be found, I believe, perfectly simple and just.

A third quotation is from *Eden Bower*, and says, "What more prize than love to impel thee?/ Grip and lip my limbs as I tell thee!" Here again no reference is given, and naturally the reader would suppose that a human embrace is described. The embrace, on the contrary, is that of a fabled snake-woman and a snake. It would be possible still, no doubt, to object on other grounds to this conception; but the ground inferred and relied on for full effect by the critic is none the less an absolute misrepresentation. These three extracts, it will be admitted, are virtually, though not verbally, garbled with malicious intention; and the same is the case, as I have shown, with the sonnet called *Nuptial Sleep* when purposely treated as a "whole poem."

The last of the four quotations grouped by the critic as conclusive examples consists of two lines from *Jenny*. Neither some thirteen years ago, when I wrote this poem, nor last year when I published it, did I fail to foresee impending charges of recklessness and aggressiveness, or to perceive that even some among those who could really *read* the poem, and acquit me on these grounds, might still hold that the thought in it had better have dispensed with the situation which serves it for framework. Nor did I omit to consider how far a treatment from without might here be possible. But the motive powers of art reverse the requirement of science, and demand first of all an *inner* standing-point. The heart of such a mystery as this must be plucked from the very world in which it beats or bleeds; and the beauty and pity, the self-questionings and all-questionings, which it brings with it, can come with full force only from the mouth of one alive to its whole appeal, such as the speaker put forward in the poem,—that is, of a young and thoughtful man of the world. To such a speaker, many half-cynical revulsions of feeling and reverie, and a recurrent presence of the impressions of beauty (however artificial) which first brought him within such a circle of influence, would be inevitable features of the dramatic relations portrayed. Here again I can give the lie, in hearing of honest readers, to the base or trivial ideas which my critic labours to connect with the poem. There is another little charge, however, which this minstrel in mufti brings against *Jenny*, namely, one of plagiarism from that very poetic self of his which the tutelary prose does but enshroud for the moment. This question can, fortunately, be settled with ease by others who have read my critic's poems; and thus I need the less regret that, not happening myself to be in that position, I must be content to rank with those who cannot pretend to an opinion on the subject.

It would be humiliating, need one come to serious detail, to have to refute such an accusation as that of "binding oneself by solemn league and covenant to extol fleshliness as the distinct and supreme end of poetic and pictorial art"; and one cannot but feel that here every one will think it allowable merely to pass by with a smile the foolish fellow who has brought a charge thus framed against any reasonable man. Indeed, what I have said already is substantially enough to refute it, even did I not feel sure that a fair balance of my poetry must, of itself, do so in the eyes of every candid reader. I say nothing of my pictures; but those who know them will laugh at the idea. That I may, nevertheless, take a wider view than some poets or critics, of how much, in the material conditions absolutely given to man to deal with as distinct from his spiritual aspirations, is admissible within the limits of Art,—this, I say, is possible enough; nor do I wish to shrink from such responsibility. But to state that I do so to the ignoring or overshadowing of spiritual beauty, is an absolute falsehood, impossible to be put forward except in the indulgence of prejudice or rancour.

I have selected, amid much railing on my critic's part, what seemed the most representative indictment against me, and have, so far, answered it. Its remaining clauses set forth how others and myself "aver that poetic expression is greater than poetic thought . . . and sound superior to sense"— an accusation elsewhere, I observe, expressed by saying that we "wish to create form for its own sake." If writers of verse are to be listened to in such arraignment of each other, it might be quite competent to me to prove, from the works of my friends in question, that no such thing is the case with them; but my present function is to confine myself to my own defence. This, again, it is difficult to do quite seriously. It is no part of my undertaking to dispute the verdict of any "contemporary," however contemptuous or contemptible, on my own measure of executive success; but the accusation cited above is not against the poetic value of certain work, but against its primary and (by assumption) its admitted aim. And to this I must reply that so far, assuredly, not even Shakspeare himself could desire more arduous human tragedy for development in Art than belongs to the themes I venture to embody, however incalculably higher might be his power of dealing with them. What more inspiring for poetic effort than the terrible Love turned to Hate,—perhaps the deadliest of all passion-woven complexities,—which is the theme of *Sister Helen*, and, in a more fantastic form, of *Eden Bower*— the surroundings of both poems being the mere machinery of a central universal meaning? What, again, more so than the savage penalty exacted for a lost ideal, as expressed in the *Last Confession*;—than the outraged love for man and burning compensations in art and memory of *Dante at Verona*;— than the baffling problems which the face of *Jenny* conjures up;—or than the analysis of passion and feeling attempted in *The House of Life*, and others among the more purely lyrical poems? I speak here, as does my critic in the clause adduced, of *aim*, not of *achievement*; and so far, the mere summary is instantly subversive of the preposterous imputation. To assert that the poet whose matter is such as this aims chiefly at "creating form for its own sake," is, in fact, almost an ingenuous kind of dishonesty; for surely it delivers up the asserter at once, bound hand and foot, to the tender mercies of contradic-tory proof. Yet this may fairly be taken as an example of the spirit in which a constant effort is here made against me to appeal to those who either are ignorant of what I write, or else belong to the large class too easily influenced by an assumption of authority in addressing them. The false name appended to the article must, as is evident, aid this position vastly; for who, after all, would not be apt to laugh at seeing one poet confessedly come forward as aggressor against another in the field of criticism?

It would not be worth while to lose time and patience in noticing minutely how the system of misrepresentation is carried into points of artistic detail,—giving us, for example, such statements as that the burthen employed in the ballad of *Sister Helen* "is repeated with little or no alteration through thirty-four verses," whereas the fact is, that the alteration of it in every verse is the very scheme of the poem. But these are minor matters quite thrown into the shade by the critic's more daring sallies. In addition to the class of attack I have answered above, the article contains, of course, an immense amount of personal paltriness; as, for instance, attributions of my work to this, that, or the other absurd derivative source; or again, pure nonsense (which can have no real meaning even to the writer) about "one art getting hold of another, and imposing on it its conditions and limitations"; or, indeed, what not besides? However, to such antics as this, no more attention is possible than that which Virgil enjoined Dante to bestow on the meaner phenomena of his pilgrimage.

Thus far, then, let me thank you for the opportunity afforded me to join issue with the Stealthy School of Criticism. As for any literary justice to be done on this particular Mr. Robert-Thomas, I will merely ask the reader whether, once identified, he does not become manifestly his own best "sworn tormentor"? For who will then fail to discern all the palpitations which preceded his final resolve in the great question whether to be or not to be his acknowledged self when he became an assailant? And yet this is he who, from behind his mask, ventures to charge another with "bad blood," with "insincerity," and the rest of it (and that where poetic fancies are alone in question); while every word on his own tongue is covert rancour, and every stroke from his pen perversion of truth. Yet, after all, there is nothing wonderful in the lengths to which a fretful poet-critic will carry such grudges as he may bear, while publisher and editor can both be found who are willing to consider such means admissible, even to the clear subversion of first professed tenets in the *Review* which they conduct.

In many phases of outward nature, the principle of chaff and grain holds good,—the base enveloping the precious continually; but an untruth was never yet the husk of a truth. Thresh and riddle and winnow it as you may,— let it fly in shreds to the four winds,—falsehood only will be that which flies and that which stays. And thus the sheath of deceit which this pseudonymous undertaking presents at the outset insures in fact what will be found to be its real character to the core.

Rossetti and the Religion of Beauty

Frederic W. H. Myers

Among those picturesque aspects of life which the advance of civilisation is tending to reduce to smoothness and uniformity we may include that hubbub and conflict which in rougher days used to salute the appearance of any markedly new influence in science, literature, or art. Prejudice—not long since so formidable and ubiquitous a giant—now shows sometimes little more vitality than Bunyan's Pope or Pagan; and the men who stone one of our modern prophets do it hurriedly, feeling that they may be interrupted at any moment by having to make arrangements for his interment in Westminster Abbey.

Now, while it would be absurd not to rejoice in this increasing receptivity of cultivated men—absurd to wish the struggle of genius sharper, or its recognition longer deferred—we may yet note one incidental advantage which belonged to the older *régime*. While victory was kept longer in doubt, and while the conflict was rougher, the advocates of a new cause felt a stronger obligation to master it in all its aspects, and to set it forth with such exposition as might best prepare a place for it in ordinary minds. The merits of Wordsworth (to take an obvious instance) were long ignored by the public; but in the meantime his admirers had explained them so often and so fully that the recognition which was at last accorded to them was given *on* those merits, and not in mere deference to the authority of any esoteric circle.

The exhibition of Dante Rossetti's pictures which now (February 1883) covers the walls of Burlington House is the visible sign of the admission of a new strain of thought and emotion within the pale of our artistic orthodoxy. And since Rossetti's poetry expresses with singular exactness the same range of ideas as his painting, and is at any rate not inferior to his painting in technical skill, we may fairly say that his poetry also has attained hereby some sort of general recognition, and that the enthusiastic notices which appeared on his decease embodied a view of him to which the public is willing to some extent to defer.

Yet it hardly seems that enough has been done to make that deference spontaneous or intelligent. The students of Rossetti's poems—taking their tone from Mr. Swinburne's magnificent eulogy—have for the most part

Reprinted from *Essays: Modern* (London: Macmillan, 1885), 312–34.

rather set forth their artistic excellence than endeavoured to explain their contents, or to indicate the relation of the poet's habit of thought and feeling to the ideas which Englishmen are accustomed to trust or admire. And consequently many critics, whose ethical point of view demands respect, continue to find in Rossetti's works an enigma not worth the pains of solution, and to decry them as obscure, fantastic, or even as grossly immoral in tendency.

It will be the object of this essay—written from a point of view of by no means exclusive sympathy with the movement which Rossetti led—to show, in the first place, the great practical importance of that movement for good or evil; and, further, to trace such relations between this Religion of Art, this Worship of Beauty, and the older and more accredited manifestations of the Higher Life, as may indicate to the moralist on what points he should concentrate his efforts if, hopeless of withstanding the rising stream, he seeks at least to retain some power of deepening or modifying its channel.

From the æsthetic side such an attempt will be regarded with indifference, and from the ethical side with little hope. Even so bold a peacemaker as the author of *Natural Religion* has shrunk from this task; for the art which he admits as an element in his Church of Civilisation is an art very different from Rossetti's. It is an art manifestly untainted by sensuousness, manifestly akin to virtue; an art which, like Wordsworth's, finds its revelation in sea and sky and mountain rather than in "eyes which the sungate of the soul unbar," or in "Such fire as Love's soul-winnowing hands distil,/Even from his inmost ark of light and dew." Yet, however slight the points of contact between the ethical and the æsthetic theories of life may be, it is important that they should be noted and dwelt upon. For assuredly the "æsthetic movement" is not a mere fashion of the day—the modish pastime of nincompoops and charlatans. The imitators who surround its leaders, and whose jargon almost disgusts us with the very mysteries of art, the very vocabulary of emotion—these men are but the straws that mark the current, the inevitable parasites of a rapidly-rising cause. We have, indeed, only to look around us to perceive that—whether or not the conditions of the modern world are favourable to artistic *excellence*—all the main forces of civilisation are tending towards artistic *activity*. The increase of wealth, the diffusion of education, the gradual decline of the military, the hieratic, the aristocratic ideals—each of these causes removes some obstacle from the artist's path or offers some fresh prize to his endeavours. Art has outlived both the Puritans and the Inquisition; she is no longer deadened by the spirit of self-mortification, nor enslaved by a jealous orthodoxy. The increased wealth of the world makes the artist's life stable and secure, while it sets free a surplus income so large that an increasing share of it must almost necessarily be diverted to some form of æsthetic expenditure.

And more than this. It is evident, especially in new countries, that a need is felt of some kind of social distinction—some new aristocracy—based on differences other than those of birth and wealth. Not, indeed, that rank and family are likely to cease to be held in honour; but, as power is gradually dissociated from them, they lose their exclusive predominance, and take their place on the same footing as other graces and dignities of life. Still less need we assume any slackening in the pursuit of riches; the fact being rather that this pursuit is so widely successful that in civilised capitals even immense opulence can now scarcely confer on its possessor all the distinction which he desires. In America, accordingly, where modern instincts find their freest field, we have before our eyes the process of the gradual distribution of the old prerogatives of birth amongst wealth, culture, and the proletariat. In Europe a class privileged by birth used to supply at once the rulers and the ideals of other men. In America the *rule* has passed to the multitude; largely swayed in subordinate matters by organised wealth, but in the last resort supreme. The *ideal* of the new community at first was Wealth; but, as its best literature and its best society plainly show, that ideal is shifting in the direction of Culture. The younger cities, the coarser classes, still bow down undisguisedly to the god Dollar; but when this Philistine deity is rejected as shaming his worshippers, æsthetic Culture seems somehow the only Power ready to instal itself in the vacant shrine.

And all over the world the spread of Science, the diffusion of Morality, tend in this same direction. For the net result of Science and Morality for the mass of men is simply to give them comfort and leisure, to leave them cheerful, peaceful, and anxious for occupation. Nay, even the sexual instinct, as men become less vehement and unbridled, merges in larger and larger measure into the mere æsthetic enjoyment of beauty; till Stesichorus might now maintain with more truth than of old that our modern Helen is not herself fought for by two continents, but rather her εἴδωλον or image is blamelessly diffused over the albums of two hemispheres.

It is by no means clear that these modern conditions are favourable to the development either of the highest art or of the highest virtue. It is not certain even that they are permanent—that this æsthetic paradise of the well-to-do may not sometime be convulsed by an invasion from the rough world without. Meantime, however, it exists and spreads, and its leading figures exert an influence which few men of science, and fewer theologians, can surpass. And alike to *savant*, to theologian, and to moralist, it must be important to trace the workings of a powerful mind, concerned with interests which are so different from theirs, but which for a large section of society are becoming daily more paramount and engrossing.

"Under the arch of Life," says Rossetti in a sonnet whose Platonism is the more impressive because probably unconscious—

> "Under the arch of Life, where love and death,
>   Terror and mystery, guard her shrine, I saw
>   Beauty enthroned; and though her gaze struck awe,
> I drew it in as simply as my breath."

Rossetti was ignorant of Greek, and it seems doubtful whether he knew Plato even by translations. But his idealising spirit has reproduced the myth of the *Phædrus*—even to the τρέφεται καὶ εὐπαθεῖ—the words that affirm the repose and well-being of the soul when she perceives beneath the arch of heaven the pure Idea which is at once her sustenance and her lord:—

> "Hers are the eyes which, over and beneath,
> The sky and sea bend on thee; which can draw,
> By sea or sky or woman, to one law,
> The allotted bondman of her palm and wreath."

For Beauty, as Plato has told us, is of all the divine ideas at once most manifest and most loveable to men. When "Justice and Wisdom and all other things that are held in honour of souls" are hidden from the worshipper's gaze, as finding no avenue of sense by which to reach him through the veil of flesh, Beauty has still some passage and entrance from mortal eyes to eyes, "and he that gazed so earnestly on what things in that holy place were to be seen, he when he discerns on earth some godlike countenance or fashion of body, that counterfeits Beauty well, first of all he trembles, and there comes over him something of the fear which erst he knew; but then, looking on that earthly beauty, he worships it as divine, and if he did not fear the reproach of utter madness he would sacrifice to his heart's idol as to the image and presence of a god."

> "This is that Lady Beauty, in whose praise
> Thy voice and hand shake still—long known to thee
> By flying hair and fluttering hem—the beat
> Following her daily of thy heart and feet,
> How passionately and irretrievably,
> In what fond flight, how many ways and days!"

There are some few hearts, no doubt, in which "sky and sea" and the face of Nature are able to inspire this yearning passion. But with this newer school—with Rossetti especially—we feel at once that Nature is no more than an accessory. The most direct appeals, the most penetrating reminiscences, come to the worshipper of Beauty from a woman's eyes. The steady rise in the status of women; that constant deepening and complication of the commerce between the sexes which is one of the signs of progressive civilisation; all this is perpetually teaching and preaching (if I may say so) the charms of womanhood to all sections of the community. What a difference in this respect has the century since Turner's birth made in England! If another Turner were born now—an eye which gazed, as it were, on a new-created planet from the very bedchamber and outgoing of the sun—can we suppose that such an eye would still find its most attractive feminine type in the bumboats of Wapping? The anomaly, strange enough in Turner's day, is now inconceivable. Our present danger lies in just the opposite direction. We are in danger of losing that direct and straightforward outlook on human loveliness (of which Mr. Millais may serve as a modern example) which notes and represents the object with a frank enjoyment, and seeks for no further insight into the secret of its charm. All the arts, in fact, are returning now to the spirit of Leonardo, to the sense that of all visible objects known to us the human face and form are the most complex and mysterious, to the desire to extract the utmost secret, the occult message, from all the phenomena of Life and Being.

Now there is at any rate one obvious explanation of the sense of mystery which attaches to the female form. We may interpret it all as in some way a transformation of the sexual passion. This essentially materialistic view is surrounded with a kind of glamour by such writers as Gautier and Baudelaire. The tone of sentiment thus generated is repugnant—is sometimes even nauseating—to English feeling; but this tone of sentiment is certainly not Rossetti's. There is no trace in him of this deliberate worship of Baal and Ashtoreth; no touch of the cruelty which is the characteristic note of natures in which the sexual instincts have become haunting and dominant.

It is, indeed, at the opposite end of the scale—among those who meet the mysteries of love and womanhood with a very different interpretation— that Rossetti's nearest affinities are to be found. It must not be forgotten that one of his most exquisite literary achievements consists in a translation of the *Vita Nuova* of Dante. Now, the *Vita Nuova*, to the vulgar reader a childish or meaningless tale, is to those who rightly apprehend it the very gospel and charter of mystical passion. When the child Dante trembles at the first sight of the child Beatrice; when the voice within him cries *Ecce deus fortior me, qui veniens dominabitur mihi*; when that majestic spirit passes, at a look of the beloved one, through all the upward or downward trajectory between heaven and hell; this, indeed, is a love which appertains to the category of reasoned affections no more; its place is with the visions of saints, the intuitions of philosophers, in Plato's ideal world. It is recognised as a secret which none can hope to fathom till we can discern from some mount of unearthly vision what those eternal things were indeed to which somewhat in human nature blindly perceived itself akin.

The parallel between Rossetti and Dante must not be pushed too far. Rossetti is but as a Dante still in the *selva oscura*; he has not sounded hell so profoundly, nor mounted into heaven so high. He is not a prophet but an artist; yet an artist who, both by the very intensity of his artistic vision, and by some inborn bent towards symbol and mysticism, stands on the side of those who see in material things a spiritual significance, and utters words of universal meaning from the fulness of his own heart. Yet he is, it must be repeated, neither prophet, philosopher, nor saint. The basis of his love is the normal emotion—"the delight in beauty alloyed with appetite, and strengthened by the alloy";—and although that love has indeed learned, in George Eliot's words, to "acknowledge an effect from the imagined light of unproven firmaments, and have its scale set to the grander orbit of what hath been and shall be," this transfiguration is effected not so much by any elevation of ethical feeling, as by the mere might and potency of an ardent spirit which projects itself with passionate intensity among things unreachable and unknown. To him his beloved one seems not as herself alone, "but as the meaning of all things that are"; her voice recalls a prenatal memory, and her eyes "dream against a distant goal." We hear little of the intellectual aspects of passion, of the subtle interaction of one character on another, of the modes in which Love possesses himself of the eager or the reluctant heart. In these poems the lovers have lost their idiosyncrasies; they are made at one for ever; the two streams have mingled only to become conscious that they are being drawn together into a boundless sea. Nay, the very passion which serves to unite them, and which is sometimes dwelt on with an Italian emphasis of sensuousness which our English reserve condemns, tends oftener to merge itself in the mystic companionship which holds the two souls together in their enchanted land.

> "One flame-winged brought a white-winged harp-player
>   Even where my lady and I lay all alone;
>   Saying: 'Behold, this minstrel is unknown;
> Bid him depart, for I am minstrel here;
> Only my strains are to Love's dear ones dear.'
>   Then said I: 'Through thine haut-boy's rapturous tone
>   Unto my lady still this harp makes moan,
> And still she deems the cadence deep and clear.'
>
> "Then said my lady: 'Thou art Passion of Love,
>   And this Love's Worship; both he plights to me
>   Thy mastering music walks the sunlit sea;
> But where wan water trembles in the grove,
> And the wan moon is all the light thereof,
>   This harp still makes my name its Voluntary.' "

The voluntaries of the white-winged harp-player do not linger long among the accidents of earth; they link with the beloved name all "the soul's sphere of infinite images," all that she finds of benign or wondrous "amid the bitterness of things occult." And as the lover moves amid these mysteries it appears to him that Love is the key which may unlock them all. For the need is not so much of an intellectual insight as of an elevation of the whole being—a rarefaction, as it were, of man's spirit which Love's pure fire effects, and which enables it to penetrate more deeply into the ideal world.

In that thin air Love undergoes a yet further transformation. The personal element, already sublimed into a mystic companionship, retires into the background. The lover is now, in Plato's words, ἐπὶ το πολὺ πέλαγος τετραμμένος τοῦ καλοῦ ; he has set sail upon the ocean of Beauty, and Love becomes the ἑρμηνεῦον καὶ διαπορθμεῦςον, the "interpreter and mediator between God and man," through whom the true prayer passes and the true revelation is made.

> "Not I myself know all my love for thee:
>   How should I reach so far, who cannot weigh
>   To-morrow's dower by gage of yesterday?
> Shall birth and death, and all dark names that be
> As doors and windows bared to some loud sea,
>   Lash deaf mine ears and blind my face with spray;
>   And shall my sense pierce love—the last relay
> And ultimate outpost of eternity?"

For thus, indeed, is Love discerned to be something which lies beyond the region of this world's wisdom or desire—something out of proportion to earthly needs and to causes that we know. Here is the point where the lover's personality seems to be exalted to its highest, and at the same moment to disappear; as he perceives that his individual emotion is merged in the flood and tideway of a cosmic law:—

> "Lo! What am I to Love, the lord of all?
>   One murmuring shell he gathers from the sand—
>   One little heart-flame sheltered in his hand.
> Yet through thine eyes he grants me clearest call
> And veriest touch of powers primordial
>   That any hour-girt life may understand."

Alas! this call, by its very nature, is heard in one heart alone; this "touch of powers primordial" is intransferable to other souls. The eyes which, to the lover's vision, "The sun-gate of the soul unbar,/Being of its furthest fires oracular," can send this message to the world only through sign and symbol; the "bower of unimagined flower and tree" is fashioned by Love in such hearts only as he has already made his own.

And thus it is that so much of Rossetti's art, in speech or colour, spends itself in the effort to communicate the incommunicable. It is toward "the vale of magical dark mysteries" that those grave low-hanging brows are bent, and "vanished hours and hours eventual" brood in the remorseful gaze of Pandora, the yearning gaze of Proserpine. The pictures that perplex us with their obvious incompleteness, their new and haunting beauty, are not the mere caprices of a richly-dowered but wandering spirit. Rather they may be called (and none the less so for their shortcomings) the sacred pictures of a new religion; forms and faces which bear the same relation to that mystical worship of Beauty on which we have dwelt so long, as the forms and faces of a Francia or a Leonardo bear to the mediæval mysteries of the worship of Mary or of Christ. And here it is that in Rossetti's pictures we find ourselves in the midst of a novel symbolism—a symbolism genuine and deeply felt as that of the fifteenth century, and using once more birds and flowers and stars, colours and lights of the evening or the dawn, to tell of beauties impalpable, spaces unfathomed, the setting and resurrection of no measurable or earthly day.

It is chiefly in a series of women's faces that these ideas seek expression. All these have something in common, some union of strange and puissant physical loveliness with depth and remoteness of gaze. They range from demon to angel—as such names may be interpreted in a Religion of Beauty— from Lilith, whose beauty is destruction, and Astarte, throned between the Sun and Moon in her sinister splendour, to the *Blessed Damozel* and the "maiden pre-elect," type of the love whose look regenerates and whose assumption lifts to heaven. But all have the look—characteristic of Rossetti's faces as the mystic smile of Leonardo's—the look which bids the spectator murmur—

> "What netherworld gulf-whispers doth she hear,
>   In answering echoes from what planisphere,
>   Along the wind, along the estuary?"

And since these primal impulses, at any rate, will remain to mankind, since Love's pathway will be retrodden by many a generation, and all of faith or knowledge to which that pathway leads will endure, it is no small part of the poet's function to show in how great a measure Love does actually pre-suppose and consist of this exaltation of the mystic element in man; and how the sense of unearthly destinies may give dignity to Love's invasion, and steadfastness to his continuance, and surround his vanishing with the mingled ecstasy of anguish and of hope. Let us trace, with Rossetti, some stages of his onward way.

The inexplicable suddenness with which Love will sometimes possess himself of two several hearts—finding a secret kinship which, like a common aroma, permeates the whole being of each—has often suggested the thought that such companionship is not in reality now first begun; that it is founded in a prenatal affection, and is the unconscious prolongation of the emotions of an ideal world—

> "Even so, when first I saw you, seemed it, love,
>   That among souls allied to mine was yet
> One nearer kindred then life hinted of.
>   O born with me somewhere that men forget,
>   And though in years of sight and sound unmet,
> Known for my soul's birth-partner well enough!"

It is thus that Rossetti traces backward the kindling of the earthly flame. And he feels also that if love be so pervading, so fateful a thing, the man who takes it upon him has much to fear. He moves among great risks; "the moon-track of the journeying face of Fate" is subject for him to strange perturbations, to terrible eclipse. What if his love be a mistake?—if he feels against his will a disenchantment stealing over the enchanted garden, and his new self walking, a ghastly intruder, among scenes vainly consecrated by an illusive past?

> "Whence came his feet into my field, and why?
> How is it that he finds it all so drear?
> How do I see his seeing, and how hear
> The name his bitter silence knows it by?"

Or what of him for whom some unforgotten hour has marred his life's best felicity, *et inquinavit aere tempus aureum?* What of the recollection that chills his freest moments with an inward and icy breath? "Look in my face, my name is Might-have-been;/I am also called No-more, Too-late, Farewell."

There is no need to invite attention to the lines which thus begin. They will summon their own auditors; they will not die till that inward Presence dies also, and there sits not at the heart of any man a memory deeper than his joy.

But over all lovers, however wisely they may love, and well, there hangs one shadow which no wisdom can avert. To one or other the shock must come, the separation which will make the survivor's afterlife seem something posthumous, and its events like the changes in a dream.

Without intruding into the private story of a life which has not yet been authoritatively recounted to us, we may recognise that on Rossetti the shock of severance, of bereavement, must have fallen with desolating force. In several of his most pregnant poems,—in the sonnets entitled *Willow-wood* most of all,—those who know the utmost anguish of yearning have listened to a voice speaking as though from their own hearts. The state of tension, indeed, which finds utterance in these sonnets is by its very nature transitory. There comes a time when most men forget. But in some hearts the change which comes over the passion of love is not decay, but transfiguration. That passion is generalised, as Plato desired that it should be generalised, though in a somewhat different way. The Platonic enthusiasm of admiration was to extend itself "from one fair form to all fair forms," and from fair forms to noble and beautiful ideas and actions, and all that is likest God. And something not unlike this takes place when the lover feels that the object of his earthly worship, now removed from his sight, is becoming identified for him with all else that he has been wont to revere—representative to him, to use Plato's words again, "of those things, by dwelling on which it is that even a god is divine." It is not, indeed, the bereaved lover only who finds in a female figure the ideal recipient of his impulses of adoring love. Of how many creeds has this been the inspiring element!—from the painter who invokes upon his canvas a Virgin revealed in sleep, to the philosopher who preaches the worship of Humanity in a woman's likeness, to be at once the Mother and the Beloved of all. Yet this ideal will operate most actively in hearts which can give to that celestial vision a remembered reality, whose "memorial threshold" seems visibly to bridge the passage between the transitory and the supernal world.

> "City, of thine a single simple door,
>   By some new Power reduplicate, must be
>   Even yet my life-porch in eternity,
>   Even with one presence filled, as once of yore;
>   Or mocking winds whirl round a chaff-strewn floor
> Thee and thy years and these my words and me."

And if sometimes this transmuted passion—this religion of beauty spiritualised into a beatific dream—should prompt to quietism rather than to vigorous action,—if sometimes we hear in the mourner's utterance a tone as of a man too weak for his destiny—this has its pathos too. For it is a part of the lot of man that the fires which purify should also consume him, and that as the lower things become distasteful the energy which seeks the higher things should fade too often into a sad repose.

> "Here with her face doth Memory sit,
>   Meanwhile, and wait the day's decline,
>   Till other eyes shall look from it—
>   Eyes of the spirit's Palestine,
>   Even than the old gaze tenderer;
>   While hopes and aims, long lost with her,
>   Stand round her image side by side,
>   Like tombs of pilgrims that have died
> About the Holy Sepulchre."

And when the dream and the legend which inspired Rossetti's boyhood with the vision of the *Blessed Damozel*—which kindled his early manhood into the sweetest *Ave* that ever saluted "Mary Virgin, full of grace"—had transformed themselves in his heart into the reality and the recollection; when Love had been made known to him by life itself and death—then he had at least gained power to show how the vaguer worship may become a concentrated expectancy: how one vanished hand may seem to offer the endless welcome, one name to symbolise all heaven, and to be in itself the single hope.

> "Ah! when the wan soul in that golden air
>   Between the scriptured petals softly blown

Peers breathless for the gift of grace unknown,—
Ah! let none other alien spell soe'er,
But only the one Hope's one name be there,—
Not less nor more, but e'en that word alone."

Enough, perhaps, has been said to indicate not only how superficial is the view which represents Rossetti as a dangerous sensualist, but also how inadequately we shall understand him if we think to find in him only the commonplaces of passion dressed out in fantastic language and Italianised allegory. There is more to be learnt from him than this, though it be too soon, as yet, to discern with exactness his place in the history of our time. Yet we may note that his sensitive and reserved individuality; his life, absorbed in Art, and aloof from—without being below—the circles of politics or fashion; his refinement, created as it were from within, and independent of conventional models, point him out as a member of that new aristocracy of which we have already spoken, that *optimacy* of passion and genius (if we may revive an obsolete word to express a new shade of meaning) which is coming into existence as a cosmopolitan gentility among the confused and fading class-distinctions of the past. And, further, we may observe in him the reaction of Art against Materialism, which becomes more marked as the dominant tone of science grows more soulless and severe. The instincts which make other men Catholics, Ritualists, Hegelians, have compelled him, too, to seek "the meaning of all things that are" elsewhere than in the behaviour of ether and atoms, though we can track his revelation to no source more explicit than the look in a woman's eyes.

But if we ask—and it was one of the questions with which we started—what encouragement the moralist can find in this counter-wave of art and mysticism which meets the materialistic tide, there is no certain or easy answer. The one view of life seems as powerless as the other to supply that antique and manly virtue which civilisation tends to undermine by the lessening effort that it exacts of men, the increasing enjoyment that it offers to them. "Time has run back and fetched the age of gold," in the sense that the opulent can now take life as easily as it was taken in Paradise; and Rossetti's poems, placed beside Sidney's or Lovelace's, seem the expression of a century which is refining itself into quietism and mellowing into decay.

Yet thus much we may safely affirm, that if we contrast æstheticism with pure hedonism—the pursuit of pleasure through art with the pursuit of pleasure simply as pleasure—the one has a tendency to quicken and exalt, as the other to deaden and vulgarise, the emotions and appetencies of man. If only the artist can keep clear of the sensual selfishness which will, in its turn, degrade the art which yields to it; if only he can worship beauty with a strong and single heart, his emotional nature will acquire a grace and elevation which are not, indeed, identical with the elevation of virtue, the grace of holiness, but which are none the less a priceless enrichment of the complex life of man. Rossetti could never have summoned us to the clear heights of Wordsworth's *Laodamia*. Yet who can read the *House of Life* and not feel that the poet has known Love as Love can be—not an enjoyment only or a triumph, but a worship and a regeneration; Love not fleeting nor changeful, but "far above all passionate winds of welcome and farewell"; Love offering to the soul no mere excitation and by-play, but "a heavenly solstice, hushed and halcyon"; Love whose "hours elect in choral consonancy" bear with them nothing that is vain or vulgar, common or unclean. He must have felt as no passing tragedy the long ache of parted pain, "the ground-whirl of the perished leaves of hope," "the sunset's desolate disarray," the fruitless striving "to wrest a bond from night's inveteracy," to behold "for once, for once alone," the unforgotten eyes re-risen from the dark of death.

Love, as Plato said, is the ἑρμηνεῦον κἀι διαπορθμεῦον, "the interpreter and mediator" between things human and things divine; and it may be to Love that we must look to teach the worshipper of Beauty that the highest things are also the loveliest, and that the strongest of moral agencies is also the most pervading and keenest joy. Art and Religion, which no compression could amalgamate, may by Love be expanded and interfused; and thus the poet may not err so wholly who seeks in a woman's eyes "the meaning of all things that are"; and "the soul's sphere of infinite images" may not be a mere prismatic fringe to reality, but rather those images may be as dark rays made visible by passing through the medium of a mind which is fitted to refract and reflect them.

A faint, a fitful reflex! Whether it be from light of sun or of moon, *sole repercussum aut radiantis imagine lunae*,—the glimmer of a vivifying or of a phantom day—may scarcely be for us to know. But never yet has the universe been proved smaller than the conceptions of man, whose farthest, deepest speculation has only found *within* him yet profounder abysses,—*without*, a more unfathomable heaven.

Dante Gabriel Rossetti

Walter Pater

It was characteristic of a poet who had ever something about him of mystic isolation, and will still appeal perhaps, though with a name it may seem now established in English literature, to a special and limited audience, that some of his poems had won a kind of exquisite fame before they were in the full sense published. *The Blessed Damozel*, although actually printed twice before the year 1870, was eagerly circulated in manuscript; and the volume which it now opens came at last to satisfy a long-standing curiosity as to the poet, whose pictures also had become an object of the same peculiar kind of interest. For those poems were the work of a painter, understood to belong to, and to be indeed the leader, of a new school then rising into note; and the reader of to-day may observe already, in *The Blessed Damozel*, written at the age of eighteen, a prefigurement of the chief characteristics of that school, as he will recognise in it also, in proportion as he really knows Rossetti, many of the characteristics which are most markedly personal and his own. Common to that school and to him, and in both alike of primary significance, was the quality of sincerity, already felt as one of the charms of that earliest poem—a perfect sincerity, taking effect in the deliberate use of the most direct and unconventional expression, for the conveyance of a poetic sense which recognised no conventional standard of what poetry was called upon to be. At a time when poetic originality in England might seem to have had its utmost play, here was certainly one new poet more, with a structure and music of verse, a vocabulary, an accent, unmistakably novel, yet felt to be no mere tricks of manner adopted with a view to forcing attention—an accent which might rather count as the very seal of reality on one man's own proper speech; as that speech itself was the wholly natural expression of certain wonderful things he really felt and saw. Here was one, who had a matter to present to his readers, to himself at least, in the first instance, so valuable, so real and definite, that his primary aim, as regards form or expression in his verse, would be but its exact equivalence to those *data* within. That he had this gift of transparency in language—the control of a style which did but obediently shift and shape itself to the mental motion, as a well-trained hand can follow on the tracing-paper the outline of an

Reprinted from *Appreciations* (London: Macmillan, 1889), 228–42.

original drawing below it, was proved afterwards by a volume of typically perfect translations from the delightful but difficult "early Italian poets": such transparency being indeed the secret of all genuine style, of all such style as can truly belong to one man and not to another. His own meaning was always personal and even recondite, in a certain sense learned and casuistical, sometimes complex or obscure; but the term was always, one could see, deliberately chosen from many competitors, as the just transcript of that peculiar phase of soul which he alone knew, precisely as he knew it.

One of the peculiarities of *The Blessed Damozel* was a definiteness of sensible imagery, which seemed almost grotesque to some, and was strange, above all, in a theme so profoundly visionary. The gold bar of heaven from which she leaned, her hair yellow like ripe corn, are but examples of a general treatment, as naively detailed as the pictures of those early painters contemporary with Dante, who has shown a similar care for minute and definite imagery in his verse; there, too, in the very midst of profoundly mystic vision. Such definition of outline is indeed one among many points in which Rossetti resembles the great Italian poet, of whom, led to him at first by family circumstances, he was ever a lover—a "servant and singer," faithful as Dante, "of Florence and of Beatrice"—with some close inward conformities of genius also, independent of any mere circumstances of education. It was said by a critic of the last century, not wisely though agreeably to the practice of his time, that poetry rejoices in abstractions. For Rossetti, as for Dante, without question on his part, the first condition of the poetic way of seeing and presenting things is particularisation. "Tell me now," he writes, for Villon's

> "Dictes-moy où, n'en quel pays,
> Est Flora, la belle Romaine"—
>
> "Tell me now, in what hidden way is
> Lady Flora the lovely Roman:"

—"way," in which one might actually chance to meet her; the unmistakably poetic effect of the couplet in English being dependent on the definiteness of that single word (though actually lighted on in the search after a difficult double rhyme) for which every one else would have written, like Villon himself, a more general one, just equivalent to place or region.

And this delight in concrete definition is allied with another of his conformities to Dante, the really imaginative vividness, namely, of his personifications—his hold upon them, or rather their hold upon him, with the force of a Frankenstein, when once they have taken life from him. Not Death only and Sleep, for instance, and the winged spirit of Love, but certain particular aspects of them, a whole "populace" of special hours and places, "the hour" even "which might have been, yet might not be," are living creatures, with hands and eyes and articulate voices.

"Stands it not by the door—
Love's Hour—till she and I shall meet;
With bodiless form and unapparent feet
That cast no shadow yet before,
Though round its head the dawn begins to pour
The breath that makes day sweet?"—

"Nay, why
Name the dead hours? I mind them well:
Their ghosts in many darkened doorways dwell
With desolate eyes to know them by."

Poetry as a *mania*—one of Plato's two higher forms of "divine" mania—has, in all its species, a mere insanity incidental to it, the "defect of its quality," into which it may lapse in its moment of weakness; and the insanity which follows a vivid poetic anthropomorphism like that of Rossetti may be noted here and there in his work, in a forced and almost grotesque materialising of abstractions, as Dante also became at times a mere subject of the scholastic realism of the Middle Age.

In *Love's Nocturn* and *The Stream's Secret*, congruously perhaps with a certain feverishness of soul in the moods they present, there is at times a near approach (may it be said?) to such insanity of realism—

"Pity and love shall burn
In her pressed cheek and cherishing hands;
And from the living spirit of love that stands
Between her lips to soothe and yearn,
Each separate breath shall clasp me round in turn
And loose my spirit's bands."

But even if we concede this; even if we allow, in the very plan of those two compositions, something of the literary conceit—what exquisite, what novel flowers of poetry, we must admit them to be, as they stand! In the one, what a delight in all the natural beauty of water, all its details for the eye of a painter; in the other, how subtle and fine the imaginative hold upon all the secret ways of sleep and dreams! In both of them, with much the same attitude and tone, Love—sick and doubtful Love—would fain inquire of what lies below the surface of sleep, and below the water; stream or dream being forced to speak by Love's powerful "control"; and the poet would have it foretell the fortune, issue, and event of his wasting passion. Such artifices, indeed, were not unknown in the old Provençal poetry of which Dante had learned something. Only, in Rossetti at least, they are redeemed by a serious purpose, by that sincerity of his, which allies itself readily to a serious beauty, a sort of grandeur of literary workmanship, to a great style. One seems to hear there a really new kind of poetic utterance, with effects which have nothing else like them; as there is nothing else, for instance, like the narrative of Jacob's Dream in *Genesis*, or Blake's design of the Singing of the Morning Stars, or Addison's Nineteenth Psalm.

With him indeed, as in some revival of the old mythopœic age, common things—dawn, noon, night—are full of human or personal expression, full of sentiment. The lovely little sceneries scattered up and down his poems, glimpses of a landscape, not indeed of broad open-air effects, but rather that of a painter concentrated upon the picturesque effect of one or two selected objects at a time—the "hollow brimmed with mist," or the "ruined weir," as he sees it from one of the windows, or reflected in one of the mirrors of his "house of life" (the vignettes for instance seen by Rose Mary in the magic beryl) attest, by their very freshness and simplicity, to a pictorial or descriptive power in dealing with the inanimate world, which is certainly also one half of the charm, in that other, more remote and mystic, use of it. For with Rossetti this sense of lifeless nature after all, is translated to a higher service, in which it does but incorporate itself with some phase of strong emotion. Every one understands how this may happen at critical moments of life; what a weirdly expressive soul may have crept, even in full noonday, into "the white-flower'd elder-thicket," when Godiva saw it "gleam through the Gothic archways in the wall," at the end of her terrible ride. To Rossetti it is so always, because to him life is a crisis at every moment. A sustained impressibility towards the mysterious conditions of man's everyday life, towards the very mystery itself in it, gives a singular gravity to all his work: those matters never became trite to him. But throughout, it is the ideal intensity of love—of love based upon a perfect yet peculiar type of physical or material beauty—which is enthroned in the midst of those mysterious powers; Youth and Death, Destiny and Fortune, Fame, Poetic Fame, Memory, Oblivion, and the like. Rossetti is one of those who, in the words of Mérimée, *se passionnent pour la passion*, one of Love's lovers.

And yet, again as with Dante, to speak of his ideal type of beauty as material, is partly misleading. Spirit and matter, indeed, have been for the most part opposed, with a false contrast or antagonism, by schoolmen, whose artificial creation those abstractions really are. In our actual concrete experience, the two trains of phenomena which the words *matter* and *spirit* do but roughly distinguish, play inextricably into each other. Practically, the church of the Middle Age by its æsthetic worship, its sacramentalism, its real faith in the resurrection of the flesh, had set itself against that Manichean opposition of spirit and matter, and its results in men's way of taking life; and in this, Dante is the central representative of its spirit. To him, in the vehement and impassioned heat of his conceptions, the material and the spiritual are fused and blent: if the spiritual attains the definite visibility of a crystal, what is material loses its earthiness and impurity. And here again, by force of instinct, Rossetti is one with him. His chosen type of beauty is one, "Whose speech Truth knows not from her thought,/Nor

Love her body from her soul." Like Dante, he knows no region of spirit which shall not be sensuous also, or material. The shadowy world, which he realises so powerfully, has still the ways and houses, the land and water, the light and darkness, the fire and flowers, that had so much to do in the moulding of those bodily powers and aspects which counted for so large a part of the soul, here.

For Rossetti, then, the great affections of persons to each other, swayed and determined, in the case of his highly pictorial genius, mainly by that so-called material loveliness, formed the great undeniable reality in things, the solid resisting substance, in a world where all beside might be but shadow. The fortunes of those affections—of the great love so determined; its casuistries, its languor sometimes; above all, its sorrows; its fortunate or unfortunate collisions with those other great matters; how it looks, as the long day of life goes round, in the light and shadow of them: all this, conceived with an abundant imagination, and a deep, a philosophic, reflectiveness, is the matter of his verse, and especially of what he designed as his chief poetic work, "a work to be called *The House of Life*," towards which the majority of his sonnets and songs were contributions.

The dwelling-place in which one finds oneself by chance or destiny, yet can partly fashion for oneself; never properly one's own at all, if it be changed too lightly; in which every object has its associations—the dim mirrors, the portraits, the lamps, the books, the hair-tresses of the dead and visionary magic crystals in the secret drawers, the names and words scratched on the windows, windows open upon prospects the saddest or the sweetest; the house one must quit, yet taking perhaps, how much of its quietly active light and colour along with us!—grown now to be a kind of raiment to one's body, as the body, according to Swedenborg, is but the raiment of the soul— under that image, the whole of Rossetti's work might count as a *House of Life*, of which he is but the "Interpreter." And it is a "haunted" house. A sense of power in love, defying distance, and those barriers which are so much more than physical distance, of unutterable desire penetrating into the world of sleep, however "lead-bound," was one of those anticipative notes obscurely struck in *The Blessed Damozel*, and, in his later work, makes him speak sometimes almost like a believer in mesmerism. Dream-land, as we said, with its "phantoms of the body," deftly coming and going on love's service, is to him, in no mere fancy or figure of speech, a real country, a veritable expansion of, or addition to, our waking life; and he did well perhaps to wait carefully upon sleep, for the lack of it became mortal disease with him. One may even recognise a sort of morbid and over-hasty making-ready for death itself, which increases on him; thoughts concerning it, its imageries, coming with a frequency and importunity, in excess, one might think, of even the very saddest, quite wholesome wisdom.

And indeed the publication of his second volume of *Ballads and Sonnets* preceded his death by scarcely a twelvemonth. That volume bears witness to the reverse of any failure of power, or falling-off from his early standard of literary perfection, in every one of his then accustomed forms of poetry— the song, the sonnet, and the ballad. The newly printed sonnets, now completing the *House of Life*, certainly advanced beyond those earlier ones, in clearness; his dramatic power in the ballad, was here at its height; while one monumental, gnomic piece, *Soothsay*, testifies, more clearly even than the *Nineveh* of his first volume, to the reflective force, the dry reason, always at work behind his imaginative creations, which at no time dispensed with a genuine intellectual structure. For in matters of pure reflection also, Rossetti maintained the painter's sensuous clearness of conception; and this has something to do with the capacity, largely illustrated by his ballads, of telling some red-hearted story of impassioned action with effect.

Have there, in very deed, been ages, in which the external conditions of poetry such as Rossetti's were of more spontaneous growth than in our own? The archaic side of Rossetti's work, his preferences in regard to earlier poetry, connect him with those who have certainly thought so, who fancied they could have breathed more largely in the age of Chaucer, or of Ronsard, in one of those ages, in the words of Stendhal—*ces siècles de passions où les âmes pouvaient se livrer franchement à la plus haute exaltation, quand les passions qui font la possibilité comme les sujets des beaux arts existaient* [those passionate centuries where souls were able to raise themselves openly to the highest exaltation, when the passions existed which make the possibility as well as the subjects of the fine arts]. We may think, perhaps, that such old time as that has never really existed except in the fancy of poets; but it was to find it, that Rossetti turned so often from modern life to the chronicle of the past. Old Scotch history, perhaps beyond any other, is strong in the matter of heroic and vehement hatreds and love, the tragic Mary herself being but the perfect blossom of them; and it is from that history that Rossetti has taken the subjects of the two longer ballads of his second volume: of the three admirable ballads in it, *The King's Tragedy* (in which Rossetti has dexterously interwoven some relics of James's own exquisite early verse) reaching the highest level of dramatic success, and marking perfection, perhaps, in this kind of poetry; which, in the earlier volume, gave us, among other pieces, *Troy Town, Sister Helen,* and *Eden Bower.*

Like those earlier pieces, the ballads of the second volume bring with them the question of the poetic value of the "refrain"—"Eden bower's in flower:/And O the bower and the hour!"—and the like. Two of those ballads—*Troy Town* and *Eden Bower,* are terrible in theme; and the refrain serves, perhaps, to relieve their bold aim at the sentiment of terror. In *Sister Helen* again, the refrain has a real, and sustained purpose (being here duly varied also) and performs the part of a chorus, as the story proceeds. Yet even in these cases, whatever its effect may be in actual recitation, it may fairly be questioned, whether, to the mere reader their actual effect is not that of a positive interruption and drawback, at least in pieces so lengthy; and Rossetti himself, it would seem, came to think so, for in the shortest of his later ballads, *The White Ship*—that old true history of the generosity with which a youth, worthless in life, flung himself upon death—he was contented with a single utterance of the refrain, "given out" like the keynote or tune of a chant.

In *The King's Tragedy*, Rossetti has worked upon motive, broadly human (to adopt the phrase of popular criticism) such as one and all may realise. Rossetti, indeed, with all his self-concentration upon his own peculiar aim, by no means ignored those general interests which are external to poetry as he conceived it; as he has shown here and there, in this poetic, as also in pictorial, work. It was but that, in a life to be shorter even than the average, he found enough to occupy him in the fulfilment of a task, plainly "given him to do." Perhaps, if one had to name a single composition of his to readers desiring to make acquaintance with him for the first time, one would select: *The King's Tragedy*—that poem so moving, so popularly dramatic, and lifelike. Notwithstanding this, his work, it must be conceded, certainly through no narrowness or egotism, but in the faithfulness of a true workman to a vocation so emphatic, was mainly of the esoteric order. But poetry, at all times, exercises two distinct functions: it may reveal, it may unveil to every eye, the ideal aspects of common things, after Gray's way (though Gray too, it is well to remember, seemed in his own day, seemed even to Johnson, obscure) or it may actually add to the number of motives poetic and uncommon in themselves, by the imaginative creation of things that are ideal from their very birth. Rossetti did something, something excellent, of the former kind; but his characteristic, his really revealing work, lay in the adding to poetry of fresh poetic material, of a new order of phenomena, in the creation of a new ideal.

RECENT STUDIES

◆

Problems of Form and Content in the Poetry of Dante Gabriel Rossetti

HAROLD L. WEATHERBY

The most significant problem, I think, in coming to an accurate estimate of Rossetti's poetry is that of the relationship between form and content. Critics have consistently found him cloying on account of two things—the sensuous nature of his material and the highly wrought, often overwrought, surface of the poetry itself, and though neither objection should hold much weight in a century which has grown accustomed to the overt sexuality of Lawrence and the difficult syntax of Eliot, Rossetti still seems unsatisfactory to many of our contemporaries. The reason, I think, is not far to seek; it rests in the fact that Rossetti often failed to work out a proper relationship between what he had to say and the way he went about saying it. This failure may be a private one—a weakness in Rossetti's poetic sensibility, but I doubt if that is the whole of it. To be sure he lacks the general stature of Tennyson, Browning, and Arnold, but so does a poet like Gerard Manley Hopkins whose work is no less complete on account of its limitations. Rossetti's difficulty is more profound and hence more interesting than any weakness of his own. It is essentially the difficulty that beset the Victorian art for art's sake movement—the failure of content, the failure of meaning, the failure of traditional symbols to function properly when they were cut loose from the belief in spiritual realities which originally produced them.

One of the most peculiar qualities of Pre-Raphaelite art is the way in which highly realistic and deliberately allegorical details are combined. One is reminded at once of Holman Hunt's *The Light of the World* in which the strikingly realistic figure of Christ holds up an equally striking but thoroughly symbolic lantern; or of Rossetti's *The Girlhood of Mary Virgin* in which the medieval Madonna is replaced by Christina, but Christina with a halo set against a conscious attempt at a medieval backdrop. Or there is *The Blessed Damozel* (painting and poem) with her warm breast against the bar of heaven. In each of these cases we are confronted with a problem of definition, for to put it quite simply neither subject nor attitude toward the subject

Reprinted from *Victorian Poetry* 2 (1964): 11–19, by permission of the journal.

lends itself to a simple analysis. In Hunt's *The Light of the World*, for instance, it is very difficult to say whether the *light* is Jesus, with his glowing halo, or the lantern which he holds; if it is the latter, with its apertures in the shapes of moons and stars, we are faced with the further difficulty of deciding what this lantern is intended to represent, and if the former, how this thoroughly untraditional figure of Christ is to be interpreted. In short, the central conception of the painting blurs.

The same problem confronts us in much of Rossetti's early poetry. In "My Sister's Sleep," for instance, the sharp details of the death scene—the firelight reflected in the mirror, the click of needles and rustle of a skirt—contribute to an impression of Zolaesque precision in the recording of life. Yet these details are set in a quasi-supernatural frame—the scraping of chairs in the room above and the peculiarly appropriate hour of the death. We are left wondering whether the poem is supposed to be a realistic portrayal of a young girl's death or whether it is a symbolic study having something vaguely to do with "Christ's blessing on the newly born!" Like Hunt's painting the poem blurs upon our vision because it lacks an integrity of focus, and yet, also like Hunt's painting, it represents an attempt at a highly formalized sort of art. Consider for a moment the last line of "My Sister's Sleep," "Christ's blessing on the newly born!" In terms of the poem itself this is precisely the right ending. It fills out the pattern, places the last thread in the tapestry, and points up very neatly the suggested parallel between the death of the sister (by implication her rebirth) and the birth of Christ. However, as soon as any sort of experience foreign to the immediate text of the poem intrudes itself, and whenever we are confronted with a symbol as rich in allusion as the birth of Christ, external experience will perforce intrude, the threads unravel. In fact the heightening of meaning which the Christmas morning setting could provide, either directly or ironically, in a thoroughly unified poem would be an immeasurable asset. However, in "My Sister's Sleep" it breaks the fabric into shreds because it is never clear exactly where the poem stands. The sharp realism of detail renders a willing suspension of disbelief impossible, but on the other hand Rossetti makes no attempt whatever to use his religious effects for an ironic purpose. It is possible for Beatrice to function in a divine context not only because she never appears in company with a set of knitting needles but (and this is a corollary) because the reality of the spiritual stands at the center of Dante's conception. Dismissing for a moment the questions of whether or what Rossetti believed, the reality of the Christian allusion in "My Sister's Sleep" is highly questionable. What we believe in here is the firelight and the rustling skirt; the Christmas morning setting looks suspiciously like decoration, like an embellishment which Rossetti adds to otherwise photographic realism in order to qualify the representation for the name of "poem"—in short, to give it a form.

By way of contrast, one is reminded of Hardy's "The Oxen":

> Yet, I feel,
> If someone said on Christmas Eve,
> "Come; see the oxen kneel,
>
> "In the lonely barton by yonder coomb
> Our childhood used to know,"
> I should go with him in the gloom,
> Hoping it might be so.

Hardy's details are no less realistic than Rossetti's; but his attitude toward the supernatural event is clearly defined. Consequently the Christmas allusion, in contrast with the presumed "facts" of the case, helps to focus the whole poem on the poignant longing which Hardy is writing about. Rossetti is neither supremely concerned with spiritual reality as is Dante, nor the loss of it, as is Hardy, but with using the machinery of it for artistic effect. Consequently he succeeds in creating a form but not in avoiding the disintegration which results from failure of meaning.

If it is objected that I have raised up in Hardy and Dante poets too radically different in quality and kind to be spoken of in the same breath, or that I have further offended by using them as cannons against a butterfly (the poem, not Rossetti), I can only plead the value of illuminating contrasts wherever they may be found. It is always tempting to compare Rossetti with his namesake, and though "My Sister's Sleep" is not really Dantesque at all, the problems which it raises do shed light upon similar problems in Rossetti's more florid Italianate poetry. One might also say "problem," for there is really a single difficulty underlying all Rossetti's failures to establish proper relationships between content and form—the unresolved question of whether or not there is such a thing as a spiritual reality. Hardy, a product of the same scientifically sceptical age as Rossetti, assumed, albeit ruefully, the non-existence of the supernatural and on the basis of such an assumption was able to write thoroughly satisfactory if somewhat limited poems. Rossetti, one feels, tried to make poetic use of the supernatural and the spiritual without ever believing in it.

A comment on Rossetti by Watts-Dunton throws some oblique light on this subject: "To eliminate asceticism from romantic art, and yet to remain romantic, to retain that *mysticism* which alone can give life to romantic art, and yet to be as *sensuous* as the Titians who revived *sensuousness* at the sacrifice of *mysticism*, was the quest, more or less conscious, of Rossetti's genius."[1] What Watts-Dunton is saying, I take it, is that Rossetti was attempting to give a sensuous form to a mystical reality in an effort to avoid total commitment to romantic subjectivism which we may suggest, at the risk of a specious generalization, was what all of the formalistic tendencies in Pre-Raphaelite art are aimed at. Or as Baum puts it: "In seeking to give expression to the real which lies behind the actual, the poet must frankly undertake to 'communicate the incommunicable,' and this he does by the use of symbols" (p. 23). This is all very well, almost an aesthetic truism, but it fails to work if the symbol is allowed to replace the reality which is symbolized. Here, as Baum admits, falls Rossetti—at least part of the time; and it is tempting to suggest (and Baum does not really consider this possibility) that his failure is as much a religious or metaphysical as it is a poetic problem. In short, to create a symbolic representation of a mystical reality which is not really believed to be real is difficult: and the problem confronts Rossetti again and again. In "The Blessed Damozel," for instance, once we attempt to transcend its purely formal attributes, it becomes very difficult to speak intelligently about the supposedly supernatural machinery of the piece. For one thing Rossetti's cosmology is hopelessly jumbled, and it becomes readily apparent that far from attempting a serious symbolic representation of heaven and earth he is using the whole scheme for something very close to the purposes of decoration. Not that he necessarily should be endeavoring to justify the ways of God to man, but cosmologies, like Christmas eves, refuse to be used indiscriminately. Traditional meanings attach themselves and demand more serious consideration than can ever be implicit in a warm breast and a few artistic tears.

All of this points to the central weakness in "The Blessed Damozel"— the problem of meaning in relationship to the reality or unreality of the supernatural. Whether we are to take the portrait literally or not (the woman, lilies, and stars comprise a portrait within the poem) is never clear. The passages in parenthesis, the lover's, presumably the poet's, thoughts, ought to provide a key for our understanding, but they are contradictory. "I saw her smile," and "I heard her tears," are balanced against "her hair / Fell all about my face . . . / Nothing: the autumn-fall of leaves." It is impossible to tell exactly what Rossetti expects us to believe or disbelieve, for the poem is neither fully committed to the supernatural ("I heard her tears"), nor ironically detached ("Nothing: the autumn-fall of leaves"). The structure of the piece is very neat, and in so far as there is a kind of abstract geometric beauty in well-constructed rhetorical and metaphoric patterns it is beautiful. But it will not sustain analysis because it has, finally, no center—no commitment to any single conception of values. We believe in the symbolic reality of Milton's cosmos even though we recognize the fact that the whole fabric is a representation, not to be taken altogether literally, of something which is to mortal sight inconceivable. But we believe in it for that very reason— because it assumes the reality of the thing symbolized. With Rossetti, on the other hand, it is never quite clear whether we have to do with anything real at all—even the falling leaves, even the grief, are artistic constructs, matters of form.[2]

It is this weakness of meaning, this lack of faith in the reality of his material, which is responsible for many of our current objections to his work. His surfaces seem overwrought, not because they are, comparatively speaking, exceedingly ornate but because there is often no solid fabric beneath them; and his love poetry seems unhealthily sensuous because the physical fact is not always redeemed by the idea. The easiest way to illustrate what Rossetti was aiming at when he failed is to cite Baum's discussion of one of his successes, or near successes:

> Sweet dimness of her loosened hair's downfall
>   About thy face; her sweet hands round thy head
>   In gracious fostering union garlanded;
> Her tremulous smiles; her glances' sweet recall
> Of love; her murmuring sighs memorial;
>   Her mouth's culled sweetness by thy kisses shed
>   On cheeks and neck and eyelids, and so led
> Back to her mouth which answers there for all:—
>
> What sweeter than these things, except the thing
>   In lacking which all these would lose their sweet:—
>   The confident heart's still fervour: the swift beat
> And soft subsidence of the spirit's wing,
> Then when it feels, in cloud-girt wayfaring,
>   The breath of kindred plumes against its feet?
>
> (House of Life XXI)

As Baum suggests, the intention in love poetry of this sort is not only to depict the human experience but to use the flesh in order to show forth the spirit (Baum, pp. 23–24). But if we read only the octave of "Love's Sweetness," it becomes amply clear what happens when the symbol is substituted for the thing symbolized. It is not that the "fleshly" passage is indecently frank and needs spiritual validation for the sake of propriety but that the content does not justify the metaphoric and syntactical elaborations. Without some validating idea to relate, "in gracious fostering union garlanded" degenerates into just so much unnecessary ornamentation. When we realize however, and the sestet as Baum notes makes the matter clear, that the "gracious fostering union" has multiple ramifications in the mysterious realms of spiritual love and that it does not simply describe a physical embrace, the linguistic complexity is validated. In fact, the sestet operates in a kind of fugal relationship to the octave and provides thereby as a point of unity for the whole sonnet the analogy of physical and spiritual experience. In a sonnet like "Through Death to Love," however, with its highly ornate imagery and virtually intolerable syntax,

> Like labor-laden moonclouds faint to flee
>   From winds that sweep the winter-bitten wold,—
>   Like multiform circumfluence manifold
> Of night's flood-tide,
>
> (House of Life XLI)

one feels again that Rossetti is simply decorating, as if he were unable, in the absence of an inherited and believed theological structure like that which sustains Dante in both his sonnets and his *Comedy*, to maintain for any extended period the mystical understanding of the relationship between body and soul which is absolutely necessary for the kind of love poetry which *The House of Life* attempts to be.

Rossetti's successes, like his failures, are not, however, limited to his sonnets or even to his love poetry. When he has a subject in which he either thoroughly believes or believes enough to engage with a thorough aesthetic commitment, he is apt to succeed admirably. In a poem like "Jenny," for instance, all Victorian objections notwithstanding, there is little trace of cloying, overwrought sensuousness. To be sure we have a realistic, even a sordid scene, rendered at times in elaborate images:

> Poor flower left torn since yesterday
> Until to-morrow leave you bare;
> Poor handful of bright spring-water
> Flung in the whirlpool's shrieking face.
> (ll. 14–17)

But there is no attempt to confuse the real and the ideal, no sentimentalizing about whoredom: "Whose person or whose purse may be/The lodestar of your reverie?" (ll. 20–21).

The gold coins which provide a metaphor, "A Danaë for a moment there," are still coins and payment to a prostitute if not for the act of prostitution; the idealizing tendency of the metaphor is countered with an honest allusion to the fact. One feels that Rossetti is deeply and honestly involved in his subject—the ugliness of prostitution in contrast with the beauty of the woman—"Poor shameful Jenny, full of grace," and it is revealing, in light of Rossetti's success in this poem, that "Jenny" does not commit him to the specific use of any sort of spiritual machinery. Consequently he is never drawn into the trap of decorating his design with symbols which fail to convince.

This withdrawal from religion as poetic artifice is carried still further in "The Burden of Nineveh" where, in fact, the very rudiments of religious thought are questioned.

> Those heavy wings spread high,
> So sure of flight, which do not fly;
> That set gaze never on the sky;
> Those scriptured flanks it cannot see;
>
> Its crown, a brow-contracting load;
> Its planted feet which trust the sod: . . .

(So grew the image as I trod:)
O Nineveh, was this thy God,—
Thine also, mighty Nineveh?

(ll. 192–200)

Nineveh's pagan burden has become London's—a thoroughly sceptical sort of idea. The poem probes at doubt, moving in something of the same direction that Arnold takes (and later in a different type of poetry, Hardy), and though the result of thorough scepticism is likely to be a very limited kind of poetry, and though we can always hope for better, it may be the only kind possible in an age like Rossetti's. Certainly it is preferable to a poetry of spiritual ornament without spiritual content. Possibly its only alternative is the extreme of romantic subjectivism in which all experience is validated by the poet's feeling, and certainly the whole movement of the age after Arnold was away from that toward its classical opposite. At any rate, Rossetti, with his dedication to form would not be likely to revert altogether to an *In Memoriam* "life drama" kind of poetry. His horizons were therefore very limited, for neither Dantesque Christian Platonism nor romantic mysticism were really available to him, and when he tried to make use of an approximation of the former, he failed—simply because he was out of his element. His only recourse, really, was to turn to a different kind of poetry altogether, poetry of a critical quality like Arnold's and Browning's, like "Jenny" and "The Burden of Nineveh."

The peculiar and perhaps unfortunate thing about Rossetti, however, is that he had a strong predilection for the supernatural, as strong indeed as his predilection for the flesh (and the two go hand in hand). The critical detachment of an Arnold or a Browning was not native to him, and though their type of poetry is probably the most successful which the last half of the century produced, it is very doubtful that Rossetti could have sustained their ironic, critical vein for any prolonged endeavor. He is far more at home with a mysteriously voluptuous woman or a legion of devils than he is with an archeological specimen or even a reasonably domesticated prostitute like Jenny. What seems to have happened is that the sceptical sensibilities of the intellectual and artistic rebellion which he led (and without laboring the biographical aspects of the matter he was never a believer himself)[3] left open to him only one channel along which his fascination with the mystical could flow—the demonic, nor is this as strange as it may seem, for death is simply one aspect of the demonic, and death for Rossetti was oppressively real. If he was not sure enough about the reality of medieval hierarchies to write convincingly of a Christian heaven, he was nevertheless capable of treating physical and spiritual disintegration with great conviction. Even in his love poetry, perhaps we should say *especially* in his love poetry, even while he strives toward the idea of a perfect union and fulfillment, there is likely to be a reversion to the opposite extreme of perfect evil. In fact the figure that fascinated him most is *la belle dame sans merci*. She is scarcely hidden by "the swift heat / And soft subsidence of the spirit's wing," and she rises to full view in a poem like "The Card Dealer" in which Rossetti's propensity for juxtaposing realistic detail with supernatural machinery works to good advantage. The atmosphere of a gaming house lends itself quite well to this vision of death whose "eyes unravel the coiled night / And know the stars at noon," but the success of the poem does not depend so much upon the technique of correlating realistic with supernatural detail as upon the fact that the reality of death and hence the validity of Rossetti's symbol, is assumed from the outset—just as the heavenly redemptive reality of Dante's Beatrice is assumed. Rossetti believed in the horror which the card dealer symbolizes; the blessed damozel and her heaven are artifice.

The same assumption of reality and consequent validity of the female death symbol gives life to "The Orchard-Pit":

> My love I call her, and she loves me well:
> But I love her as in the maelstrom's cup
> The whirled stone loves the leaf inseparable
> That clings to it round all the circling swell,
> And that the same last eddy swallows up.

We are not far here from *The Picture of Dorian Gray*, and we can speculate upon the apparent fact that art must have a morality, even if it be that of demonism. If scepticism deprives poetry of a god in which it can believe strongly enough to render as a valid symbol, it may either have to revert to a morality based upon the divinity of passion (and consequently of death) or else confine itself forever to the straitened limits of Arnoldian critical canons.

This is certainly not the last word on Rossetti—only an estimate based on what seem to me the most characteristic features of his poetry. Some of his best work I have not even mentioned—"The White Ship" for instance in which Rossetti tells a good story and tells it well; or the highly ornate but very beautiful "The Stream's Secret"; or the humorous epigrammatic vein of "There's a female bard, grim as a fakier / Who daily grows shakier and shakier" ("On Christina Rossetti"). But all of these (and many more) simply indicate that Rossetti was capable both of variety and intensity, genuinely a poet, capable of rendering feeling as language. It is too often, though, exactly that and no more—just good *poetry*; he wrote only a few good *poems*. For despite his conscious efforts at the creation of poetic forms, his content, which in the final analysis is the only thing that can validate form, often failed him. Or he failed it.

Notes

1. Quoted from Watts-Dunton in the introduction to D. G. Rossetti, *The House of Life*, ed. P. F. Baum (Cambridge, Mass., 1928), p. 27—hereafter cited as Baum. (Italics mine).

2. Note that both "My Sister's Sleep" and "The Blessed Damozel" deal with purely fictitious situations and that the inspiration of the latter is largely owing to Poe, Bailey and certain early Italian poets. In short its whole conception is artistic, which may explain its tendency toward mere artifice. See notes in D. G. Rossetti, *Poems, Ballads and Sonnets*, ed. P. F. Baum (New York, 1937).

3. For one of Rossetti's few comments on Christianity see Oswald Doughty, *Dante Gabriel Rossetti, a Victorian Romantic* (New Haven, 1949), p. 575.

Rossetti's Significant Details

Jerome J. McGann

Despite the salutary, if modest, revival of interest in Pre-Raphaelite art and poetry in recent years, Dante Gabriel Rossetti and his associates remain a suburban concern of most nineteenth-century scholars. Students generally continue to follow the opinion laid down by that group of critics who, coming into prominence after World War I, made their views apparent principally by their indifference. Behind this position was the conviction that Pre-Raphaelite art and poetry only pretended to exactness: despite the wealth of detail on page and canvas, the Pre-Raphaelites rarely achieved a true artistic precision. This attitude has never been seriously questioned since, nor has the neglect of the PRB been appreciably lifted. When, for example, Dante Gabriel Rossetti's work is examined, we generally hear the traditional complaint: "A care for finish of style and polish of phrasing takes the place of a scrupulous effort at definition of meaning." Harold Weatherby's recent essay on Rossetti is largely a continuation of this melancholy long withdrawing roar. Even a mildly sympathetic critic like Graham Hough finds in Rossetti's poetry "the mere romantic confusion of unrelated notions that could only have made sense if fitted into some coherent scheme of belief."[1]

W. W. Robson's main line of attack is made upon what he (accurately, if superciliously) calls Rossetti's "Pre-Raphaelite . . . idiosyncrasies of style," for example, the "curious trick of particularizing." He cites the Blessed Damozel's three lilies and seven stars and goes on to quote several passages from "My Sister's Sleep" to show "the particularity of sensory detail, of which the thematic relevance is not obvious" (p. 355). Robson is objecting to the same things which elicit apologies from sympathetic readers like Graham Hough and provoke critics like Harold Weatherby to attack: Rossetti's failure to distinguish "between his imaginative mythology and what he regards as theological truth"; or, in an alternative phrasing, the "unhealthily sensuous" detail in a love poetry where "the physical fact is not always redeemed by the idea."[2] This basic objection can take many forms but it always comes back to the question of apparently irrelevant detail, and to the problematical status of Rossetti's Christian images and allusions. Because both of these

Reprinted from *Victorian Poetry* 7 (1969):41–54, by permission of the journal.

issues in Rossetti's poetry are intimately tied up with the nature of Pre-Raphaelitism in general, I think it important to consider them again.

Robson and Weatherby both attack "My Sister's Sleep." Robson quotes stanzas four, seven, and eight to illustrate his charge of irrelevant detail. He cannot see, for example, the point of the "cold moon" or the tropes associated with it. Weatherby goes further. He does not object to "the sharp details of the death scene," the "Zolaesque precision in the recording of life," but to the relation of these "realistic" elements to the "quasi-supernatural" details that flit through the poem and that appear to culminate in the last line. "We are left wondering whether the poem is supposed to be a realistic portrayal of a young girl's death or whether it is a symbolic study having something vaguely to do with 'Christ's blessing on the newly born!' " (p. 12). Thus "My Sister's Sleep" epitomizes one of the fundamental vices of Pre-Raphaelitism: a refusal to choose between realism and symbolism, or, alternatively, between a secular and a religious point of view.

Perhaps a genuine confusion would exist if we assumed Rossetti to be the speaker of the poem. But we know that the family is wholly imaginary, so that if we look for Rossetti it must be at one remove from the brother in the poem. Understanding this helps to explain a good deal. The brother shares the piety of his mother because they share the same milieu. Rossetti stands apart, observing. All the realistic details accumulate to form a picture of a Victorian tragedy, which is to say, of course, a sentimental tragedy. The son watches the mother with an ideal respect, and the mother attends the dying girl with a deep yet composed sympathy. She prays for her daughter but is careful not to disturb the girl's rest. If she is alert to the arrival of Christmas she seems even more concerned for her daughter's purely physical comforts. Thus, the blessing at the end does not point to a religious truth, does not serve the symbolic function that it might, but rather emphasizes the emotional state of the mother and son, the measure of comfort that they derive from a traditional religious truth at a moment of deep personal loss.

These facts reinforce the reader's sense that the mother's religious impulses are directed more toward works of mercy than toward contemplative acts, and more toward corporal rather than spiritual works of mercy. Nothing that the mother and son do or say suggests the religious attitudes which invest Dante's poetry, for example, or even Herbert's or Vaughan's. A more human, not to say homely, quality pervades the responses of the mother and her son.

But "My Sister's Sleep" is not a slice of nineteenth-century life. Detailed though it is, the poem is scarcely "Zolaesque." For one thing, the situation is too special, too idealized, and this fact brings us back to Rossetti in *propria persona*. Even though he is not the poem's speaker, we always know he is with us, and not only from the poem's contrived dramatic circumstances. Those details objected to by Robson further exemplify Rossetti's self-conscious manipulation of his materials. Like Swinburne, Morris, and certain of the Romantics, Rossetti was an accomplished master of the literary ballad, a poetic form which is subjective and lyrical in its effects but objective and narrative in its traditional form. "My Sister's Sleep" is not a literary ballad, but it is like that peculiar genre in that it ought to have complete dramatic objectivity but doesn't. Despite all the sharp detail, the figures in Rossetti's poem are distillates. They represent Rossetti's conception of a certain kind of personality who can maintain religious ideas and forms and yet whose essential worthiness has little to do with these things. The mother is an ideal figure not because she is pious, and not in spite of her piety, but because her strictly human feelings—both for her family and her traditions—are deep and committed.

Rossetti creates this impression by constantly subordinating the specifically religious details in the poem to the "realistic," or at least a-religious, details. Harold Weatherby sees this clearly when he says: "What we believe in is the firelight and the rustling skirt; the Christmas morning looks suspiciously like decoration" (p. 13). But Weatherby misinterprets the status of the religious imagery in supposing it to have a merely decorative function. As he is himself aware, none of the religious details will yield a precise religious meaning, none of them will symbolize. Yet religious imagery must do this if it is to suggest transcendentals. Similarly, the contrived religious situation itself refuses to be explicated in terms of religious symbolism. For this reason Weatherby finds it vague. On the contrary, the very refusal of the traditional materials to operate in an expected way is so startling that it forces us to see the importance which Rossetti attaches to the pure, and non-symbolic, detail. What Weatherby calls Rossetti's "realism" is, as he sees, the poem's primary value; what he does not see is that the surprising manipulation of the traditional imagery contributes to this result.

This fact is graphically shown in stanzas four to eight where Rossetti concentrates the poem's most sensational images. The management here seems to me brilliant. In the first three stanzas Rossetti introduces the religious motif definitively, but he also surrounds it with such a weight of purely physical details that its integrity is undercut. After leaving the religious idea out of stanza three altogether, Rossetti reintroduces it into stanza four in a minor key.

> Without there was a cold moon up,
> Of winter radiance sheer and thin;
> The hollow halo it was in
> Was like an icy crystal cup.

These tropes have an inherent religious urgency which is only increased by the context, by the religious motif present from the first line. The stanza is an artistic triumph because it succeeds in sterilizing completely the religious potency of the images. Rossetti's art here is highly self-conscious: he wants us to seek and fail to find the religious "meaning" in his stanza, and failing to find it, to recognize the purely sensational value of the lines. By this we are brought to an unexpected experience. Phenomena—things, people, places, images—are restored to a kind of innocence. Saved from their overlay of traditional symbolism, the items of experience can again be, as it were, simply themselves.

The succeeding stanzas reemphasize this fact. Stanza five offers a series of images which have no symbolic potential at all. When we encounter the symbolically suggestive tropes at the end of stanzas six and seven, then, we come to realize that Rossetti does not want us to symbolize, indeed, is teaching us how to respond immediately rather than to seek for meanings. Like the "halo" and the "crystal cup," these later images are purified of any possible religious content which they vaguely suggest. They bravely resist all attempts at spiritual exegesis. Stanza eight epitomizes the entire process: the silence, so complete, isolates the noise of the silk dress and thereby focuses our attention wholly upon it. We cannot push beyond the immediate experience to some deeper content awaiting exposure below. Significance is in the sensation, and the "idea" redeemed by the poem is exactly that. In this way does the poem so effectively evoke the feeling of grief: Rossetti keeps the scene uncontaminated by intellectual significances, emphasizes its sensational aspects, thence the emotional drama, and ultimately the fundamentally affective quality of the mother's and son's thoughts.

A huge cultural gap separates this work from the intellectual passions of the poets of the sixteenth and seventeenth centuries. Nevertheless, Rossetti's poem is itself basically intellectual in the sense that he does not want his reader simply to respond to the poem's sentimental drama. Rather, the poem basically seeks to tell us how to renew our capacity for fresh experience. Rossetti accomplishes this by manipulating his materials in a startling way: thereby we are not only driven to a new perspective, we are also forced to a clear consciousness of the process as it happens. Like all symbolic modes, Christian understanding depends upon a depth of tradition: all new experience is referred to the preexisting myth. If, then, an artist invokes the framework of a traditional symbolism but consciously renders it inoperative, his audience is forced to regard the medium of the symbology in a totally new way. This is what Rossetti does in "My Sister's Sleep" and elsewhere. By at once undermining a more traditional set of responses and driving us toward unexpected impressions, Rossetti makes us understand what it means to undergo a fresh experience, or—as Shelley would have said—to have the veil of familiarity torn away.

A poem like "The Woodspurge" illustrates Rossetti's purposes very well. The opening stanza describes the poet's sense of grief over some unnamed event. His sorrow was so extreme that it extinguished his consciousness, and he gave himself up completely to his environmental stimuli: "I had walked on at the wind's will— / I sat now for the wind was still." He carelessly hung his head between his knees, but then found that his complete submissiveness to external impulses brought an unexpected remedy.

> My eyes, wide open, had the run
> Of some ten weeds to fix upon;
> Among those few, out of the sun,
> The woodspurge flowered, three cups in one.
>
> From perfect grief there need not be
> Wisdom or even memory:
> One thing then learnt remains to me,—
> The woodspurge has a cup of three.

The three-in-one detail seems another of Robson's irrelevant images, and insofar as we allow it to evoke any trinitarian ideas, it is one indeed. But the rest of the poem, and in particular the last stanza, extinguishes any such notion. Thus, when the three-in-one detail is completely freed of its possible religious connotations we suddenly realize the enormous relevance of the flower's non-symbolic fact. At that time and in that place this poet gained a measure of relief from a simple act of observation. No conceptualized knowledge or wisdom was involved, either before or after. The poem hints at the mystery which Rossetti felt in the mere fact of precise sensory perception and in the hidden resources of the simple human organism. From the event he does not preserve an idea or significant intellectual insight. Only the image of the woodspurge remains, yet one understands the radical importance of such a remnant. It is a modest yet graphic reminder that unless you approach the external world in as complete an innocence as possible life will shrink up and die. In the woodspurge Rossetti rediscovers the mystery of the world, and the fact that he carries the image of the flower around with him rather than some symbolic or intellectual content like that just abstracted from it is his guarantee (within the poem's implied drama) that he will never lack sources of inspiration. For us as readers, the poet's woodspurge is at once the sign of his innocent powers and a token of the magical potential in any objective datum, natural or otherwise.

Although "The Paris Railway-Station" (from "A Trip to Paris and Belgium") does not involve any startling metamorphoses of religious symbology, it does rely upon another kind of shock effect, just as it raises in another way Rossetti's conception of the artist's responsibility to objective detail, general environment, and his own sensations. The poem is framed by witty observations on why travelers through France always seem to be delayed by the passport authorities ("to baffle thieves and murderers"). Rossetti then describes a scene which he and Holman Hunt witnessed while their own trip was held up.

the other day
In passing by the Morgue we saw a man
(The thing is common, and we never should
Have known of it, only we passed that way)
Who had been stabbed and tumbled in the Seine
Where he had stayed some days. The face was black,
And, like a negro's, swollen; all the flesh
Had furred, and broken into a green mould.

Now, very likely, he who did the job
Was standing among those who stood with us
To look upon the corpse. You fancy him—
Smoking an early pipe, and watching, as
An artist, the effect of his last work.

The details of the scene are deliberately itemized in a sensational way in order to give us an extreme lesson in observation and sensory responsiveness. We do not want to look at such ugliness, but Rossetti presents his picture with such a detached air that the details become as it were idealized. The appearance of the corpse is purified of our stock emotional responses and returned to our sight in a condition of phenomenal innocence. Rossetti underlines his point by transferring to his hypothesized murderer the attitude of artistic indifference which his own description so perfectly illustrates. The passage and its "point" remind one of Keats's frequent pronouncements upon poetic disinterestedness:

May there not be superior beings amused with any graceful, though instinctive attitude my mind may fall into, as I am entertained with the alertness of a Stoat or the anxiety of a Deer? Though a quarrel in the streets is a thing to be hated, the energies displayed in it are fine; the commonest Man shows a grace in his quarrel—By a superior being our reasoning[s] may take the same tone—though erroneous they may be fine—This is the very thing in which consists poetry; and if so it is not so fine a thing as philosophy—For the same reason that an eagle is not so fine a thing as a truth.[3]

Keats's decision in favor of philosophy is one which Rossetti would not make; in this, as always, he takes the Keatsian position to the extreme. The reason that Rossetti would rest content with the eagle has already been shown in "The Woodspurge": the image has a perfect integrity, and because its existence is for Rossetti the ground of all thought, its primacy must be confirmed. The artist's province is the image, and insofar as he concerns himself with philosophy he damages his art. To achieve his idealities the artist must be true first of all to experience, not ideas: he must be open and totally responsive. This attitude—no more and no less—is the basis of Rossetti's notorious aestheticism.

Oswald Doughty, still our most reliable commentator on Rossetti, points out the relation between the idea of receptivity in the Pre-Raphaelite and Keats's predilection for passivity and indolence. He quotes Rossetti's sonnet "Blessed Idleness," which concludes with the following lines:

> Be thou loth to rack
> And hack thy brain for thought which *may* lurk there
> Or may not. Without pain of thought, the eyes
> Can see, the ears can hear, the sultry mouth
> Can taste the summer's flavour. Towards the South
> Let earth sway round, while this my body lies
> In warmth, and has the sun on face and hair.

The preeminence of the sensory life here scarcely needs comment. Doughty quotes the sonnet to illustrate how close Rossetti is to Keats in trusting to a "creative lethargy." For Rossetti, out of such moments of sensuous openness springs the "idealizing, *inner* dream . . . of the imagination," the "lotus land of his heart's desire where sensuous beauty, peace, languor, sadness, pleasure, mingle to form for him a ravishing harmony of flesh and spirit."[4]

Thus, Rossetti is not a "nature" poet in the strict sense, for his interest in sensory experience is confined by his idealizing program: "Whatever the apparent theme, Rossetti as poet or painter is evidently excited more by the physical beauty of his material than by the intellectual structure. But this was not due to any genuine visual interest in the material of the external world, such as Holman Hunt's Pre-Raphaelite principles exacted. He was only interested in material things when they entered his pictures, formed a part of his design" (Doughty, p. 93). But Rossetti's "design" is completely a-religious and non-supernatural in the ordinary senses of those words. Everywhere his poetry undermines its Christian traditions, puts the ancient imagery to entirely new, and pagan, uses. His belief in the human sensorium drove him to adventure in the deep mysteries of visibility, and to insist upon a new sort of transcendental: the exaltation of the exactly perceptual above heaven and hell alike, above spirit and nature.

This central theme in Rossetti's poetry makes "The Blessed Damozel" the epitome of his art. Doubtless *The House of Life* is a greater work, but everything in that sequence is implied in the early lyric. The poem's subject is Eros, the love-longing of a recently deceased and emparadised lady for her lover stranded on earth, and his yearning toward her. Formally the poem is written from this side of paradise, yet the burden of the lyric—witness the long poem within a poem sung by the damozel—has to do with the lady's passionate desire to be reunited with her lover. This is why she leans out over "the gold bar of heaven." But her story is framed by the parenthetical statements of her earthly lover, whose loneliness is the image of hers just as her desire to be reunited mirrors his.[5] The poem concludes with the lovers still separated and the damozel weeping behind "the golden barriers."

As everyone knows, "The Blessed Damozel" idealizes purely human love: the process is effected by using the Christian and spiritual images to define the passions of the earthly lovers. Recognizing the centrality of this situation in Rossetti's poetry, Graham Hough argues that Rossetti was generally unable to accommodate his symbolism to his themes. "Perpetually tormented by the irreconcilability of the unsensual love he had idealised and the love of the senses, he tries to identify them. . . . He simply turns his own confused and all too human conception of love into the highest value, and calls it God" (p. 80). The texts Hough works with are not from "The Blessed Damozel," but they might as well be. He quotes the following two passages to illustrate the alleged "confusion":

> How shall my soul stand rapt and awed,
> When, by the new birth borne abroad
> Throughout the music of the suns,
> It enters in her soul at once
> And knows the silence there for God.
> ("The Portrait")

> The soul I know not from thy body, nor
> Thee from myself, neither our love from God.
> (The House of Life, V)

These passages recall several from "The Blessed Damozel," for example, the stanza where the lover interrupts the damozel's song.

> (Alas! We two, we two, thou say'st!
> Yea, one wast thou with me
> That once of old. But shall God lift
> To endless unity
> The soul whose likeness with thy soul
> Was but its love for thee?)

But none of this seems to me unclear or ill-defined. What the lovers want is

> Only to live as once on earth
> With Love, only to be,
> As then awhile, for ever now
> Together, I and he.

In the earlier stanza Rossetti plays with the idea of unity, for if the earthly lovers want to be "one" as they once were "of old," this means they want a union that also insures sexual separation and individual identity. The Christian idea of "endless unity" where the sexual personality is annihilated in the embrace of Divine Love is here being wittily transformed. The Rossetti lover will allow no distinction between soul and body, so that the traditional concept of "endless unity" has to give way to Rossetti's concept. Lovers will be "one" in the sense that they are one on earth: they are united by their mutual love, by the fact that two individuals acknowledge each other's splendor rather than their own. For Rossetti, their relationship is "Love" (another witty transformation of a technical Christian term), and this Love cannot exist without the sexual separation which both makes it possible and impossible.

This fundamental paradox about Rossetti's ideal of sexual love is the reason why the lovers remain separated by the "golden barriers." The perfect human love which they praise and long for is embodied in the world of the Blessed Damozel. Human sexual love is "golden" but also (and by definition) an eternal barrier to any complete identity of the lovers' personalities. But of course they would not have their glorious relationship without that separation. Rossetti is doing here no more than what many other nineteenth-century artists did (witness *Tristan und Isolde*): he is replacing Love as agapé with Love as eros. Surely it is gratuitous to say that such an idea is "confused," or to suggest that Rossetti is committing some sort of artistic impropriety by declaring human love the most divine thing he can conceive. To argue in this way is to deny him his poetic premises.

But Rossetti's lovers do not merely suffer. They would if their goal were self-annihilation, but it is not. Rossetti's lovers want to be united "for ever" in heaven the way they were "awhile" on earth. If such a goal ensures their eternal separation, it also establishes the sexualized lover's ideal of an endless succession of deeper attachments and encounters. This is what the damozel is telling us when she sings:

> And I myself will teach to him,
> I myself, lying so,
> The songs I sing here; which his voice
> Shall pause in, hushed and slow,
> And find some knowledge at each pause,
> Or some new thing to know.

The exact meaning of these lines will perhaps be clarified if we set them beside passages from some other poems where the same situation is being treated. "Spheral Change" describes a lover's reactions when he enters "this new shade of Death." His beloved is there, but when he seeks to approach her she is "gone before I come." The poem then concludes:

> O dearest! while we lived and died
> A living death in every day,
> Some hours we still were side by side,
> When where I was you too might stay
> And rest and need not go away.

O nearest, furthest! Can there be
At length some hard-earned heart-won home,
Where,—exile changed for sanctuary,—
Our lot may fill indeed its sum,
And you may wait and I may come?

In other words, can we find (or make) a heaven that is as good as the earth, where lovers can count upon being together for "some hours," and where the poet can be sure that his beloved will wait for him when he comes to her?

"Insomnia" repeats the theme in a different way. The first two stanzas describe how lovers draw "a little nearer yet" to each other by day and night, awake and dreaming. The lines

Our lives, most dear, are never near,
Our thoughts are never far apart,
Though all that draws us heart to heart
Seems fainter now and now more clear.

perfectly illustrate the problem with Rossetti's Eros-Love. Aware of the contradiction, Rossetti's lover asks in the last stanza:

Is there a home where heavy earth
Melts to bright air that breathes no pain,
Where water leaves no thirst again
And springing fire is Love's new birth?
If faith long bound to one true goal
May there at length its hope beget,
My soul that hour shall draw your soul
For ever nearer yet.

The final line completes the poem brilliantly, for in that "home" of the imagination Eros is fulfilled—not in the sense that Eros is satisfied and longing thereby ended, but in the sense that Eros is perfected. Heaven becomes a place where Love is eternally coming "For ever nearer yet."

That last stanza shows Rossetti again at work recasting traditional Christian images. Its first four lines seem to present an orthodox picture of a spiritual heaven opposed to a fleshly earth. But the stanza's conclusion overturns that traditional way of thinking, for if "heaven" becomes a matter of "For ever nearer yet" and no more, then the meaning of "soul" necessarily becomes humanized ("Thy soul I know not from thy body") and all the other spiritual concepts are similarly affected. To a Rossetti lover, the body becomes not "heavy earth" but "bright air." All human emotions take on not a transcendental meaning but a transcendental value.

This habit of thought governs "The Blessed Damozel" and all its famous array of images. Drawn from a Christian tradition in which a sharp division was enforced between heaven and earth, the old ideas and symbols are transubstantiated (Rossetti would have approved that image) in his erotic poem. Though aware of this aspect of Rossetti's art, Graham Hough criticizes him for it. Rossetti's poetry, he says, "inaugurates that period of emotional unrest in which satisfaction is sought in the traditional religious symbolism, but is not found, since the symbols have been emptied of almost all their traditional religious content" (p. 81). But he speaks as if this change happened *to* Rossetti, as if it were a casual thing, or at least an accidental misstep. This is not so: Rossetti consciously strove to purify the religious symbols of their inherited content. Harold Weatherby's objection to Rossetti is like Hough's except that he sees the deliberateness and disapproves, apparently on principle: "Traditional meanings attach themselves" to traditional imagery, he says, "and demand more serious consideration" (p. 14). Yet surely Rossetti deals reverently with the tradition he is using for his own novel purposes. Certainly he is more reverent toward the traditions he employs than Swinburne often is.

I have already discussed Rossetti's methods for transforming his orthodox materials with a new usefulness, but the point is sufficiently important to repeat with respect to "The Blessed Damozel." Almost any stanza will do for illustration.

> When round his head the aureole clings,
> And he is clothed in white,
> I'll take his hand and go with him
> To the deep wells of light;
> As unto a stream we will step down,
> And bathe there in God's sight.

As we have already seen, a picture like this possesses a symbolic potential by virtue of the tradition which lies behind it; yet Rossetti's technique is such that he completely insulates the picture and thereby annihilates the symbolism. Is not this poet one of Marianne Moore's hoped-for " 'literalists of the imagination'—above insolence and triviality [who] can present for inspection 'imaginary gardens with real toads in them' "? The point of Rossetti's erotic imagery is strictly its sensational quality. Pre-Raphaelite lovers walk about this very unchristian heaven because to do so is to experience a sequence of wonders, unexpected marvels or spendid well-known sights. A stately pleasure dome, Rossetti's heaven exists only to increase the lovers' experience of their situation, of their relationship. If we insist upon asking what the place symbolizes, the answer is surely "Love," that is, Eros. In her imagination the damozel sees herself and her lover exploring the mysteries of their relationship, finding "some knowledge at each pause, Or some new thing to know." The sensational imagery, then, defines the human quality of their paradise at the same time that the spiritual tradition behind the images suggests the transcendental value which is now attributed to purely human love. More than that, the startling transformation process which the imagery itself undergoes in the poem is fundamental to the work. This transformation—the purification of the imagery—is the locus of our emotional reactions (we are, and are supposed to be, surprised by it). Always associated with the lovers' paradise, these imagistic "stunners" (as Rossetti would say) come to represent the sense of wonder which the damozel and her lover are constantly experiencing. Thus the images are the perfect equivalent of Rossetti's divinized human love: sensational in effect and sublime in value. By purifying his Christian imagery Rossetti raises it to the level of the marvelous, creates it anew, makes it a beautiful, unknown quantity.

We may legitimately object to Rossetti's poetry on philosophic grounds. It is conceivable that his ideas about love, being thoroughly agnostic and even pagan, are naive, especially if we examine those ideas in the context of the Christianity which he is so deliberately using for his own purposes. What does not seem legitimate, however, is the more customary charge that his poetry has no precise meaning. To call "the central weakness" in "The Blessed Damozel" "the problem of meaning in relationship to the reality or unreality of the supernatural" is to expose not a fault in Rossetti but a failure on the critic's part to understand what the poet was doing.[6] "The Blessed Damozel" has nothing whatever to do with such a problem and to raise it is to ensure an oblique reading of the poem. Rossetti's ideal never admits a distinction between an order called nature and one called supernature. He uses a tradition which does make such a distinction because through it he can clarify his own very different ideas.

When critics say that Rossetti's artifice is unredeemed by an idea, or that it is beauty without any firm conceptual basis, one may be justifiably puzzled. Both Weatherby and Hough make these charges, yet both also show that they understand at least the broad outlines of Rossetti's message. The point seems to be that they do not approve his message, that they consider it trivial, unprofound. But to see human sexual love as one of man's highest ideals, the value equivalent of a "supermundane" experience within a wholly non-transcendental frame of reference, does not seem to me either vague or trivial. The fact that Rossetti's Eros-Love must by its nature avoid any absolute fulfillments does not make it any less sublime (or actual) an experience nor his artistic rendering of it necessarily "confused." On the point of craftsmanship, I think we have seen that the poetry achieves a careful integration of themes and techniques, at least in the works under discussion here. One cannot be as definite about the purely substantive issue. A sensibility more committed to moral and rational absolutes than to artistic ones will likely not think much of Rossetti's poetry. Rossetti will seem an aesthete because he places a higher value on images than on concepts. The heavy emphasis placed upon the thematic aspects of literature during the past four decades—the emphasis upon the sort of "interpretation" which Susan Sontag has recently declared "against"—helps to explain why Rossetti has been so long out of favor. Critics schooled in this method seek to define their absolutes not at the surface but below it, not in the apparition but the concept. Rossetti does not fare well in such school because he forces the reader to attend to the surface, insists that the greatest significance lies there, unburied. He does not want deep readers, which is not to say that he does not demand intelligent ones.

If, then, Rossetti and his Pre-Raphaelite brothers (and sisters) cannot be fully recovered without some shift in current tastes and critical perspectives, at least we can clarify some of the issues. Rossetti's poetry is not vague, his imagery is not merely decorative, his themes are not manifestly trivial: insofar as these points have been substantiated by this discussion my purposes have been achieved.

Notes

1. W. W. Robson, "Pre-Raphaelite Poetry," *From Dickens to Hardy, Pelican Guide to English Literature VI*, ed. Boris Ford (London, 1958), p. 358; Harold L. Weatherby, "Problems of Form and Content in the Poetry of Dante Gabriel Rossetti," *VP*, II (1964), 11–19; Graham Hough, *The Last Romantics* (London, 1947, 1961), p. 77. Subsequent references to these works are where possible incorporated into the text.

2. Hough, p. 80; Weatherby, p. 15.

3. *The Letters of John Keats*, ed. Hyder E. Rollins (Cambridge, Mass., 1958), II, 80–81.

4. Oswald Doughty, "Rossetti's Conception of the 'Poetic' in Poetry and Painting," *Transactions of the Royal Society of Literature of the United Kingdom*, NS XXVI (1953), 97.

5. See the fine discussion of this matter by Paul Lauter, "The Narrator of 'The Blessed Damozel,' " *MLN*, LXXIII (1958), 344–348.

6. Weatherby, p. 14.

Love, Unity, and Desire in the Poetry of Dante Gabriel Rossetti

STEPHEN J. SPECTOR

I

Perhaps the most elegant formulation of the core problem of Romanticism is Earl R. Wasserman's statement that Wordsworth, Coleridge, Keats, and Shelley "all face the central need to find a significant relationship between the subjective and objective worlds."[1] The poetry of Dante Gabriel Rossetti, like that of many of his fellow Victorians, constitutes both an articulation and a critical examination of this problem. But whereas the Romantics were able, at least at times, to exult because they discovered powers within the self that allowed them to connect with the external world, the self in Rossetti's poetry, despite its strenuous attempts, is most often unable to bridge the gap between the subjective and the objective worlds. The Romantics were able to forge new epistemologies based upon what they conceived to be the creative powers of the self, powers which they most often designated in their metapsychological systems as the Imagination. In contrast, Rossetti's poetry displays a self that is really conscious only of itself; its most characteristic action, unlike the creative act of the Romantic Imagination, is one of tautological sterility. His poetry resembles the poetry of the Romantics in that both involve a centripetal journey into the interior of the self, but unlike the Romantics, Rossetti investigates a self that is unable to reverse its course and make the centrifugal journey that leads back to the external world.

That this is so is surprising, because Rossetti's poetry is, above all, love poetry; and love, of course, is usually a means of escaping the prison of the self. Traditionally love provides a way for the self to escape its own limitations; love is the most significant mode of human relationships which are interpersonal and therefore in direct contrast to the predicament where the self is locked in subjective isolation. Traditionally the lover feels that the ground of value is not in himself, but in the beloved, or in a reciprocal relationship between himself and his beloved. Love, because it validates the reality of something outside of the self, becomes the basis for a significant

Reprinted From *ELH* 38 (1971): 432–58. Reprinted by permission of the author and the Johns Hopkins University Press.

relationship between the subjective and the objective worlds, even if the world outside is only the beloved, which is, of course, frequently the case. (In poetry this familiar situation is usually marked by an imagery or a symbolism in which the beloved is a microcosm of the whole world or of a significant aspect of the external world, such as nature or the heavens.) Love, paradoxically, by affirming the alterity of the beloved, establishes the integrity of the lover. The relationship between lover and beloved that is established is a victory over alienation, and Shelley's famous words in *A Defence of Poetry* are a perfect expression of this idea: "The great secret of morals is love; or a going out of our own nature, and an identification of ourselves with the beautiful which exists in thought, action, or person, not our own."[2]

What is distinctive and disturbing about much of Rossetti's most accomplished poetry is that the traditional function of love is reversed: love, instead of liberating the self, actually increases the subjective isolation of the lover. Lovers like Aloÿse (the heroine of "The Bride's Prelude"), Rose Mary, and the hero of "A Last Confession" become increasingly trapped within themselves because of love. Instead of embracing wholeheartedly an optimistic religion of love, Rossetti is consistently engaged in its demystification; he reveals not only the illusory nature of love, but also the ways that love itself actually generates illusion.

Rossetti shows that love, or indeed any intense emotion, often tends to increase the isolation of the self, because the self, in such moments, cannot escape from being aware of its own intense feeling. As love becomes more intense, as it becomes passion, the lover can feel only his own passion; the beloved becomes more and more unknowable. Love, which begins with the perception of the beloved and the hope that the beloved will become the locus of a ground of value outside of the self, and therefore an escape from the pain of subjective isolation, ends with the lover feeling an even greater sense of isolation. As passion increases, the lover becomes more and more aware, not of the beloved, but of his own increasingly agitated mind and heart, a heart that beats louder and louder until it is the only reality he can perceive. Love, instead of being a mode of intersubjectivity, becomes another mode of subjectivism.[3]

Because the lover who is trapped with his own passion is unable to truly know the beloved, Rossetti's poems often are built around situations that are inherently ironic. Statements made by the lovers are rarely accurate representations of reality. Rossetti manages irony most deftly, especially in his longer poems, in which the falsity of the lover's statements, especially in relation to the beloved, is revealed gradually. For example, "Rose Mary," "A Last Confession," and "The Bride's Prelude" are poems which are based upon the ironic misapprehension of the beloved by the lover. Rose Mary never learns that her betrothed, Sir James of Heronhaye, for whom she dies, actually does not love her at all; the idealistic speaker of "A Last Confession" allows his passion for a young girl to distort his perception of her so totally that he can see her only as a Virgin or a whore, rather than as the ordinary adolescent she really is; Aloÿse, overcome by feelings which her convent education left her helpless to understand, is deceived and seduced by the treacherous Lord Urscelyn.

In the poems cited above, the dramatic situations are complexly ironic; the isolation of the lover not only prevents him from knowing the beloved, but it also makes the lover unknowable to others. Rose Mary's mother, for example, initiates the tragic action because she does not know the most important fact about her daughter, that she is no longer "pure," and therefore unable to use the magic glass. The hero of "A Last Confession," because of his passion, is a mystery to both the priest to whom he makes confession and to the girl with whom he had lived for eleven years. And Aloÿse keeps her love secret from her brothers and father until the disaster is irreversible; the substance of the poem is Aloÿse's revelation to Amelotte (and to the reader) of herself as a totally different person from what Amelotte thought her to be.

While the irony in these poems is complex, it is presented clearly. But in "Jenny" and "The Blessed Damozel" the irony is more ambiguous and therefore more difficult to interpret. The major problem is that it is difficult to delimit the point of view of the speaker; but this should not prevent the reader from perceiving the irony in the poems.

In "The Blessed Damozel" the reader is faced with the problem of determining whether or not the whole poem, as Paul Lauter asserts, "is concerned with the bereaved lover's mind."[4] Lauter's point, which I think is correct, is that the Blessed Damozel does not exist as an independent voice in the poem; instead, her speech is a projection of the bereaved lover's desire, it is what he imagines and hopes she would say if she could. We can see in "The Blessed Damozel" one of the essential situations in Rossetti's poetry— the isolated, separated lover expressing his desire for unity with his beloved. The vision of heaven inhabited by a warm-breasted damozel is properly understood as a wish-fulfilling dream in the mind of the earthly lover. The heart of the poem is the ironic conflict between the speaker's very earthly bodily desire, which he unconsciously reveals, and the tradition that heaven is a place of heavenly, disembodied souls, a tradition which is ironically emphasized by the speaker's religious language.

In "Jenny" the most difficult interpretational problem is to determine to what extent the speaker is being presented ironically. But we can see that one source of irony is the fact that the speaker has no knowledge at all of Jenny's mind, even though he pretends to read her thoughts. Let us examine the following lines:

> Why, Jenny, as I watch you there,—
> For all your wealth of loosened hair,

> Your silk ungirdled and unlac'd
> And warm sweets opened to the waist,
> All golden in the lamplight's gleam,—
> You know not what a book you seem,
> Half-read by lightning in a dream!
>
> (37)[5]

First, there is the obvious irony that the young man is unable to accept his sexual attraction for what it is: it is clear that Jenny, with her warm and open sweets, does not really look like a book to the young man. But it is appropriate that this particular young man, who has just come from his own room which is "full of books" (36), employs such a metaphor to describe Jenny. To him, and the social class which he represents, Jenny is not a person with a consciousness; rather, she is merely a book, a statistic, an academic problem. By describing Jenny as a book the young man not only denies her reality as another consciousness, he also tries to deny her reality as a sexual being. The poem, then, is a dramatization of the complete separation of the speaker from Jenny; and the more he pretends to have knowledge of her, the more ironic the poem becomes.

As we have noted, love frequently leads to the isolation of the lover, thereby inverting the traditional function of love and upsetting the hopes and expectations of the lover. Also, we can see that Rossetti demonstrates that as the intensity of love increases, the greater becomes the isolation of the self. In the ballads "Eden Bower" and "Sister Helen" Rossetti explores the self-absorbed intensity of love which has been raised to such a high degree of intensity that it has turned into hate; Rossetti's comments about these poems in "The Stealthy School of Criticism" are revealing: "What more inspiring for poetic effort than the terrible Love turned to Hate,—perhaps the deadliest of all passion-woven complexities,—which is the theme of 'Sister Helen,' and, in a more fantastic form, of 'Eden Bower'—the surroundings of both poems being the mere machinery of a central universal meaning?" (620). Both Sister Helen and Lilith are entrapped by the web of "passion-woven complexities"—webs which they spin out of their own passions. In both ballads Rossetti achieves hypnotic rhythmical patterns that reflect the self-hypnotized states of his heroines.

In "Sister Helen" Rossetti presents the isolating effects of passion in a way analogous to the method he employs in "The Bride's Prelude" and "A Last Confession": in all three poems the narrator-lover speaks to another person who cannot understand him. The speakers treat their auditors as innocent children who cannot possibly understand the emotions described. Of course the auditors may indeed understand the speakers, just as the reader may, but the crucial point is that the speakers feel that they are completely separate from the rest of humanity; in fact, all three feel that they are damned, that they have taken an irreversible step placing themselves forever outside the human community. In "Sister Helen," the heroine is completely inaccessible to the brothers, father, and wife of Keith of Ewern; even her own brother can only listen uncomprehendingly. Her relationship to her brother (always addressed as "Little Brother") is analogous to Aloÿse's relationship to Amelotte, and the speaker's relationship to the priest in "A Last Confession."

To say that Rossetti's problem describes the self locked in subjective isolation does not mean that the beloved is not present in his poetry. However, the lover never enters into the beloved's consciousness; indeed, the beloved exists, not as another mind, but as a beautiful object. The relationship between the lover and the beloved is not a relationship between subject and subject, rather, it is a relationship between subject and object. The lover is first attracted by the physical attributes of the beloved; the real basis of attraction, therefore, seems to be either sexual or aesthetic or a combination of the two. The lover's perception of the physical attributes of the beloved is followed swiftly by a dangerous, irresistible attraction to the beloved. Often the danger of this attraction is expressed by the lover's feeling that he is being absorbed into the beloved; his self is being destroyed by his attraction for the beloved. In "Body's Beauty" (LXXVIII),[6] Rossetti reveals that the genesis of attraction, even where physical beauty is the most obvious element in that attraction, is never merely physical. While Lilith's attractions are, of course, mainly physical, she is attractive for a more profound reason: she exists in isolation. Her deadly attractiveness is due to the fact that she seems not to be at all interested in relating to anything outside of herself, and so she makes men even more aware of their own isolation, an isolation that they must attempt to overcome:

> And still she sits, young while the earth is old,
> And, subtly of herself contemplative,
> Draws men to watch the bright web she can weave,
> Till heart and body and life are in its hold.

Clearly, the more that Lilith seems to be self-absorbed, the more the lover will attempt to break down the barriers between them, and the more he attempts to become united with her, the more imprisoned he will be. And, ironically, the prison, though it is woven by Lilith's hair, is ultimately a prison of his own construction: it is the prison of his own impotent desire. Rossetti's own comments to Thomas Gordon Hake make his intent clear: "You ask me about 'Lilith'—I suppose referring to the picture-sonnet. The picture is called 'Lady Lilith' by rights . . . and represents a *Modern Lilith* combing out her abundant golden hair and gazing on herself in the glass with that self-absorption by whose strange fascination such natures draw others within their own circle. The idea which you indicate (viz: of the perilous principle in the world being female from the first) is about the most essential notion of the sonnet."[7]

II

The lover's desire for unity with his beloved is best understood as the most important manifestation of man's overarching desire to be united to something outside of himself, especially God. Love is not generated by regard for another person, but by the universal desire to heal the wound of existence. Rossetti, beginning with the perception that the world is fragmented, could not find any sign on earth that there was a God, or any transcendental power, that bound men together or connected the isolated self to something, like nature or society, that was beyond the restrictive circle of self-consciousness. However, in a typically Victorian posture, Rossetti hoped that some transcendent power existed, that after death he would find the unity he was denied on earth, even though he could not put any real faith in such a hope. When Ford Maddox Brown's son, Nolly, died, Rossetti wrote to the bereaved father: "Now the mist of death has risen and covers it all. Is it still behind the mist, or really gone for ever? I, for one, cannot but hope" (*Letters*, III, 1319). The mist that separates life from death in this passage is really a metaphor for the separation of God and man; it is another version of the image of the hidden God which occurs so frequently in Victorian literature and which is perhaps best known in Tennyson's "In Memoriam":

> O for thy voice to soothe and bless!
> What hope or answer, or redress?
> Behind the veil, behind the veil.
>   (LVI, 26–28)

Like Tennyson, Rossetti hoped that the separateness of earthly existence was only illusory, that somewhere there was a realm of complete unity which man simply was unable to perceive from his earthly vantage point.[8]

The hope for a transcendental unity pervades Rossetti's thought, and it may be examined most conveniently in "The Cloud Confines," a poem which, as Rossetti wrote to William Bell Scott on 13 August 1871, was "meant to deal with important matters" (*Letters*, III, 976). In fact the poem was so important to Rossetti that at one time he speculated about using it as the last section of his masterpiece; in a letter of 8 November 1873 to Franz Hüffer he wrote: "What do you think of putting 'The Cloud Confines' at the end of {The} *House of Life* section, to which it belongs?" (*Letters*, III, 1229).

In one sense "The Cloud Confines" is a catalogue of various modes of experiencing isolation. The image with which the poem begins is another version of the veil/mist image: man is imprisoned on earth, cut off from the heavens and from the realm of transcendence by clouds of seemingly infinite depth. Man searches the sky but only "wild shadows are shown, / Deep under deep unknown / And height above unknown height" (219). Because the clouds will not part man is separated from any knowledge of his origins or of his destiny; and, therefore, he is also separated from any significant knowledge of himself. Isolated in the confused present and cut off from both his past and his future, man's position is bleak:

> Our past is clean forgot,
> Our present is and is not,
> Our future's a sealed seedplot. . . .
>
> (220)

Only if man were able to perceive the transcendental reality, only if man were able to know God, would he be able to know his own, hopefully divine, self. Within the confines of this cloud-enclosed earthly existence, however, both the world and man's self are shrouded in inscrutable darkness:

> The day is dark and the night
> To him that would search their heart;
> No lips of cloud that will part
> Nor morning song in the light. . . .
>
> (219)

In the last stanza Rossetti returns to the image of darkness which begins the poem; once more the feeling of isolation is accompanied by the sensation of being lost in darkness. A final image of the darkness of the inscrutable sky and sea sums up Rossetti's ontological and epistemological confusion: he cannot find meaning in the song of the sea (symbolizing earthly time); and the heavens (symbolizing eternal time) are silent. Both the sky and the sea are therefore essentially the same; and in an image which recurs frequently in Rossetti's poetry, they merge together in darkness:

> The sky leans dumb on the sea,
> Aweary with all its wings;
> And oh! the song the sea sings
> Is dark everlastingly.
>
> (220)

And in "The Card-Dealer" we find that not only are the sky and the sea in darkness, but that the land is dark also. Man lives "Within a vain strange land," which is, in words that echo Job, "A land of darkness as darkness itself / And of the shadow of death" (174).

Rossetti, however, could never relinquish the hope that some transcendent reality did exist, even if he could not find it or see any evidence of it. Like so many Victorians, he vacillated between moments of faith and doubt, and this vacillation is recorded in the difficulties he experienced with the refrain of "The Cloud Confines." The refrain that he published is highly ambiguous, and Rossetti meant it to be that way.

> Still we say as we go,—
> 'Strange to think by the way,
> Whatever there is to know,
> That we shall know one day.'
>
> (219)

Obviously this leaves open the possibility that perhaps there will be nothing to know; after death there may be nothing because there may not be any reality other than the meaningless darkness of sea and sky. And there is another complication in this stanza; "strange" may refer to the intuition that one day we will know the ultimate truth, whatever that is; or, "strange" may refer to the very fact that we *think* that eventually we will know the answer to the riddle of existence. In other words, our faith and hope are strange and mysterious; they are mysterious because they exist even though there seems to be no basis for them.

At one time Rossetti decided to conclude with a statement affirming the essential unity of God and man, a unity which would last after death:

> And what must our birthright be?
> Oh, never from thee to sever,
> Thou Will that shalt be and art,
> To throb at thy heart for ever,
> Yet never to know thy heart.
>
> (Letters, III, 990)[9]

Even in this affirmative statement of faith we can see the ambivalence that Rossetti always felt about God; at the height of his faith he could not believe that he would ever know God's heart: he would always be estranged from knowledge of transcendental reality.

Rossetti's comments to William Bell Scott (August, 1871) about this stanza are most intriguing; they constitute perhaps the single most elaborate statement of his philosophical and religious thinking that is to be found in his writings, and these comments also throw light on a rather peculiar aspect of Rossetti's ideas about unity: "I don't go with your objection to the wind-up as contradictory. It is *meant* as the possible answer to the question. I cannot suppose that any particle of life is *extinguished*, though its permanent individuality may be more than questionable. Absorption is not annihilation; and it is even a real retributive feature of the special atom of life to be reembodied (if so it were) in a world which its former ideality had helped to fashion for pain or pleasure. Such is the theory conjectured here" (Letters, III, 989–90).

Upon writing these words Rossetti must have been struck by the realization that no quatrain, no matter how artfully contrived, could possibly express such a theory; perhaps, looking back at what he had just written, he concluded that his theory was not clear even to himself. At any rate he decided to change the quatrain; he concludes to Scott: "But I believe I am of opinion with you, perhaps, that it is best not to try to squeeze the expression of it into so small a space, but rather to leave the question quite unanswered" (*Letters*, III, 990). And so Rossetti proposed another version of the last stanza:

> What words to say as we go?
> What thoughts to think by the way?
> What truth may there be to know?
> And shall we know it one day?
> (*Letters*, III, 990)

The important thing about Rossetti's "theory" is that it posits two modes of existence, which we might designate as an earthly mode and a transcendental mode. The earthly mode is merely a phase through which the "special atom of life" passes; this special particle comes from its supernal home, passes through its earthly phase, and then is absorbed back into the transcendental realm, where it recovers its original identity. In its original state the soul, of course, is part of a total cosmic unity; in "The Birth-Bond" (XV) the lover intuits that his attraction for his beloved is rooted in their original prenatal unity:

> Even so, when first I saw you, seemed it, love,
> That among souls allied to mine was yet
> One nearer kindred than life hinted of.
> O born with me somewhere that men forget,
> And though in years of sight and sound unmet,
> Known for my soul's birth-partner well enough!

And the cyclical return to an original unity is also described in "The Heart of the Night" (LXVI):

> Alas, the soul!—how soon must she
> Accept her primal immortality,—
> The flesh resume its dust whence it began?

It is apparent that Rossetti's theory is another version of the familiar, traditional Christian doctrine of the immortality of the soul: the soul originates in the divine, passes through earthly life, and returns to God—the source and origin of the variety and multiplicity of creation. And the theme of a lost prenatal identity is the subject of many poems, including, of course, Wordsworth's "Intimations" ode and Yeats's "Among School Children"; and, even more striking is the resemblance of Rossetti's theory, with its emphasis on the "atom" of life, to the atomic theory of the universe elaborated by Poe in *Eureka*. But the significant fact is that all of these poets have in common the notion that there is an original unity from which life comes and to which the soul will someday return, but that on earth man is alienated from his own identity, and therefore the original unity can only be intuited or glimpsed. Finally, it must be remembered that this theory is, to Rossetti, only a theory: his belief in it is highly equivocal, as is shown by the fact that he finally, in "The Cloud Confines," decides to "leave the whole question open" (*Letters*, III, 1005). Nevertheless, if Rossetti does entertain any cosmic myth, the notion of a transcendental realm of original unity has a central place in it.

III

If it is remembered that essential unity is a mode of existence which is located, if at all, only in some supernal realm, one of the most disconcerting aspects of Rossetti's poetry becomes explicable: the fact that the lover's desire for unity is often expressed as if it were a desire for death. Indeed, the desire for unity is most often voiced by a living lover who waits for death in the hope that after death he will enter the transcendental realm and achieve absolute unity with his beloved there. Many poems about unity, such as "The Stream's Secret," "The Song of the Bower," "The Portrait," "The Blessed Damozel," "Spheral Change," "Parted Presence," "A Death-Parting," "Alas So Long!," "Insomnia," and many of the *House of Life* sonnets (especially the climactic "Willowwood" series) are not about the *experience* of unity at all; rather, they are about the *desire* for unity on the part of the totally separate self.

If we examine Rossetti's descriptions of the state of unity in love, we find that its most significant feature is the absence of the fundamental dimensions of human experience. The drive towards the state of unity almost always includes the tendency to exclude space and time in an effort to approximate supernal reality. While space and time are the fundamental attributes of earthly existence which the lover tries to negate, other important attributes which he also attempts to banish are sound, light, and movement. The conditions of the lovers' state of unity, therefore, are usually: a compressed and enclosing space, a timeless moment (often designated "Love's Hour"), darkness, stillness, and silence.[10] While these conditions of absence are usually copresent, it will be useful to examine them separately.

The space in the state of unity is most often a sanctuary or a shelter, and it is a special instance of the compressed space which is so typical of the space in Rossetti's poetry.[11] The sanctuary is an appropriate image because it reflects the lover's feeling of protection in the state of unity and the fact that his desire is to shut out the external world. The isolated lover in "The Stream's Secret," for example, looks forward to that hour when he will be united with his beloved in the silent shelter ("our nest") of her presence:

> Beneath her sheltering hair,
> In the warm silence near her breast,
> Our kisses and our sobs shall sink to rest;
> As in some still trance made aware
> That day and night have wrought to fulness there
> And Love has built our nest.
>
> (115)

In "Love Enthroned" (I), the first sonnet in *The House of Life*, the ideal space of Love is presented. In the octave Rossetti enumerates "all kindred Powers the heart finds fair": Truth, Hope, Fame, Youth, and Life. These are presented so that the reader assumes that they are attendants grouped around the throne at the court of Love. But Love is not to be found in the same space with the attributes of earthly existence; instead, we find at the turn of the sonnet that our expectations are upset:

> Love's throne was not with these; but far above
> All passionate wind of welcome and farewell
> He sat on breathless bowers they dream not of. . . .

Once more we see that the ideal location of Love is an enclosed space, a "breathless bower" which is specifically located above Life. The space where Love is enthroned is defined by what is excluded from that space, not what is present there. This is to be expected because, as we have seen, unity exists only in a realm which is the polar opposite of earthly life. Therefore it is appropriate that Love's throne is above Life, in a lifeless ("breathless") space which may be found only by abandoning Life and entering a realm which is similar to the realm of Death.[12] In the next sonnet, "Bridal Birth" (II), the lovers look forward to the day when they will be truly united by Love; but that can occur only after they die. Paradoxically, their ultimate marriage will take place after they experience "Death's nuptial change." Rossetti's lovers are epitomized by the bereaved lover in "Spheral Change," who, as Dante and Petrarch hoped to be reunited with Beatrice and Laura, hopes that after death he can rejoin his beloved, and at last have his "exile changed for sanctuary" (236).

Often, as in the stanza quoted above from "The Stream's Secret," the beloved's hair creates the sheltered space; and frequently, the beloved's hair also serves to keep out light, creating a space which is not only sheltered but also shadowed. In fact, "shadowed" and "shelter" seem to be interchangeable words throughout much of Rossetti's poetry. The darkness of the sanctuary beneath the beloved's hair is brought out clearly in "Love's Lovers" (VIII): "Thine eyes gray-lit in shadowing hair above"; in "Love-Sweetness" (XXI): "Sweet dimness of her loosened hair's downfall / About thy face"; in "The Love Letter" (XI), in which the lover envies the letter which is "Warmed by her hand and shadowed by her hair"; and in "Venus Victrix" (XXXIII), in which the poet-lover's page is "gold-shadowed in thy hair." The sheltering hair, darkness, and compressed space are all combined in "At Last":

> Cling round me, sacred sweetness, hold me fast;
> Oh! as I kneel, enfold mine eyes even there
> Within thy breast; and to Love's deepest lair
> Of memory bid thy soul with mine retreat,
> And let our past years and our future meet
> In the warm darkness underneath thine hair.[13]

A distinguished French critic, Henri Talon, has also noticed Rossetti's penchant for clouding or shadowing the beloved's "glimmering visage"; after asking "pourquoi cette dilection du clair-obscur,"[14] he draws attention to the fact that in the state of unity contraries are joined—light and dark coexist. But the distinctive feature of the state of unity is the tendency towards the conditions of death, the aspiration for absorption into a non-human transcendental realm. Of course light is present there, usually light generated by the beloved's eyes, but light is dominated by darkness. What Rossetti usually excludes from the sanctuary is the light of the sun, which, as in "The Bride's Prelude," is often a symbol of actuality. In "Heart's Haven" (XXII) Love exists as a paradoxical, magical balancing of light and dark for the lovers, to whom he is "our light at night and shade at noon." But Love's function is also to protect their haven, a function which he fulfills when he "turns away / All shafts of shelterless tumultuous day."

Perhaps no other aspect of the state of unity illuminates and underscores the fact that it is essentially a state of absence so much as its tendency to be a state of silence; or, if there is sound, it is not the sound of the human voice but the music of the spheres. The separated lover in "The Stream's Secret," for example, looks forward to the moment when he and his beloved will with "closed lips in closed arms a silence keep" (115). When they finally achieve "One love in unity" (116) there will be no need for words: "Each on the other gazing shall but see / A self that has no need to speak" (116). The silence which pervades the sanctuary of love is, of course, the same kind of silence that is found in the silence of death. Silence is a condition in which there is no discord; all separate and discordant sounds are reduced to a perfect unity. But silence, while it is a perfect expression of absolute unity, is non-human, precisely because it is absolute: for a lover to desire silence is for him to desire the obliteration of both himself and his beloved. Thus, Rossetti's lovers, when they express their desire for unity in silence, also reveal their desire to leave this earth; and so the bereaved lover in "The Portrait" hopes that after death he might be united with his beloved when his reborn soul "enters her soul at once / And knows the silence there for God!" (170).[15]

IV

The straining desire for unity and the anguish of separation are the emotional poles which dominate Rossetti's consciousness. In *The House of Life* the essential structure of the poem is determined by the change from existence with love to existence without love—after the Old Love dies and the poet-lover is severed from the New Beloved. Rossetti himself, in a notebook entry addressed to the reader of *The House of Life*, wrote: "The 'life' involved is neither my life nor your life, but life representative, as tripled with love and death" (638). His intention, then, is to examine life and its relationship to two great influences, two facts of existence which become the ground of all consciousness, transforming every aspect of perception and awareness—love and death. The centrality of love and death is also indicated, it should be remembered, by the fact that Rossetti entitled the sixteen *House of Life* sonnets, which he published in the March, 1869 *Fortnightly Review*, "Of Life, Love, and Death: Sixteen Sonnets."

The first part of *The House of Life* presents and examines the state of unity achieved through love, which we have just examined. But even in the first thirty-five sonnets the tenuousness of the state of unity is repeatedly underscored by the fact that it is a state of paradox. For a brief moment all the contradictions of existence are seemingly bound together—light and dark, night and day, sky and sea, sound and silence, past and future, stasis and movement, all coexist. But these contraries inevitably fall apart, just as the lover and the Beloveds are separated, and time triumphs. The two central events of the poem, the death of the Old Love and the parting with the New Beloved, are only the most dramatic manifestations of the collapse of the state of unity, and both events, therefore, have the same significance to the poet-lover and to the meaning of the whole poem. In a sense *The House of Life* is a poem with a single modulation; the shift from the static, sheltered world of unity and love to the changing, exposed world of disunity and death; the shift from the stillness of the bower to the wandering, aimless journey of the isolated self which, after "Secret Parting" (XLV) and "Parted Love" (XLVI), becomes the dominant motif of the poem; the shift from Edenic innocence and happiness to purgatorial anguish. In the world of *The House of Life* this shift is simply an inexplicable fact of existence, an inevitable consequence of the passage of time: nothing within man, no fact of human nature, no Original Sin is responsible for the expulsion from the Edenic bower, and this inexplicable fact is the starting point for Rossetti's perception of reality.

One way to trace the shift from the state of love's unity to the state of separation, and to reveal the significance of that shift, is to examine Rossetti's subtle handling of a few selected images. One aspect of *The House of Life* which has struck many commentators is the homogeneity of the language throughout the entire poem, not only in terms of syntax and diction, but also in terms of imagery. The same images which appear in the earliest sonnets recur throughout the poem, but over the course of the sequence they undergo a sea-change, and we can trace the shifting significance of such images as light, dark, sky, sea, reflection, music, and silence. Out of the large number of possible image complexes which play an important role in *The House of Life*, I have chosen to examine two which seem especially rich, the images of the horizon-line and the mirror. In both cases imagistic strands which we have already seen in isolation are woven together, revealing and creating larger patterns of meaning, and contributing to the consistency of the whole poem.

The constant, straining aspiration for transcendence is felt throughout *The House of Life*, where, as in "The Cloud Confines," the supreme desire of the self is to find its true home. Since there seems to be no home on earth, one theme which is almost always present is the hope that beyond the clouds there is some supernal reality in which the self might rediscover its original identity after death. Often, the horizon-line is the symbol of the mystery and attraction of the realm beyond human experience. This is an especially appropriate symbolism because the horizon-line is in reality an inextricable union of the sea, the symbol of earthly existence (and specifically the symbol of human time), and the sky, the symbol of the supernal (and specifically the symbol of eternity). The heart of the mystery is that there is no way to determine whether the horizon-line, which is what man sees at the extreme limit of his vision, is actually the sky or the sea or a mixture of both; in other words, man does not know whether the object of his farthest sight is human or divine.

The poem which Rossetti chose for the crucial final position in the *Poems*, 1870 version of *The House of Life*, was "The Sea-Limits," in which once more the limits of human knowledge and experience are compared to the limits of man's perception of the sea. The "sea's listless chime" is "Time's self" "made audible" (191); this perception of the endless and repetitive sound of the sea, a sound analogous to the sound of humanity, where each culture and each individual repeats the eternal cycle of birth and death, is as far as the human understanding of time, space, and destiny can reach. At the end of the sea there is only the impenetrable beyond; man cannot see beyond the horizon-line:

> Secret continuance sublime
> Is the sea's end: our sight may pass
> No furlong further. . . .
>
> (191)

The sound of the sea is the chiming of the bell which must toll for all men; to perceive the meaning of the sound of the sea is to know your earthly destiny; but the sky offers no clue about the meaning of its infinity: "Last utterly, the whole sky stands,/Grey and not known, along its path" (191). As in "The Cloud Confines," the sky in "The Sea-Limits" is silent; the only sound audible is the roar of the sea which is identical to the sound of the voices of men who wander in the dark woods of earthly existence.[16] The life of each man is like the life of each wave, and the sound of humanity is the sound of the rise and fall of each life within the sea of life:

> Listen alone beside the sea,
> Listen alone among the woods;
> Those voices of twin solitudes
> Shall have one sound alike to thee:
> Hark where the murmurs of thronged men
> Surge and sink back and surge again,—
> Still the one voice of wave and tree.
>
> (191)

In *The House of Life* there are two sonnets in which the horizon-line is the crucial symbol, "The Lovers' Walk" (XII) and "The Monochord" (LXXIX).[17] Both of these sonnets repay close examination because they are good examples of Rossetti's most condensed style, displaying his stylistic virtuosity and his capacity for complex thought. Moreover, the contrast between "The Lovers' Walk" (XII), one of the most positive of the early love sonnets, and "The Monochord" (LXXIX), a most difficult poem situated near the mid-point of the "Change and Fate" section, provides a microcosmic view of the overarching movement in *The House of Life* generally. First, let us examine "The Lovers' Walk":

> Sweet twining hedgeflowers wind-stirred in no wise
> On this June day; and hand that clings in hand:—
> Still glades; and meeting faces scarcely fann'd:—
> An osier-odoured stream that draws the skies
> Deep to its heart; and mirrored eyes in eyes:—
> Fresh hourly wonder o'er the Summer land
> Of light and cloud; and two souls softly spann'd
> With one o'erarching heaven of smiles and sighs:—
> Even such their path, whose bodies lean unto
> Each other's visible sweetness amorously,—

> Whose passionate hearts lean by Love's high decree
> Together on his heart for ever true,
> As the cloud-foaming firmamental blue
> Rests on the blue line of a foamless sea.

In this sonnet the informing idea is the absolute unity of the two lovers; with consummate artistry Rossetti manages a series of implied similes describing the lovers' unity. Each single term of each simile is in itself an image of union, and by yoking the two terms together in simile, Rossetti creates a unity of two unities. For example, the hedgeflowers are twined together and therefore natural symbols of unity; and they are bound by simile to the entwined hands of the lovers. This proliferation of unities is not merely a static catalogue, however. The sonnet embodies the fact that the desire for unity is always accompanied by the aspiration for the transcendental, because the only true unity exists, not on earth, but beyond. As in "Silent Noon" (XIX), the movement is away from the terrestrial and towards the heavens. First, there are images of earth and nature—the hedgeflowers and glades of the first two similes; then, beginning with the third simile, the comparison of the sky's reflection in the stream to the reciprocal reflection of the lovers' eyes, the ascension begins; finally, in the fourth and final double simile of the octave, the earth is completely left behind.

The sestet brings us back to the image of the horizon-line. The entire sestet, one of Rossetti's most beautifully handled conceits, is a comparison of the path, which is simultaneously taken and made by the lovers, with the horizon-line. Because the lovers walk so closely together, their steps are completely intermingled, and so their path is virtually one path—it is impossible to say whether the path has been formed by the lover or by his mistress. Their unity is therefore symbolized by the line which their path forms, and their unity is compared, with perfect appropriateness, to the line formed by the meeting point of the sky and the sea—the horizon-line. The lines made by the lovers and the horizon-line are therefore complementary images of inexplicable unities; moreover, the comparison of the lovers' unity to the unity of sea and sky fulfills the movement of the octave, and the significance of the lovers' path is now fully realized: their unity is an earthly version of the ultimate unity of the human and the divine. Indeed, the final two lines are perhaps the closest Rossetti ever comes to a complete and adequate poetic embodiment of the unity of earth and heaven: the sky, because it is "cloud-foaming," is partially transformed into the sea; and the sea, because it is "foamless" and blue, is partially transformed into the sky. Finally, the interpenetration of sky and sea is completed by the criss-cross pattern formed by the words "foaming" and "blue" in line thirteen and "blue" and "foamless" in the final line: "As the cloud-foaming firmamental blue/Rests on the blue line of a foamless sea."

While the early love-sonnets, like "The Lovers' Walk," do possess a vision of unity, it is apparent that the idea of unity is only expressed through tremendous strain; the extravagance of the conceits in "The Lovers' Walk" is in itself some indication of the effort required to realize the conception in concrete terms. When we reach "The Monochord" (LXXIX) the theme is still unity and the image is still the horizon-line; but now the speaker is completely alone—he is a "separate wave" in the sea of life. The moment of earthly union has passed and he meditates on the possibility of the existence of some supernal region in which he would recover the unity he has lost. Here is the sonnet:

> Is it this sky's vast vault or ocean's sound
> That is Life's self and draws my life from me,
> And by instinct ineffable decree
> Holds my breath quailing on the bitter bound?
> Nay, is it Life or Death, thus thunder-crowned,
> That mid the tide of all emergency
> Now notes my separate wave, and to what sea
> Its difficult eddies labour in the ground?
> Oh! what is this that knows the road I came,
> The flame turned cloud, the cloud returned to flame,
> The lifted shifted steeps and all the way?—
> That draws round me at last this wind-warm space,
> And in regenerate rapture turns my face
> Upon the devious coverts of dismay?

"The Monochord" (LXXIX) has always been a puzzle to critics, who usually agree with William Rossetti's opinion that it is the "most obscure" of the *House of Life* sonnets.[18] The title itself has caused a great deal of confusion. William quotes a dictionary definition which says that a monochord is " 'an instrument of one string, used to ascertain and demonstrate the several lengths of the string required to produce the several notes of the musical scale' " (pp. 240–41). But William does not see any way that the musical instrument figures in the poem: "Evidently, however, the word Monochord is not here applied in this literal sense, but may rather indicate 'the power of music in eliciting and meting out the emotions of the human soul' " (p. 241). Baum agrees with William's estimate of the obscurity of the sonnet and with his interpretation of the title as having only a vague relevance to the sonnet itself: "the sonnet expresses the power of music to raise the great questions of existence, Life and Death, with their application to the individual existence; and also, while introducing a mood of introspection, to soften old memories and present pain. It is a prime example of poetry striving towards the condition of music—and almost ceasing to be intelligible."[19]

However, as I shall attempt to demonstrate, the title is more than tangentially related to the sonnet; in fact, it is the underlying image of the whole of the first quatrain, which, for convenience, I will quote again:

> Is it this sky's vast vault or ocean's sound
> That is Life's self and draws my life from me,
> And by instinct ineffable decree
> Holds my breath quailing on the bitter bound?

The horizon-line again figures crucially because an actual monochord is presented imagistically in this quatrain as an instrument whose single string is, in fact, the horizon-line (the "bound" or boundary in line four), which is strung over a sounding box which is either (and this is the question to be pondered) the vaulted sky or the ocean. Thus Rossetti creates an ambiguous image; there are two possible monochords, each a mirror of the other, depending on whether the sky or the sea forms the sounding box of the monochord. Obviously the same question which is posed by the horizon-line itself is posed again, and that question is really, as we have seen, ontological: what is the ultimate ground of reality ("Life's self") of which everything, each separate "life," is a part—what is the music to which all creation moves?

The sound created by the vibration of the horizon-line produces a sympathetic vibration in the speaker, whose own voice (his "breath") sounds in harmony with the horizon-line. His own voice is sounded without his will ("by instinct ineffable decree") because he cannot help but respond to that which is identical to himself, and so he finds his soul held "quailing on the bitter bound." The speaker's soul has been set in movement, which he experiences, in an extension of the musical metaphor, as a kind of rhapsody ("regenerate rapture"); but he is not able to decide what his experience ultimately signifies. The duality inherent in the horizon-line is never resolved; the speaker never knows whether his individual self vibrates sympathetically to the sound of a transcendental, eternal reality (the sky), or if he is merely responding to the sad music of the mortal sea of life.

In the next quatrain, as if he has become aware of the vastness of his query, Rossetti restates the question raised in the first quatrain, but he deepens the breadth and significance of the question:

> Nay, is it Life or Death, thus thunder-crowned,
> That 'mid the tide of all emergency
> Now notes my separate wave, and to what sea
> Its difficult eddies labour in the ground?

We can see that Rossetti has framed his question with more precision. If "Life's self" is the sky, then the overarching power which "notes" his "separate wave" (his separate self) assures him eternal life, because then the reality to which he responds and of which he is a part is a supernal, eternal reality. On the other hand, if "Life's self" is the sea, then he is in harmony only with the transient and the earthly—all aspects of which are doomed to death. There is no answer to such a mystery, of course. The whole sonnet is simply a series of four parallel and unanswerable questions—the tension caused by the uncertainty of the ultimate identity of the self and the universe is never resolved, although the very fact that the self has responded to something is, at this point in *The House of Life*, enough to cause a subtle shift in emotion, signalled by the difference between the self "quailing" in the first quatrain, to the suggestion of joy ("regenerate rapture") in the final tercet. The simple fact that the self still has the power to respond, that it is capable, as Rossetti wrote in his own copy of *Poems*, 1870, of "that sublimated mood of the soul in which a separate essence of itself seems to oversoar and survey it"[20]—that is sufficient ground for joy.

We have already seen the mirror as a symbol of unity in "The Lovers' Walk" (XII): "An osier-odoured stream that draws the skies Deep to its heart; and mirrored eyes in eyes. . . ." In this sonnet the stream, a mirror reflecting and embracing the sky, illustrates the unity of the natural and divine; and the implied simile, comparing the reflection of the sky in the stream to the mutual reflection of the lovers' eyes, establishes a three-fold unity of the natural, the divine, and the human. The mirror imagery here is clearly another variation of the union of sky and water which we have examined in the image of the horizon-line; both images represent the presence of a harmonizing principle in the universe, a kind of natural *concordia discors*. The imagery of reflected eyes and reflected sky in water is shown in all its positive glory in "The Lovers' Walk" (XII), where all of the contraries of existence are magically bound together; and the privileged, infinite moment of "Mid-Rapture" (XXVI) is captured in the imagery of reflection also:

> What word can answer to thy word,—what gaze
> To thine, which now absorbs within its sphere
> My worshipping face, till I am mirrored there
> Light-circled in a heaven of deep-drawn rays?

But even in the earliest *House of Life* sonnets the precariousness of the privileged moment is apparent to the poet-lover. In "Lovesight" (IV), a poem which accurately predicts many of the later developments in *The House of Life*, and which, Baum reports,[21] Rossetti at one time planned to use as the first sonnet in the series, the image-cluster of water, eyes, and mirror appears in a darker mode; the lover exclaims:

> O love, my love! if I no more should see
> Thyself, nor on earth the shadow of thee,
> Nor image of thine eyes in any spring. . . .

Of course this is exactly what occurs when the unity sought by the lover is shattered by death and separation. In the "Willowwood" series the motif of the mirroring eyes and the mirroring spring is fully and ironically orchestrated. Nowhere is the change from the harmony and unity of the early sonnets to the discord and isolation following the loss of love clearer than in the "Willowwood" group.

The "Willowwood" sonnets record the obsessive nature of the desire for unity and the fact that the desire becomes even more obsessive after separation. The vision of the beloved, which is conjured up by the speaker's memory in the first sonnet of the group only to disappear in the last sonnet, is bitter and mocking. After his vision the lover is left alone, united not with his beloved, but with Love himself, the personification of an emotional force which haunts him and will not set him free. While it is true that, as Baum writes, the "vision in Willowwood, with its grief and ecstasy, has given him something like the catharsis of tragedy,"[22] that catharsis is only momentary. In the sonnets which immediately follow "Willowwood," "Without Her" (LIII) and "Love's Fatality" (LIV), the lover plunges back into the desolation of isolation and returns to his obsessive desire.

The central images in the "Willowwood" series are the mirrored reflections on the water of the well which stands in the middle of the dark woods. The initial impulse to drink at the well arises from the desire to quench the anguished thirst of separation, the well representing, in this aspect, as it traditionally does so often, the source of being—and the desire to drink its waters is the desire to recover wholeness. But that desire proves vain and the unity which is achieved is only illusory: the bubbling image of the beloved is only the projection of the isolated lover's desire. He attempts to recapture the same kind of unity which is embodied in the mirror images of "The Lovers' Walk" (XII) and "Mid-Rapture" (XXVI); but the mirrored eyes of his beloved that appear on the surface of the well's water are only hallucinations. The union created by the kiss of the lover and the watery image of his beloved is as fragile as the air-bubbles floating on the water, to which her lips are compared.

From another point of view the "Willowwood" sonnets do describe a special kind of anguished unity: the union of the lost beloved and the lover in the lover's mind—within his memory. Ironically the lover's deepest desire after he has attained this kind of union is for absolute separation; more than anything he hopes that he might free himself from the bondage of "half-remembrance," that the well-water, like the water of Lethe, will enable him to forget his dead love; as Love sings: "Better all life forget her than this thing, / That Willowwood should hold her wandering!" (LI). The lover experiences a momentary triumph because the haunting image of the beloved is finally exorcized and the painful union of the kiss is severed:

So when the song died did the kiss unclose;
And her face fell back drowned; and was as grey
As its grey eyes; and if it ever may
Meet mine again I know not if Love knows.

(LII)

But this exorcism does not bring peace. In the very next sonnet, "Without Her" (LIII), the imagery of mirrow, sky, and water is repeated, but now there is no reflection of the beloved at all: "What of her glass without her? The blank grey / There where the pool is blind of the moon's face." Rossetti has returned to the doubling of images which he used in "The Lovers' Walk" (XII), but now the doubled images depict isolation and separation. The final four lines of "Without Her" (LIII) are themselves a dark mirror of the images of the lovers' unity in "The Lovers' Walk" (XII); the lover's dark depression is mirrored by the darkness caused by the severance-ruling cloud—his heart is a wanderer shadowed, not by his beloved's hair, but by the confining cloud of mortality:

A wayfarer by barren ways and chill,
Steep ways and weary, without her thou art,
Where the long cloud, the long wood's counterpart,
Sheds doubled darkness up the labouring hill.

The mirror symbolism of *The House of Life* brings us back to the problem of subjectivism in Rossetti's poetry. Inherent in the metaphor of the beloved's eyes as a mirror is the irony that the lover never sees his beloved when he looks into her eyes; instead, he sees his own reflection. When the mirror is removed, when the Old Love dies and the New Beloved leaves, the lover is lost. Without a beloved his personality disintegrates because she has been his means of sustaining an identity; and so, the "Willowwood" group and many of the following sonnets, like "A Superscription" (XCVII) and "He and I" (XCVIII), express the theme, as Henri Talon puts it, of "l'absence d'intégration psychologique."[23] Above all, then, the lover's quest for unity with the beloved is a quest to validate his own self. His goal is the same as the one sought by Chiaro dell' Erma, the artist-hero of "Hand and Soul," whose spiritual journey ends with the appearance of a beautiful woman who says to him: " 'I am an image, Chiaro, of thine own soul within thee. See me, and know me as I am' " (553). Chiaro learns that his duty is to know his own self and to make it manifest through art in order to add to the glory of God, because his soul is divine and part of the ultimate unity. By painting a portrait of his soul Chiaro will therefore create a mirror of God. The advice of his divine soul-image is another version of the Victorian doctrine of work as voiced by Carlyle and Ruskin, but it also brings us back to the heart of Rossetti's conception of unity:

"Give thou to God no more than He asketh of thee; but to man also, that which is man's. In all that thou doest, work from thine own heart, simply; for his heart is as thine, when thine is wise and humble; and he shall have understanding of thee. One drop of rain is as another, and the sun's prism in all: and shalt thou not be as he, whose lives are the breath of One? Only by making thyself his equal can he learn to hold communion with thee, and at last own thee above him. Not till thou lean over the water shalt thou see thine image therein: stand erect, and it shall slope from thy feet and be lost. Know that there is but this means whereby thou mayst serve God, with man:—Set thine hand and thy soul to serve man with God."

(554–55)

Chiaro is ultimately able to accept his self because he recognizes that it is an instrument of God's. His self is validated by its miraculous connection with the divine, which assures him that he is indeed part of a transcendental unity. But in *The House of Life* there is no divine intervention, and the beloved is only the reflection of the lover's own self, a self which is never certain that it has any connection with God. The fact that the beloved never exists as another consciousness, that she is only a mirror for the lover, is only another proof that he is unable to escape from the prison of subjectivism. Without God the self needs some other ground of value outside itself in order to be sustained, and by denying the alterity of his beloved, by using her merely to reflect himself, the lover destroys his own best hope for salvation.

Notes

1. "The English Romantics: The Grounds of Knowledge," *Studies in Romanticism*, 4 (1964), 33.
2. In *The Complete Works of Percy Bysshe Shelley*, ed. Roger Ingpen and Walter E. Peck (New York and London, 1965), VII, 118.
3. Northrop Frye's comments in *A Study of English Romanticism* (New York, 1968) are pertinent to this point: "The tragic hero of Romanticism is usually a tragic lover, and here again it is an excess of consciousness, which isolates the lover instead of uniting him to his beloved, that causes the tragedy. What begins as love ends in frustration, torment, or suicide" (p. 42).
4. "The Narrator of the Blessed Damozel," *MLN*, 73 (1958), 344–48. Here is the crux of Lauter's argument: "We can see how the entire poem, not merely the parentheses, is concerned with the bereaved lover's mind. 'The Blessed Damozel carries Poe's examination of the deluded lover to the point at which the delusion—the Damozel in heaven—is presented as the reality, and the reality—the grieving lover—as a passing, shadowy parenthesis" (p. 347).
5. *The Works of Dante Gabriel Rossetti*, ed. William Michael Rossetti (London, 1911). Numbers in parentheses after quotations refer to page numbers in this text.
6. Quotations from sonnets in *The House of Life* are from Paull Franklin Baum's edition (Cambridge, Mass., 1928). Roman numerals after titles refer to sonnet numbers in this text.

7. *Letters of Dante Gabriel Rossetti*, ed. Oswald Doughty and John Robert Wahl, 4 vols. (Oxford, 1965–67), II, 850. Hereafter cited as *Letters*.

8. Rossetti's position is therefore another instance of the Victorian predicament described by J. Hillis Miller in *The Disappearance of God: Five Nineteenth Century Writers* (Cambridge, Mass., 1963).

9. Rossetti also proposed this stanza to his brother on 10 September 1871 (*Letters*, III, 1003) and Thomas Gordon Hake on 11 September of the same year (*Letters*, III, 1005); in the letter to William he writes: "On one short thing I have done, not meant to be a trifle, I want your advice about the close. I copy it herewith, and the form of the last four lines there given is the one I incline to adopt—thus, you see, leaving the whole question open. But at first I had meant to answer the question in a way, on the theory hardly of annihilation but of absorption." The last sentence is muddled, but clearly Rossetti means to say that the proposed stanza affirms his belief in the theory that the soul is reabsorbed into some original state of unity, as opposed to the possibility that the soul is completely destroyed after death.

10. In "The Concept of the Infinite Moment in *The House of Life*," *Victorian Newsletter*, No. 28 (Fall 1965), 4–8, J. L. Kendall is right, it seems to me, when he states: "The 'Love-world' of Rossetti's infinite moment is very small, very exclusive" (p. 6). But I think he misses the point when he continues: "But what it includes is all that matters anywhere; what is excluded is the imperfect, the incomplete, the irrelevant, and hopefully, the illusory" (p. 6). What are excluded, despite Kendall's hopes that they are illusory, are the conditions of earthly reality. Perfection and completeness exist, not in life, but in death. The "infinite moment," as Kendall says, is a "transcendent moment" (p. 6), and it exists as a telos for the aspiration to escape from earthly life.

11. Sanctuaries formed by two lovers abound. Examples may be found in "A Last Confession," "The Blessed Damozel," "The Stream's Secret," "Spheral Change," and "Last Fire"—and in *The House of Life*, "Love Enthroned" (I), "Bridal Birth" (II), "Love's Testament" (III), "Love's Lovers" (VIII), "Heart's Haven" (XXII), and "Her Gifts" (XXXI).

12. While it is often asserted that Love is also enthroned above Death (for example, see Douglas J. Robillard, "Rossetti's 'Willowwood' Sonnets and the Structure of *The House of Life*," *Victorian Newsletter*, No. 22 [Fall 1962], p. 8), it is not clear if Death is present as one of the "kindred powers"; the only mention of Death is in line eight: "And Life, still wreathing flowers for Death to wear." The important thing to remember, in any case, is that Love's bower is lifeless.

13. "At Last" was never published during Rossetti's lifetime and it is omitted from all editions of Rossetti's *Works* or *Collected Poems*. Oswald Doughty published it in *A Victorian Romantic: Dante Gabriel Rossetti*, 2nd ed. (London, 1960), p. 398.

14. "Dante Gabriel Rossetti: Peintre-Poète dans *La Maison de Vie*," *Études Anglaises*, 19 (1966), 3.

15. There are many wonderful expressions of the silent moment, but perhaps the best is "Silent Noon" (XIX). See also "Youth's Antiphony" (XIII): "What while Love breathed in sighs and silences / Through two blent souls one rapturous undersong." In "The Birth-Bond" (XV) the closeness of siblings is described in terms of silence: they "Shall for the other have, in silence speech."

16. In "The Cloud Confines," as we have seen, "The sky leans dumb on the sea" (220).

17. The horizon-line also figures in "The Portrait" (X), where the "perfect whole of the lady's 'inner self' is described as a horizon-line: "The very sky and sea-line of her soul." The sky and the sea are also present in a difficult quatrain in "Soul's Beauty" (LXXVII) in the description of Lady Beauty's eyes: "Hers are the eyes which, over and beneath, / The sky and sea bend on thee,—which can draw, / By sea or sky or woman, to one law, / The allotted bondman of her palm and wreath."

18. *Dante Gabriel Rossetti as Designer and Writer* (London, 1889), p. 240.

19. Baum, pp. 187–88.

20. Cited by Baum, p. 187.
21. *Ibid.*, p. 70.
22. *Ibid.*, p. 143.
23. *D. G. Rossetti: The House of Life: quelques aspects de l'art et des themes* (Paris, 1966), p. 39.

"The Bitterness of Things Occult": D. G. Rossetti's Search for the Real

JOHN P. MCGOWAN

In his *Autobiography*, Yeats claims that Dante Rossetti, "though his dull brother did once persuade him that he was agnostic," was a "devout Christian."[1] This description is wildly inaccurate, yet it indicates one way to read Rossetti's poetry. Rossetti accepts the traditional Christian notion that man confronts a created world which contains within it certain universal meanings. The artist's task is to uncover those meanings and to present them to an audience, a task which involves a certain amount of interpretation. Rossetti's problem is that he cannot get the world to speak to him; its meanings continually elude him, so that his poetry is unable to present the real fashioned in such a way as to make its true meaning evident. His poetry keeps falling away from the real and the universal toward the poet's personal experiences. This failure to find an adequate poetic subject might be attributed to Rossetti's lack of talent or lack of faith, but his struggles also suggest the predicament of the post-Romantic Victorian poets who found that the sources of Romantic poetry were no longer fruitful. The result is a poetry (which includes some excellent poems) constructed out of a recognition of its own failure, a poetry which undermines its own validity in face of the reality it has failed to express. Despite all the poet's efforts, reality keeps secret from him its hidden meanings.[2]

An early sonnet, "St. Luke the Painter" (later incorporated into *The House of Life* LXXV), describes a Christian aesthetic, one in which art "rends the mist / Of devious symbols," finding in "sky-breadth and field-silence" the way to God. Rossetti aligns himself with this art which acts to make apparent the meaning of experience, and accepts the priestly role given to the artist. Lamenting the fact that modern art "has turned in vain / To soulless self-reflections of man's skill," the poet piously hopes that art will return to that time when it was "God's priest." Art must learn to "pray again."

Two consequences of this Christian aesthetic should be noted. First, a thing is never its appearance merely: there is always something beyond or beneath what is present to the senses, and the artist searches out this deeper

Reprinted from *Victorian Poetry* 20 (1982): 45–62, by permission of the journal.

significance. William Rossetti characterized "the intimate intertexture of a spiritual sense with a material form" as "one of the influences which guided the [Pre-Raphaelite] movement."[3] Holman Hunt would certainly have agreed with this statement, as well as with the aesthetic of "St. Luke the Painter." Hunt thought that the advantage of faithfulness to nature in pictorial representation was that such accuracy would make the symbolic import of the represented image more apparent.[4]

The inability to identify meaning simply as appearance, the need to represent the thing so that qualities not on the surface are manifested, leads to the second important feature of a Christian art: the identification of art with prayer. Luke is honored because he "first taught Art to fold her hands and pray" and the poet's hope is that art will learn to "pray again." The artist prays that hidden meanings might be revealed to him.

Resistance to Yeats's characterization of Rossetti as a Christian is based on Rossetti's having abandoned, after the early poems and paintings, specifically Christian themes or any adherence to Christian dogma. But Yeats's comment is true to Rossetti's retention, throughout his career, of his conviction in significances beyond sense and the need for "prayerful" poems. The problem becomes how to gain access to those hidden meanings. Hunt's belief that attention to physical detail reveals spiritual significance is, of course, derived from Ruskin, but this theory works only in the context of religious faith. Rossetti lacks Hunt's faith, if not the desires faith can satisfy, and his art strives to develop satisfactory means of access other than faith to the spiritual. Long after his art has been stripped of any Christian trappings, the poem as prayer remains one of Rossetti's stocks in trade.

> What thing unto mine ear
> Wouldst thou convey,—what secret thing,
> O wandering water ever whispering?
> Surely thy speech shall be of her.
> Thou water, O thou whispering wanderer,
> What message dost thou bring?
>
> (ll. 1–6)

"The Stream's Secret" (from which this stanza is taken) presents Rossetti at his most listless. The poet's passive stance is broken only by the voicing of his plea, but even that action is languidly performed, and continually announces its imminent end. The poet hopes his own words will spur the stream to talk, to divulge its secret. He waits anxiously for his own voice to be replaced by the stream's. But in vain. "Still silent? Can no art / Of Love's then move thy pity? Nay" (ll. 199–200). The stream retains its secret, and the discouraged poet stops speaking to cry, adding his tears to the stream's "cold" water. This poem is hardly Rossetti at his best or most attractive, but it embodies that despair which gave rise to charges of morbidity. The poet, immersed in Dante and the Romantics, goes to nature to find an intimation (a symbol) of the larger significances which give experience meaning, and only finds dead material things which resist his prayer, remain silent, and refuse incorporation into art.

"The Woodspurge" is a famous example of how nature is dead for Rossetti in a way that it was not for Dante or the Romantics.[5] The woodspurge's "cup of three" reminds the reader of the Christian synthesis which did unite the individual to the world around him, but the point of the poem is that this union no longer exists. The poet remains totally isolated in his grief, just as the individuality of the woodspurge remains inviolate despite the speaker's investigation. The poem might almost be read as a repudiation of the Ruskinian aesthetic adopted by Hunt. The poet has gone to nature and looked with care at the particular thing, and the result is neither an awakening of faith nor a feeling of greater participation in some unity which includes both poet and flower.

In "Jenny" it is not the natural world, but another person, who faces the speaker as an alien reality which he cannot get to speak. The speaker stops several times to inquire of the sleeping prostitute: "Whose person or whose purse may be / The lodestar of your reverie?" (ll. 20–21); "I wonder what you're thinking of" (l. 58). Jenny, asleep, is unable to answer, and so the speaker supplies the answers himself, offering what he imagines her thoughts must be.

Nothing could more completely distinguish Rossetti from the Romanticism of Wordsworth than this failure to find a voice beyond himself. The speaker of "Jenny" is a scholar or writer who has hidden from the world in his "room . . . full of books" (ll. 22–23). On this night he has escaped from his study to confront "life" and cull a lesson from the confrontation, much as Wordsworth does from his meeting with the leech gatherer. But Rossetti's speaker, far from gaining new insights from his encounter, spends the night only with his own thoughts. His habit of self-involved meditation results in Jenny's playing the same role as a book to him. "You know not what a book you seem, / Half-read by lightning in a dream!" (ll. 51–52). Of course, the leech gatherer only fosters an intensely personal meditation in Wordsworth as well, but the difference is that Wordsworth finds in the encounter a way to transcend himself, to change the current of his thoughts. Rossetti's speaker achieves no such transcendence. Jenny is subsumed entirely into him, another manifestation of his thoughts.[6]

The futility of his thoughts, their emptiness and unreality, overcomes the speaker at various times in the poem: ". . . my thoughts run on like this / With wasteful whims more than enough" (ll. 56–57); "Let the thoughts pass, an empty cloud!" (l. 155). The reality of Jenny lies before the speaker, but he is painfully aware that her "truth" has escaped him.

> Come, come, what use in thoughts like this?
> Poor little Jenny, good to kiss,—
> You'd not believe by what strange roads
> Thought travels, when your beauty goads
> A man tonight to think of toads!
> Jenny, wake up . . . Why there's the dawn!
>
> (ll. 298–302)

"Thought," travelling by "strange roads," strays from the real. Everything returns the speaker to the prison of self. The absence of sexual union in the poem points toward the absence of any corresponding spiritual union. Many of the sexual puns which would describe the situation also adequately describe the speaker's failure to effect a union between thought and reality, self and other. This meeting has been sterile; the speaker has not penetrated this incomprehensible other being whose thoughts remain completely unknown to him. These parallels between the physical and epistemological planes are suggested by the ending of the poem.

> And must I mock you to the last,
> Ashamed of my own shame,—aghast
> Because some thoughts not born amiss
> Rose at a poor fair face like this?
> Well, of such thoughts, so much I know:
> In my life, as in hers, they show,
> By a far gleam which I may near,
> A dark path I can strive to clear.
>
> (ll. 383–390)

This passage is difficult because the reference of "thoughts" is ambiguous. Two readings are possible, each of which illuminates certain important features of Rossetti's poetry. The first possibility is that the "thought" which "shames" the speaker is lust, and he mocks Jenny because she has fostered that emotion in him. Much of the poem has focused, in no flattering terms, on "man's changeless sum / Of lust" (ll. 278–279). The last lines suggest, then, that the speaker (in Wordsworthian fashion) has formed a new resolution. The experience of lust has intimated to him (the "far gleam") the existence of love, a state which he might attain by "clearing" the "dark path" of base desires. (The path's darkness also indicates his ignorance and inexperience.) The speaker leaves Jenny to go seek love. We might call this the "Wordsworthian" or "optimistic" reading. Although union with this particular woman is impossible, the speaker has recognized that physical love is an analogue of spiritual love, and that through physical love he can move toward the realm of spiritual love. Love can be the solution to the radical split between self and other. The dead world can be brought to life by love, and much of Rossetti's later poetry explores both how physical love either symbolizes or leads to spiritual love, and how love serves to connect self to the world.

This "optimistic" reading must be qualified, however, since the poem does not exhibit a Wordsworthian confidence that any substantial contact with Jenny has been made. The second possible reference of "thoughts" (l. 385) is to the meditations contained in the poem. The speaker's shame is his chagrined awareness that, characteristically, his night with the prostitute was spent in "thought," not in bed. He recovers his self-pride by asserting his difference from Jenny, an assertion cemented by his placing the coins in her hair. Both the speaker and Jenny are thinking beings whose thoughts "show" the "far gleam" of a purity beyond this world's degradation, but the speaker sticks to his image of Jenny as "thoughtless" (l. 7) to suggest that only he will follow the "gleam" and clear the "dark path." The speaker leaves Jenny and her physical world behind to retreat into the realm of pure thought. The poem reveals a strong disgust with the bestial in man, so the final choice of purity by the speaker, even when seen as partly a defensive reaction to his inability to participate in Jenny's world, is not a total surprise.

While the reader's ironic understanding of the speaker's limits is deliberately set up by Rossetti, the tensions explored in the poem are Rossetti's as well as the protagonist's. At times able to find in the physical an analogue for the spiritual, at other times Rossetti can only see the physical and the spiritual as complete opposites. The speaker's attitude toward Jenny, with its strange mixture of sympathy and contempt, accurately reflects Rossetti's own confusions over the exact relations of thought to life. He longs for the correspondences between thought and world found by the Romantics. But those correspondences elude him, and the world constructed by thought seems far superior to the dead world discovered by the senses.[7] However, Rossetti is rarely able to effect a retreat into pure thought with a clear conscience. He still believes in a reality which exists independent of thought, and which is also stronger than thought. If Rossetti's difficulty in finding a home in nature distinguishes him from the Romantics, his uneasiness with residence in the halls built by imagination equally demonstrates his separation from the moderns.

Poem after poem places the speaker in a position of readiness from which he strains to catch the message he is persuaded the world must hold. In "Love-Lily" the speaker's "life grows faint to hear" the approach of a "spirit" who "on my mouth his finger lays" and "shows" the silenced poet the "Eden of Love." "The Sea-Limits" is another listening poem, with "secret continuance sublime" identified as the sea's song. The poet here exhorts his readers to listen not only to the sea but also to a shell "which echo[es] . . . the whole sea's speech." When he emphasizes listening to the world, Rossetti's conception of poetry can be likened to this shell. Poetry should "echo" the voice of the world, not introducing personal or solipsistic reveries, but presenting the meanings of a world all men live in. The word "echo," which appears in many Rossetti poems, suggests a perfect harmony, a faithful reproduction of something given to the poet.[8] Yet an echo is secondary and weaker than the original sound. Rossetti seems determined to find meaning in the external world rather than in a world created by imagination, even when it means accepting a secondary and passive voice for the poet. However, his voice is weakest, not when he echoes truths present in nature, but when he laments that the secret of life's meanings is being kept from him. "The bitterness of things occult" remains the greatest burden he must bear.[9]

That thoughts exist separate from the actual significance of reality afflicts Rossetti's notion of art. Far from being an "aestheticist" in the sense that he wishes art to have no relation to life, Rossetti continually bemoans art's failed attempts to embody the real. His poetry points the way toward modern "aestheticism" only insofar as it contemplates art's difficulties in reaching beyond itself and becoming real. In "Jenny" the speaker tries to imagine how Jenny's "true nature" might be portrayed by an artist. How would "Raffael" or "Leonardo" have painted the prostitute? The beautiful women painted by these masters showed to "men's souls" what "God can do" (11. 238–240), but the artist who would portray Jenny must show a beautiful face which reveals the evil men have done while still showing that God cherishes the fallen woman. Such a portrait, the speaker concludes, could not be painted, for reasons which seem archetypally Victorian: religious doubt and the audience's prudery. How could an artist portray God's love for the sinner when he has "no sign" that such love exists. "All dark. No sign on earth / What measure of God's rest endows / The many mansions of his house" (11. 247–249). This failure to see a way to paint Jenny is followed by the lament: "If but a woman's heart might see / Such erring heart unerringly / For once! But that can never be" (11. 250–252). The flat despair of the second sentence falls limply after the soaring hope of the first. Even where reality could be made to speak, the cherished respectability of the Victorian audience would insure that the revealed meanings would never be heeded.

The relation of art to the real is complicated further when, continuing his lament that no Victorian audience would allow itself to contemplate the reality of Jenny, the speaker describes her as

> a rose shut in a book
> In which pure women may not look,
> For its base pages claim control
> To crush the flower within the soul.
> (ll. 253–256)

This passage, on one level, links Victorian prudery to the horror of Jenny's existence. Society condemns Jenny to a particular life and death by turning on her, and yet this same society is hypocritical enough to claim that the book which would present Jenny faithfully will corrupt "pure" women.[10]

More interesting in terms of the argument presented here is how this passage develops the relationship between art and life. The metaphor of the rose which is killed when it is pressed into a book suggests that the artist kills reality when he transforms it into art. Has the poet not taken the "rose," Jenny, and shut her into his own book? Making Jenny the subject of a poem is an extension of the process by which the speaker has attributed all his own thoughts to the sleeping prostitute. Art is substituted for reality just as the speaker's thoughts were substituted for Jenny's. Everything—God's silence, society's fragmentation and prudery, the speaker's solipsism, and the poet's imposition of form and interpretation—conspires to leave life's secrets inviolate and to identify art as merely the domain of personal reveries.

Both poems entitled "The Portrait" consider how the artist, through his art, appropriates reality and controls the meanings it reveals.[11] In the sonnet, the poet-painter glories in his ownership of the real.

> Let all men note
> That in all years (O Love, thy gift is this!)
> They that would look on her must come to me.

The form the portrait painter has given to his love is how she will exist for others from this point on. The earlier poem is more troubled by the hubris implied by the artist setting up his art as the sole point of access to a particular reality. The poem opens by establishing that where art is, reality is no longer. "This is her picture as she was." And the reader learns that "only this, of love's whole prize / Remains." The painting is so lifelike that the poet can cry, "'Tis she!," but he quickly qualifies this ecstasy: "though of herself, alas! / Less than her shadow on the grass / Or than her image in the stream." The limitation of Art is that while it may faithfully represent the real, it always remains only a representation of the object represented. The portrait is what remains of the poet-painter's love, but these remains are incomplete since the painting has not captured "what is secret and unknown, / Below the earth, above the skies." Not only does the loved one's life elude the artist's attempt to capture it, but the portrait also fails to convey some "mystery" about the loved one which "takes counsel with my soul alone." Because the material image is not the living woman, the essential, spiritual truth about her is not conveyed.

It might seem a long way from the "living woman" of this poem to the "dead, thoughtless" prostitute of "Jenny." But these two ways of characterizing the other are linked for Rossetti. Jenny is dead insofar as the artist must enliven her to make her suitable material for poetry. The speaker has interpreted her, created an image of her in his thoughts, tried to imagine her reality. But, in doing all this, he worries that he has crushed the "rose" of the actual Jenny. The mystery which transcends the painted image of the woman in "The Portrait" addresses the same fear that the woman presented in art is only the artist's recreation of the real in terms of his art. Even where it means belittling his art, Rossetti needs to assert the existence of a reality which is other than the artist and his imagination.

In fact, "The Portrait" implies that life and art are inimical, that the living thing is never art, that art only holds images of the dead. The poem narrates how the two lovers first exchanged vows of love. The "next day" the poet-painter remembers his ecstasy and decides he "must make them all [his] own / And paint this picture." He begins the task immediately.

> And as I wrought, while all above
>   And all around was fragrant air,
> In the sick burthen of my love
>   It seemed each sun-thrilled blossom there
> Beat like a heart among the leaves.
> O heart that never beats nor heaves,
>   In that one darkness lying still,
>   What now to thee my love's great will
> Or that fine web that sunshine weaves?

The speaker's feeling that all nature is alive as he paints is juxtaposed with the fact of the loved one's death. The "sick burthen" of his love is the need to make the previous day's perfection all his "own" by freezing it in a painting. The cause of the woman's death is never given, but the poet-painter's attempt to capture her in art results in his having exchanged her for the portrait with which he is left. The poem implies a choice between life and art. Where one is, the other is not. And since for Rossetti life comes first, the work of art becomes merely a surrogate for the reality which inspires it.

The last four stanzas continue this opposition between art and life, but the poet wavers as to which is most desirable. Reality is associated with "day" and "light," art with "darkness" and "night." Only in art can the speaker retain his memory of that once perfect love.

> For now doth daylight disavow
>   Those days,—nought left to see or hear.
> Only in solemn whispers now
>   At night-time these things reach mine ear.

Art, existing in the realm of dream, memory and night-time, remains a repository for contents which the harsh light of reality disavows. The speaker, preferring night-time, "delay[s] his sleep till dawn." But he cannot live entirely in the night world; the dawn is inevitable.

> And as I stood there suddenly
> All wan with traversing the night,
> Upon the desolate verge of light
> Yearned loud the iron-bosomed sea.

Implacable ("iron-bosomed") and desolate, reality returns, usurping the speaker's reveries and memories. The better world the poet establishes in art, the more satisfying realm of night in which desires are fulfilled in dream and imagination, must yield to the cold light of day. Reality both gives birth to the need to imagine something better than the real *and* acts to deny that imagined world's validity. The very fact that reality raises the question of meaning and then refuses to answer it makes the poet retreat to an artistic world full of significance. At the same time, the poet begins to suspect that the answer to the question of meaning is that reality is inimical to human desires.[12] Rossetti's acceptance that there exists a reality independent of the self and its desires, and that art should depict that reality, necessitated his submission to the "bitterness of things occult."

The poet's goal in *The House of Life* is to ground personal experience in reality by finding in emotion and the loved woman symbols of general truths about Love, Life, Hope, and those other personified abstractions which occupy these sonnets alongside the detailed descriptions of individual things. Of *The House of Life* Rossetti wrote; "To speak in the first person is often to speak most vividly; but these emotional poems are in no sense 'occasional.' The 'life' involved is life representative, as associated with love and death, with aspiration and foreboding, or with ideal art and beauty. Whether the recorded moment exists in the region of fact or thought is a question indifferent to the Muse, so long only as her touch can quicken it" (Doughty, p. 379). Rossetti knew very well that he had trouble effecting this movement from the particular to the general, and we must take this statement as one of desire not of achievement, but there can be little doubt that the sonnets address this concern directly.

The importance of love for Rossetti lies in its seeming ability to elevate personal experience into the realm of the archetypal. The loved woman embodies all life and all truth. In "Heart's Hope" (V) the poet tells his readers that "one loving heart" can "signify" to "all hearts all things," that the present spring can represent "other Springs gone by." The poet dedicates himself to the task of symbolizing absent things and meanings in these given particulars; the woman serves as the symbol for which the religious poet has been seeking. The way in which the symbols work is left vague, but the poet claims to have experienced moments of "instantaneous penetrating sense." Dawn, birth, and imagery of spring dominate this sonnet, as they do many of Rossetti's happier love poems when he feels that love is granting him an insight into and union with a world beyond himself. The meaning of things dawns on the poet as he perceives the loved one: he is born into a new world which now makes sense to him. And this insight validates his art. The sonnet begins by asking, "what word's power" will allow the poet to realize and embody his new-found knowledge. However, "Heart's Hope," it should be noted, is set almost entirely in the subjunctive mood and stands as a statement of the poet's projects and hopes, not of what he has already accomplished.

There is no need to doubt that love (be it for Lizzie Siddal, Janey Morris, or any other woman) granted Rossetti a sense of being at home in a world in which the bitterness of hidden meanings was, at least temporarily, assuaged. But the success of much of the love poetry need not blind the reader to the problems the poet encounters in trying to make his love experiences "signify all things."[13] The woman in these poems is often enough a shadowy figure, and she is almost always as silent as Jenny. (In fact, the emphasis on physical description turns the woman into a virtual icon, to remind the reader of Rossetti's other career as a painter.) Often the woman becomes a mystery herself, rather than a transparency through which all meanings are revealed, and the poet is reduced to contemplating a reality which excludes him, which he cannot know. Of "True Woman" (LVI) he writes:

> How strange a thing to be what Man can know
> But as a sacred secret! Heaven's own screen
> Hides her soul's purest depth and loveliest glow.

More than any individual poem, however, the structure of *The House of Life* as a whole reveals Rossetti's uneasiness with immersion in personal experience. The poems move from the personal to the non-personal, from happy moments with the loved one to memories of her and meditations on the general significance of love after death.[14] Most readers will agree that the sonnets of Part I, "Youth and Change," are better than those of Part II, "Change and Fate," but what is interesting is Rossetti's compulsion to relinquish his celebration of an individual love experience to write the more general poems of the second part. Rossetti is uneasy with the personal unless he can attach general significance to it, and so he consciously designs his sonnet sequence to move from the particular to the general.

Even in the first part, "Youth and Change," the harsh realities of change and death break in to show the youth that something beyond him exists. The beauty of a poem like "Silent Noon" (XIX) depends not only on its evocation of a perfect moment, but also on its suggestion of that moment's fragility. The lovers have succeeded in escaping for a brief instant (while the sun stops overhead) a reality which is indifferent to their needs.[15] *The House of Life* as a whole sequence denies the possibility of resting in the particular or in the moment, pleasant as such resting might be. Reality always crashes in and reestablishes a less satisfactory, but more real, world.

The sonnets often isolate intense moments but then work to reincorporate such moments into the general continuity of time.[16] Rossetti's sonnet on the sonnet describes his attempt to capture moments of "instantaneous penetrating sense."

> A Sonnet is a moment's monument,—
> Memorial from the Soul's eternity
> To one dead deathless hour.

The moment is both "dead" and "deathless" because it is past, lost forever, and yet the significance it offers, taken from the "eternal" realm which is the soul's domain, is timeless, always true. Art can "memorialize" that eternal significance. Here, then, is one solution to "the bitterness of things occult." Moments of revelation illuminate the true meaning of things in the world, and art can record these momentary insights.[17]

Twentieth-century readers are familiar enough with the consequences of an aesthetics of the moment. Inevitably, emphasis on the moment leads to a discontinuity between moments of revelation and the uninformative daily life of "habit" and "oblivion" (to use Proust's terms). Often enough, this aesthetic leads to a celebration of art's superiority to life, since art affords these glorious moments. Certainly some of Rossetti's sonnets find in the moment the only pleasures life offers. In "Severed Selves" (XL) the lovers look forward to the hour of reunion, "an hour slow to come, how quickly past,— / Which blooms, fades, and only leaves at last / Faint as shed flowers, the attenuated dream." In this poem, life itself seems a dream when compared to passion's intense hour. Rossetti is close at times to Pater's advocation of concentrated moments of intense feeling, and to identifying those moments as the most real things ever encountered, with the resultant acceptance of art, which captures and sustains those moments, as more real than life.

But Rossetti exists on the Victorian side of Pater and it is the tension between art and life, along with the conviction that life is more real, which constitutes Rossetti's poetry. While the moment is an end in itself for Pater, and turns life into art for Proust, it exists for Rossetti as an exception, a wonderful but somewhat unreal escape from the boredom and pain of the everyday. A poet whose experience of radical discontinuities generates in him a desire for continuity, Rossetti will only be satisfied when the particular touches on the general. He strives to make the personal a fit subject for the public, art express the nature of the real, and the moment take its place in a temporal sequence. Whenever the particular cannot be linked to these larger frameworks, Rossetti suspects that these smaller entities do not partake of the real, and are only figments of the imagination.

Many of Rossetti's poems yield these figments, sponsored by desire, in the face of a reality which overwhelms the poet's aspirations. The poet who has been unable to get reality to speak when he pleads for it to do so discovers the voice of reality when it denies him what he wants. Recognizing reality in this resistance to his desires, the poet submissively yields.[18] The "Willowwood Sonnets" (XLIX–LII) provide one example. The poet sits with "Love" by a well, listening for the "certain secret thing" Love has to tell. Turning Love's lute-playing into the "passionate voice" of his dead beloved, the poet is granted a vision of the lady in the water of the well. Now that the poet is absorbed in this vision, Love begins to sing, yet the message is a despairing one: "Your last hope lost, who so in vain invite / Your lips to that their unforgotten food." Love's advice is to forget the past since memory only causes the poet to feed longings which can never be satisfied. With the end of Love's song, the face seen in the well falls "back drowned," and the poet is alone once more. The reality which disperses his vision is a reality incompatible with the human desire for permanence.

It seems odd that when, uncharacteristically, Rossetti succeeds in getting a voice outside the self to speak, the message is so often dismal. The poet has begged life, reality, to reveal itself and its deepest meanings to him, and on the few occasions his request bears fruit, the lesson is that life's laws and man's hopes inevitably conflict.

> There came an image in Life's retinue
>   That had Love's wings and bore his gonfalon:
>   Fair was the web, and nobly wrought thereon,
> O soul-sequestered face, thy form and hue!
> Bewildering sounds, such as Spring wakens to,
>   Shook in its folds; and through my heart its power
>   Sped trackless as the immemorable hour
> When birth's dark portal groaned and all was new.
>
> But a veiled woman followed, and she caught
>   The banner round its staff, to furl and cling,—
>   Then plucked a feather from the bearer's wing,
> And held it to his lips that stirred it not,
> And said to me, "Behold, there is no breath:
> I and this Love are one, and I am Death."

In the octave of "Death and Love" (XLVIII), the "image" from "Life's retinue" possesses the poet utterly, granting him a "power" which he likens to being present at the mysterious origin of all life, the primal Spring. That origin is an "immemorable hour," its fundamental reality seemingly guaranteed by its transcending any incorporation into human memory or speech. Even when granted an insight into reality far beyond what he has enjoyed before, the poet can only distinguish "bewildering sounds." The mysteries here strain the poet's ability to articulate them.

In the sestet, the full consequences of this revelation become apparent. Even to have penetrated this far into "Life's retinue" is to have gone beyond the limits of the human, to have moved toward death. "Death" might be read metaphorically here. The poet could be saying that union with another in love, which results in the birth of new life (a child, his poetry), also involves a death to self which makes the new life possible. Tied as it is to birth, death here might even take on its Elizabethan, sexual meaning, with the "power" which possesses the poet being sexual passion. But the brutal and bare statement, "Behold, there is no breath," denies all metaphorical readings. The creative union the poet has hoped to find in love, a union beyond self with the real, is declared as identical to death: "I and this Love are one, and I am Death." Denied any experience of union in life, Rossetti comes to believe union can only be found in death.

Such a conclusion would seem preposterous if it were not for the evidence of the poems. The sonnets were written over a period of years, so they are not consistently gloomy. But a poem like "Michelangelo's Kiss" (XCIV) states clearly Rossetti's conviction that no satisfactory union will be experienced in this life: ". . . even thus the Soul, / Touching at length some sorely-chastened goal, / Earns oftenest but a little." After such failure, the only question remains: "What holds for her Death's garner? And for thee?" At times, Rossetti welcomes the bitterest message of reality—the necessity of death with its annihilation of all hopes for this life—because at least this action to end life proves that the reality he seeks is out there. Determined to prove reality exists and is meaningful, Rossetti can find in the forces that thwart him a confirmation that something exists beyond self. Rossetti's need to yield his own desires and his imaginative art to a transcendent reality explains the presence of death, even the worship of and wish for it, in his poems. At times he even identifies himself with this overwhelming force. In "The Monochord" (LXXIX) he considers how "Life's self," imagined as the "sky's vast vault or ocean's sound," "draws my life from me," pulling his small self back into a larger, universal self. And the poet's ambiguous response to this dissolution is expressed by his experiencing "regenerate rapture" at the very moment he perceives the "devious coverts of dismay." In death, the poet's isolation, his sojourn in what one poem calls the "cloud's confines," will end, and he will participate in the reality he never quite penetrated during his lifetime. With death will come complete knowledge of the meaning of things occult: "Strange to think by the way, / Whatever there is to know, / That we shall know one day" ("The Cloud Confines"). In "The Portrait" that demystifying death is imagined as a birth into union and knowledge.

> How shall my soul stand rapt and awed,
> When, by the new birth borne abroad
> Throughout the music of the suns,
>   It enters in her soul at once
> And knows the silence there for God!

A longing for death because it will rectify the painful ignorance of life would seem proof enough of a poet's failure to fashion through his art some sustaining meaning. But Rossetti's failure is both more complete—and more poignant. He cannot even affirm death wholeheartedly, because he does not know if it will satisfy the desire for union. Along with the poems which call on death as the solution are those poems which wonder if death, too, might cheat his hopes. "Cloud and Wind" (XLIV) contemplates the horrible possibility that death only reveals "that all is vain / And that Hope sows what Love shall never reap." Death might only be a "sleep" which "Ne'er notes" the very things the poet hopes to witness. Ignorant even here, Rossetti is forced back to prayer, pleading:

> That when the peace is garnered in from strife,
> The work retrieved, the will regenerate,
> This soul may see thy face, O lord of death!
> (LXVI)[19]

Notes

1.   (New York, 1953), pp. 188–189.
2.   The word "secret" recurs throughout Rossetti's poetry, revealing the poet's belief that some truth or meaning exists, which is being kept from him.
3.   Quoted from John Dixon Hunt, *The Pre-Raphaelite Imagination 1848–1900* (London, 1968), p. 129.
4.   Carol Christ (*The Finer Optic* [Yale Univ. Press, 1975], pp. 56–62) discusses in detail how the Pre-Raphaelites, especially Hunt, understood the interconnection between "truth to Nature" and the functioning of individual objects as symbols.
5.   McGann uses "The Woodspurge" as one example of his thesis that "Rossetti does not want us to symbolize," and he deliberately divests objects of meanings beyond themselves so that the reader is "restored to a kind of innocence" of immediate response (p. 233). Obviously, McGann's understanding of Rossetti directly contradicts the interpretation being offered here, which sees the resistance of natural objects to a symbolic reading as an indication of the poet's desire to find such meanings, a desire which is often not satisfied. For another discussion of this particular poem and the "resistance" of details to interpretation, see *The Finer Optic*, pp. 40–44.
6.   Writing on "Jenny," both James Paul Seigel (" 'Jenny': The Divided Sensibility of a Young and Thoughtful Man of the World," *SEL*, 9 [1969], 677–694) and James G. Nelson, ("The Rejected Harlot: A Reading of Rossetti's 'A Last Confession' and 'Jenny,' " *VP*, 10 [1972], 123–130) discuss the speaker's distance from the woman, and the irony (set up by Rossetti) of his failure to make any significant contact with her.
7.   The fullest description of Rossetti's separation of himself from the everyday world of Victorian England is Jerome Buckley's "Pre-Raphaelite Past and Present: The Poetry of the Rossettis" in *Victorian Poetry*, Stratford-upon-Avon Studies No. 15 (London, 1972), pp. 123–138.
8.   Some poems which use the image of the "echo" are "Plighted Promise," "Farewell to the Glen" (LXXXIV), "A Day of Love" (XVI), "Stillborn Love" (LV), "Adieu," and "The Cloud Confines."
9.   The lines quoted are from the sonnet written for the painting "Our Lady of the Rocks" by Leonardo da Vinci. Florence Saunders Boos (*The Poetry of D. G. Rossetti* [The Hague, 1976], pp. 224–228) offers a detailed reading of this interesting poem.

10.   That "Jenny" would find a place within "a book in which pure woman may not look" reads like an anticipation of the "fleshly poet" controversy. See Seigel (pp. 677–680) for Rossetti's apprehensions about the reception this poem would receive.

11.   The longer poem "The Portrait" is one of Rossetti's earliest poems; written in 1847, it was heavily revised for *Poems* (1870). The sonnet "The Portrait" is number X of *The House of Life*.

12.   Edward Said, in chapter 4 of *Beginnings* (New York, 1975), discusses nineteenth-century literature in terms of an oscillation between "authority" and "molestation." Writers of the period were searching for an "authority" beyond self to justify their artistic visions, and are concerned about the "author" who sets himself up as creator of a world. Said finds in the novels of the period characters, such as Lydgate in *Middlemarch* and Ahab in *Moby Dick*, who try to create worlds out of themselves and who are finally "molested" by a reality which is larger than their individual visions. These characters embody urges found in the authors themselves, and nineteenth-century writers usually work to assure that their visions are "authorized" by the very nature of things; in other words, the authors align themselves with the forces that "molest" the character's desires. The suggestion here is that Rossetti's poetry reveals a similar need to "molest" the poet's more extravagant desires, and for reasons similar to those outlined by Said.

13.   The fullest description of love's place in Rossetti's poetry is Stephen Spector's excellent essay "Love, Unity and Desire in the Poetry of Dante Gabriel Rossetti," *ELH*, (1971), 432–448. Spector sees love as one expression of Rossetti's overwhelming need "to bridge the gap between the subjective and objective worlds" (p. 432), but he concludes that love does not afford such unity and that Rossetti's poems are about "the desire for unity," not the "experience of unity" (p. 443). If McGann is the critic whose understanding of Rossetti is most distant from that presented here, Spector's views are the most similar.

14.   There has been a series of studies of the structure of *The House of Life* over the past fifteen years. The quick outline presented here is drawn from Robert D. Hume's "Inorganic Structure in *The House of Life*," *PLL*, 5 (1969), 282–295, and especially Houston A. Baker, "The Poet's Progress: Rossetti's *The House of Life*," *VP*, 8 (1970), 1–14.

15.   Spector (pp. 445–446) offers a wonderful evaluation of these moments of escape in Rossetti's love poems and how they generally combine light and dark, suggesting that the peace of escape is also a retreat from the world into death.

16.   George P. Landow, " 'Life touching lips with Immortality': Rossetti's Typological Structures," *SR*, 17 [1978], 247–265) argues at length (see esp. pp. 258–261) for the view presented here that isolated moments in Rossetti are always finally related to a larger temporal framework.

17.   John Dixon Hunt ("A Moment's Monument: Reflections on Pre-Raphaelite Vision in Poetry and Painting" [in Sambrook, pp. 243–264]) offers an excellent discussion of the adherence to an aesthetics of the moment by various writers and artists associated with the Pre-Raphaelite movement. The argument here, of course, is that Rossetti does not find the moment all sufficient. For another discussion of the functioning of the moment, specifically limited to a consideration of Rossetti's poetry, see Stanley M. Holberg, "Rossetti and the Trance," *VP*, 8 (1970), 299–314.

18.   Apart from the Willowwood sonnets and "Death and Love" (discussed here), only six other poems in *The House of Life* introduce a transcendent voice: "Love's Bauble" (XXII), "The Morrow's Message" (XXXVIII), "Love's Fatality" (LIV), "Love's Last Gift" (LIX), "The Love-Moon" (XXXVII), and "The Sun's Shame" (XCIII). Of these, only "Love's Bauble" and "Love's Last Gift" could be considered "positive" in any way.

19.   This essay was first written as part of an NEH Summer Seminar on Victorian and Modern Poetics directed by Carol Christ at the University of California at Berkeley. Thanks are due to the Endowment, and to Professor Christ and members of the seminar who read and helped in the revision of an early draft.

Aestheticism to Experience:
Revisions for *Poems* (1870)

DAVID G. RIEDE

By the time he returned to the writing of poetry at the end of 1868, Rossetti had been all but silent for well over a decade. During this period he had established himself as an artist—not gaining widespread public recognition, since he refused to exhibit, but acquiring a number of wealthy patrons and considerable renown within artistic circles. The reasons for the revival of his poetic ambitions are not entirely clear, though a number may be suggested. First, he began having trouble with his eyes and feared going blind, as his father had done. Painting became temporarily impossible and, he feared, might become permanently so, but perhaps he could turn to poetry. In addition, he was continually encouraged by his friends, particularly by William Bell Scott, to write and to publish, and he himself had always viewed poetry as a higher art than painting. Besides, his financial success as a painter seems to have soiled the art, as he saw it—he painted "pot-boilers" for "tin," but he would write poetry in a more lofty spirit of dedication to Art. And as a diary entry by William Rossetti suggests, it is likely that he was beginning to feel inadequate as a painter, and to hope that he might achieve immortality in the sister art: "He seems more anxious just now to achieve something permanent in poetry than in painting—in which he considers that at any rate two living Englishmen, Millais and Jones, show a higher innate *executive* power than himself."[1] Perhaps most important of all, he began to see more of Jane Morris in 1868, and for the first time since the death of Lizzie he was passionately in love, so a new source of inspiration was available to him.[2]

But for whatever reason, in the late fall of 1868 Rossetti began writing poetry again, and he was soon determined to publish a volume. To this end he began looking through his earlier poems and revising them. Many of them were not available to him, however, since in his grief and remorse at Lizzie's death he had buried the sole copies of many poems in her coffin. In order to have enough material for a substantial volume, he arranged for the

Reprinted from David G. Riede, *Dante Gabriel Rossetti and the Limits of Victorian Vision* (Ithaca, N.Y.: Cornell University Press, 1983), 77–103. Copyright © 1983 by the Cornell University Press. Used by permission of the publisher.

exhumation of the coffin, and in October 1869 the poems were retrieved. He greatly revised these poems, as well as the other early works, combined them with the new poems, and finally went to press with his first original volume of poetry in April 1870.

The shape of Rossetti's career and his long struggle to find his own voice have long been overlooked because his extensive revisions of early poems have been neglected—even in chronological studies of Rossetti's development, critics have frequently attributed poems like "The Blessed Damozel" and "The Portrait" to the late 1840s without, apparently, realizing that lines cited as written in, say, 1847, were not in fact written until 1869. "The Portrait," for example, a radically transformed version of a poem written in 1846 or 1847, clearly belongs, formally and thematically, to the year 1869, yet the best of the chronological studies of Rossetti places it in 1847.[3] Such haphazard dating encourages the impression, which Rossetti was always eager to foster, that the poet emerged full-blown as a precocious master in 1847, and obscures the important point that *Poems*, 1870, represented not merely a collection of early and middle works, but a new departure, in which the Art-Catholic themes are eliminated and new themes are consolidated. And finally, ignoring the revisions leads to a false estimation of the nature of the 1870 volume by undervaluing the great labor Rossetti exerted to achieve a uniform level of craftsmanship and, more important, a consistent thematic outlook. He conscientiously labored to make *Poems*, in his own words, "studied work, where unity is specially kept in view."[4]

The most important of Rossetti's revisions were designed to eliminate any impression of religious faith in his book. William Bell Scott, who noted that Rossetti "had never thought of pietistic matters except as a sentiment," observed that by 1853 even the sentiment was no longer part of Rossetti's inspiration, that by this time "the spirit that had made him choose 'Songs of the Art-Catholic' as a general title died out."[5] Rossetti, however, was not content merely to let the spirit die out, but took active steps to make certain that he could not be regarded as an adherent of Christian faith. In 1865, for example, he wrote to the fervently Christian James Smetham to inform him not only that he was not a believer, but that even discussion of Christianity was "painful" to him.[6] And in 1869 he expressed his chagrin that most of his early work revealed a "mental condition" that was "discouragingly angelic," and suggested that he would now write "better things."[7] His revisions for 1870 were, for the most part, designed to eliminate the "angelic."

While preparing his poems for publication, Rossetti was especially eager to mitigate the effect of the "Art-Catholic" poems "Ave" and "My Sister's Sleep." He was so eager to kill the Art-Catholic that he "hesitated much to print *Ave*, because of the subject." Nevertheless he "thought it well done, and so included it," though he gave prolonged consideration to accompanying it with a note described by Swinburne as "disclaiming a share in the blessings purchased by the blood of your Redeemer."[8] The note was intended to claim that the Christianity of the speaker was entirely dramatic: "This hymn was written as a prologue to a series of designs. Art still identifies herself with all faiths for her own purposes: and the emotional influence here employed demands above all an inner standing-point."[9] Though Rossetti revised "Ave" extensively, he could not possibly eliminate its Christianity, but he could, and did, eliminate Christian faith from other poems. He did not particularly want to include "My Sister's Sleep" in the volume at all, but felt compelled to because it had recently been publicly praised.[10] Once committed to it, he radically transformed it, sending the revised draft to his brother with the comments that "The thing is very distasteful to me as it now stands, and I have quite determined on all changes made in pen and ink. In pencil I indicate a very radical change in the omission of two more stanzas which would eliminate the religious element altogether."[11] In fact Rossetti eliminated four of the original nineteen stanzas, including two following stanza nine in which the speaker and his mother pray, and two following stanza six in which the speaker finds clear religious consolation:

> Silence was speaking at my side
>   With an exceedingly clear voice:
>   I knew the calm as of a choice
> Made in God for me, to abide.
>
> I said, "Full knowledge does not grieve:
>   This which upon my spirit dwells
>   Perhaps would have been sorrow else:
> But I am glad 'tis Christmas Eve."[12]

The poem, published in 1870, contains a reminiscence of this idea in stanza thirteen: "I heard / The silence."[13] But without the earlier stanzas the phrase has no specifically Christian significance. In 1850, however, the phrase had been italicized, emphatically underscoring the "religious element" near the end of the poem. Except for several stylistic revisions, the only other alteration Rossetti made in the poem was to change the image of an "altar-cup" to a secular "icy crystal cup" (*Poems*, 97), so eliminating even the sense that the speaker's range of associations was influenced by Christianity.

The revisions of "My Sister's Sleep" were clearly intended to eliminate the "religious element," but they transform the poem entirely in other ways as well. The early poem is a straightforward religious lyric, whether or not Rossetti himself believed in its consolation. It exhibits no special psychological insight, but only a traditional Christian point of view. The close observation of detail, for which the revised poem is justly celebrated, had been present but subsumed in the Christian idea. In the 1870 version, the details are unmediated by a mythic structure and must carry their own significance. Consequently, the poem becomes a psychological lyric in which close observation itself reveals the speaker's state of mind. Without the intellectual conception of a redeeming faith, the speaker must seek significance in direct experience, in sensory observation heightened by emotional stress. As Richard Stein has said, the "subject is consciousness itself, the hyperaesthesia experienced under the pressure of strong emotion."[14] Even though the last stanza is overtly religious, ending with "Christ's blessing on the newly born" (*Poems*, 98), the effect, in the absence of explicit Christian faith earlier in the poem, is to reinforce the reader's sense of the mother's and son's psychological groping for meaning. Jerome McGann has rightly said that "the blessing at the end does not point to a religious truth, does not serve the symbolic function that it might, but rather emphasizes the emotional state of the mother and son, the measure of comfort that they derive from a traditional religious truth at a moment of deep personal loss."[15] Rossetti changed the lyric from one that adopted the "inner standing-point" of the Christian to one that reveals the psychological pressures that lead to such an "inner standing-point." The revised poem is about unmediated experience, sensory experience, rather than about the fruits of experience, the faith evolved from human need. And of course the 1870 poem is darker, more somber, more skeptical than the early version. In this respect the revisions of "My Sister's Sleep" characterize Rossetti's consistent attempt, in preparing the 1870 *Poems* for the press, to treat all experience directly, to be a "fleshly" poet to the extent that the experiences of the senses are direct and unquestionable, though not necessarily consoling. In a sense, the revised "My Sister's Sleep" is a poem about the body, whereas the early version had been about the soul.

Aside from some sonnets for his own pictures, the only other poem in the 1870 volume that was, or seemed, explicitly Christian in theme and treatment was "The Blessed Damozel." This poem, more than any other, has given Rossetti his reputation for astonishing precocity, a reputation not wholly unearned, since the early versions are very fine, but somewhat exaggerated, since several inconsistencies and crudities were eliminated as the poem was repeatedly revised before 1870. The revisions were mostly for the sake of structural coherence or stylistic felicity, but some change the meaning and tone of the poem radically. Four stanzas about the rigors of religious faith and the peace and serenity of heaven were deleted from the 1850 version, and three entirely new stanzas were added by the time it was republished in 1870.[16] The general effect of the revisions and additions was to change the "Dantesque" heavens,[17] as Leigh Hunt called them, to heavens of more fully human love, to incorporate autobiography, and to add sorrow.[18] Two simple revisions characterize the changed tone. In 1850 the damozel had asked of Christ

> To have more blessing than on earth
> In no wise; but to be
> As then we were,—being as then
> At peace. Yea, verily.[19]

But in 1870 she asks not for peace, but specifically for earthly love:

> Only to live as once on earth
> With Love,—only to be,
> As then awhile, for ever now
> Together, I and he.
>
> *(Poems*, 6)

Similarly, the earthly lover had pondered, in 1850, his worthiness in the eyes of the Lord, but in 1870, at the same point in the poem, he recognizes explicitly that he loves not God, but the damozel:

> But shall God lift
> To endless unity
> The soul whose likeness with thy soul
> Was but its love for thee?
>
> *(Poems*, 5)

The hope in these lines for the bare possibility that earthly love may be continued after death has little to do with any Christian heaven, but it places the poem thematically with poems written in 1869 and 1870. "The Stream's Secret" (1869–70) and many of the sonnets for *The House of Life* express the same faint hope, without Christian overtones. The stanza added to "The Blessed Damozel," then, helps to fit the poem into the volume without disturbing its overall thematic unity. Even in the early version, of course, "The Blessed Damozel" had not represented a genuinely spiritual view of heaven—the damozel had always been hot-blooded enough to warm the gold bar of heaven, and the emphasis had always been on human love. But the version printed in *The Germ* had sufficient religious trappings at least to suggest "Dantesque heavens" and genuine faith, whereas the 1870 version, despite its retention of medieval religious symbolism, more fully emphasizes human love and religious doubt. Reading the 1850 version, we scarcely doubt that the lovers will be reunited, but reading the 1870 poem, we are tempted to associate the damozel's assertion, " 'I wish that he were come to me, / For he will come,' she said" (*Poems*, 5), with the despairing assertion of Tennyson's Mariana, "Then said she, 'I am very dreary, / He will not come,' she said" (ll. 81–82). As is true of "My Sister's Sleep," the revision replaces faith with skepticism, optimism with pessimism, and expresses not the "inner standing-point" of the Christian, but the grief that leads to adopting it.

Rossetti's revisions went beyond merely eradicating the impression that he himself was a Christian. The changes he made in "My Sister's Sleep" and "The Blessed Damozel" were necessary in part because those poems might be taken as utterances of a personal faith, but also because they needed to be compatible with other poems in the volume. "The Staff and Scrip," an old-fashioned ballad telling of a medieval love story, could easily include Christian belief as part of the dramatic framework, but even this poem was revised to show a darker and more skeptical view of Christianity. The story remained essentially unchanged; a pilgrim in a far-away land offers his services in war to Queen Blanchelys, whose lands have been ravaged. He is armed by the queen, sends his staff and scrip to her for safe keeping, and wins a battle for her, though despite the prayers of the queen and her court, he is killed. The queen dies ten years later, and is reunited with the pilgrim in heaven. "The Staff and Scrip" was not as extremely revised as other poems in the volume, partly, perhaps, because it was so impersonally conventional, but the few revisions make it a more somber poem. One stanza in the first published version of 1856, which had described the pilgrim's "joy to fight,"[20] for example, was replaced by a far gloomier stanza:

> Born of the day that died, that eve
>   Now dying sank to rest;
> As he, in likewise taking leave,
>   Once with a heaving breast
>   Looked to the west.
>
> (*Poems*, 30)

Not only are the images of the dying day and evening ominous, but the suggestion of natural cycles, the natural perspective, implies a view of mortality without conjuring up ideas of redemption. In fact, the religious element is altogether more ambivalent in the revised poem, as a stanza added to the description of the queen and her court in prayer and fasting illustrates:

> Lo, Father, is thine ear inclin'd
>   And hath thine angel pass'd?
> For these thy watchers now are blind
>   With vigil, and at last
>   Dizzy with fast.
>
> (*Poems*, 31)

The addition emphasizes the idea, already latent in 1856, that the ascetic ritual is faintly ridiculous, blunting the senses of the watchers but irrelevant to the fortunes of the pilgrim. Other revisions, though slight, undercut the idea of true love between the queen and pilgrim by emphasizing the queen's willingness to send the pilgrim to his death. Originally, the queen comments ambiguously on the broken sword of the slain pilgrim:

> "O soft steel that could not withstand!
> O harder heart unstay'd,
>   That pray'd and pray'd!"[21]

In 1870 the ambiguous "O harder heart" is clarified with the change to "O my hard heart" (*Poems*, 32). In the following stanza the queen commenting on the "bloodied banner" (*Poems*, 32) had originally said, "Fair flew these folds, for shame, To guide Death's aim!,"[22] but in 1870 "these folds" was replaced with "my web," underscoring the queen's complicity in the pilgrim's death. The first of these changes was made, apparently, in the interest of clarity, but the second radically alters the tone. The effect is to change the characterization of the queen, who now appears less a wronged but innocent maiden, and more a fatal woman. Her character has been adjusted to become comparable with such *femmes fatales* of the 1869 writings as Lilith in "Eden Bower" and Helen in "Troy Town." The important point, I think, is that Rossetti's stylistic revisions were necessarily written from his sensibility of 1869 and 1870, and so necessarily change the tone of the poem—this one and others. And in the process of eliminating awkward or ambiguous passages, Rossetti gained an altered insight into the poems and consequently changed other passages to express his more mature view.[23]

"The Staff and Scrip" had always, from its earliest conception, been an ironic comment on chivalry and religion, but as the added emphasis on the uselessness of religion suggests, the irony is much sharper in the revision. Changes made in a stanza near the end of the poem make this very clear. In 1856, Rossetti had written:

> And she would wake with a clear mind
> That letters writ to calm
> Her soul lay in the scrip; and find
> Pink shells, a torpid balm,
> And dust of palm.[24]

The sheer silliness of the religious objects she finds where she had sought human love was certainly intended to be ironic, but Rossetti revised the stanza as though to be certain no one missed the point. In the early version the queen's inspection of the scrip is apparently habitual, but in the revision she examines it only once, evidently on the night of her death:

> And once she woke with a clear mind
> That letters writ to calm
> Her soul lay in the scrip; to find
> Only a torpid balm
> And dust of palm.
>
> (*Poems*, 33)

The word "Only" now emphasizes the queen's distress, and more significant still, her death, described two stanzas later, now seems related to the disappointment attendant upon her single inspection of the scrip. The closing lines of the poem, addressed to the pilgrim, had also been ironic from the start:

> Not tithed with days' and years' decease
> He pays thy wage He owed,
> But in light stalls of golden peace,
> Here in His own abode,
> Thy jealous God.[25]

The religious consolation is clearly ambivalent, as the conjunction "But" implies by suggesting that the terms were not exactly what the pilgrim had in mind, and as the negative connotations of the phrase "Thy jealous God" confirm. Nevertheless, in 1870 Rossetti reinforced the irony, substituting the phrase "with imperishable peace" for "in light stalls of golden peace" and so replacing a vision of heaven with an image that may connote nothing more than the eternal rest of clodlike death. The poem and its revision indicate that though Rossetti was inclined to be ironic about religion by 1856, by 1870 he was adopting a tougher, more unmistakable tone.

"The Burden of Nineveh," conceived as early as 1850 and first published in 1856, was revised for 1870 in much the same ways as "The Staff and Scrip." "The Burden of Nineveh" was plainly conceived from the start as an ironic comment on religion since its concern, the common nineteenth-century one most familiar from Heine, Nietzsche, and Swinburne, is the changing of the gods. The poet contemplates a statue of a "winged beast from Nineveh," recently brought to London, envisions its past as a religious idol, realizes that though all else of Nineveh is long dead, its God survives, and concludes ironically with the thought that some future archaeologist may dig up the beast, "a relic now / Of London not of Nineveh," and so

> shall hold us for some race
> That walked not in Christ's lowly ways,
> But bowed its pride and vowed its praise
> Unto the God of Nineveh.
>
> (*Poems*, 18)

The ironic point that Christianity is no more, and possibly far less, enduring than the religion of Nineveh was abundantly clear in the 1856 version, but there the tone had been light-hearted and whimsical, opening, for example, with

> I have no taste for polyglot:
> At the Museum 'twas my lot,
> Just once, to jot and blot and rot
> In Babel for I know not what.[26]

The most obvious point of Rossetti's revisions was to remove such hilarity; the opening lines became

> In our Museum galleries
> To-day I lingered o'er the prize
> Dead Greece vouchsafes to living eyes,—
> Her art for ever in fresh wise.
> From hour to hour rejoicing me.
>
> (*Poems*, 14)

The most immediate effect of the altered tone is that the irony must now be taken more seriously—the tone of the whole poem is changed. Characteristically, however, the change in tone becomes a change in substance as well; in making stylistic changes Rossetti saw a deeper significance in his poem than he had originally put there, and so changed his entire conception. The opening emphasis on the endurance of art and its refreshing quality draws attention to the relic of Nineveh not just as the god of a dead civilization, but as a living work of art. The idea inherent in Rossetti's original conception, that man's works live on though his faiths die, is now clearly enunciated. Again, Rossetti revised the poem to articulate his skepticism more clearly, but in doing so he found a replacement for religion in art.

The nature of Rossetti's revisions for 1870 is still more clear in one of the volume's most radically revised poems, "The Portrait," adapted from an 1847 poem called "On Mary's Portrait Which I Painted Six Years Ago." The poem had originally been a dramatic monologue, in which an auditor had been clearly implied from the opening two words, "Why yes,"[27] to the concluding question, but Rossetti eliminated the auditor and consequently eliminated the dramatic setting. The effect was to make the poem less a casual utterance and, as with the changes made to "The Burden of Nineveh," to make the tone more serious and contemplative. Further, the elimination of the dramatic framework makes the poem seem more personal and introspective. In addition to the formal change, from dramatic monologue to introspective lyric, the tone was made more somber by the removal of passages about the beloved in life and increased emphasis on the loneliness of the poet-painter and on the inadequacy of the portrait as a substitute for the living woman. The portrait, in 1870, remains a wonderful likeness, but it is now

> alas!
> Less than her shadow on the grass
> Or than her image in the stream.
>
> (*Poems*, 73)

The various revisions, as Robert N. Keane has said, reveal a poet "taking an imaginative, youthful poem of light and love and turning it into a darker,

more melancholy poem filled with suggestive allusions to the personal experience of the mature poet."[28]

Not surprisingly, the increased sadness of the poem results from an
increased skepticism. In 1847 the inadequacy of the portrait, its transformation of a "Once joyous" brow to one "grown stately,"[29] had been an image
of hope. Looking into the eyes of the portrait, the speaker thought of the
eyes of the woman in death, and envisaged her as serene and wise in an
afterlife:

> And if I look into the eyes
> I think they are quite calm and wise;
> For while the world moves, she knows how.[30]

In 1870 the beloved is no longer in a heaven of omniscience, but lying in
dark death, oblivious to the speaker's sorrow:

> O heart that never beats nor heaves,
> In that one darkness lying still,
> What now to thee my love's great will
> Or the fine web the sunshine weaves?
> *(Poems, 74)*

The faith in an afterlife in 1847, moreover, had been specifically Christian,
a belief expressed in the suggestion that the past union of lovers had been a
type of heavenly peace, as Rossetti's simile makes clear:

> So, along some grass-bank in Heaven,
> Mary the Virgin, going by,
> Seeth her servant Rafaël . . .[31]

In general, the quasi-Christian mysticism of 1847 was replaced with a melancholy awareness that only the artifact and the memories it inspires remain of
the beloved. The revised poem, nevertheless, concludes with a vision of a
Christian paradise that had not been present in the early poem:

> Here with her face doth memory sit
> Meanwhile, and wait the day's decline,
> Till other eyes shall look from it,
> Eyes of the spirit's Palestine,
> Even then the old gaze tenderer:
> While hopes and aims long lost with her
> Stand round her image side by side,
> Like tombs of pilgrims that have died
> About the Holy Sepulchre.
> *(Poems, 75)*

The stanza at first seems to anticipate union with the beloved in heaven, but actually the poet is looking back, in memory, not ahead, and the beloved remains only an image. Even the long-lost hopes and aims are not fulfilled in death—they merely become, like the beloved, artifacts. Much more sadly than in "The Burden of Nineveh," Rossetti has replaced faith with art, realizing all the while that the substitution can offer only small consolation.

Other revisions also help to align "The Portrait" with the other poems of the 1870 volume. As in "The Blessed Damozel" and many of the sonnets for *The House of Life*, heaven was revised, Keane has pointed out, to represent no more than union with the lady's soul—God himself is left out.[32] More striking, the Christian myth has been replaced with the personal symbolism that pervaded Rossetti's poems from the mid-1850s onward. Conventional faith gives way to strange personal forebodings, which are symbolized here and in many other of Rossetti's poems of this period, by imagery of *döppelgangers*, echoes, and mirror images. In 1847, for example, the mystic glade represented in the painting was filled with "wet dew, / And red-mouthed damsels meeting you"[33] but in 1870 the glade is far stranger, characterized by "old dew, / And your own footsteps meeting you" (*Poems*, 73). And Rossetti added to the poem a description of past love that exactly corresponds to imagery used throughout "The Stream's Secret" and *The House of Life*, especially the "Willowwood" sonnets. In those poems the speaker looks into or drinks from a reflecting pool, or sits beside one with his beloved. The myth of Narcissus and Echo is consistently evoked, with the neoplatonic notion that both the reflection in the water and the echo are images of the soul. The lines added to "The Portrait" play on at least one of these ideas, and symbolically suggest the others:

> And with her
> I stooped to drink the spring-water,
> Athirst where other waters sprang;
> And where the echo is, she sang,—
> My soul another echo there.
>
> (*Poems*, 74)

Since he regarded his volume as "studied work, where unity is specially kept in view," Rossetti would, I think, have expected that the symbolism here would be seen in the light of his other allusions to Narcissus and Echo throughout the book. In any case, the image here reinforces the image of the portrait as a mirror (present in both 1847 and 1870), the image of *döppelganger* selves, and the image of "her shadow on the grass / Or . . . her image in the stream." The cumulative effect within the poem is to strengthen the sense of mystery, of things unreal, or at least insubstantial—suggestive shadows, reflections, echoes—without abandoning actual observations and experience. In short, the vaguely mystical, gothic imagery that had been too literary and perhaps too confused and confusing in Rossetti's early works was finally becoming effective in expressing genuine personal emotion. As in other poems, the revised version of "The Portrait" discards assertions of faith, and replaces them with an account of the mystery and wonder, inspired by grief, memory, and art, that leads to assuming a faith. Like the other poems, "The Portrait" was revised to replace speculation with experience.

Precisely the same can be said of the revision of "Nocturn" to "Love's Nocturn." In the version written in 1854 the speaker is in love with the idea of love, and pleads for a dream that will bring him the image of an imagined lover. The seventh stanza, eliminated entirely in 1869, indicates plainly that the speaker sought not one particular lover, but a platonic ideal of Love:

> As, since man waxed deadly wise
> Secret somewhere on this earth
> Unpermitted Eden lies,—
> So within the world's wide girth
> Hides she from my spirit's dearth,—
> Paradise
> Of a love that cries for birth.[34]

But in 1869 such idealizing of the form without the substance, the wish for experience rather than the thing itself, was no longer adequate, so revisions and added stanzas both make it clear that a specific flesh-and-blood lover is envisioned and change the tone, as in "The Portrait," to one of deeper melancholy and more distressing eeriness:

> Vaporous, unaccountable,
> Dreamland lies forlorn of light,
> Hollow like a breathing shell.
> Ah! That from all dreams I might
> Choose one dream and guide its flight!
> I know well
> What her sleep should tell to-night.
> (*Poems*, 7)

The fantasy of "dreamland" remains at the center of the poem, but now the dream is put to the service of sensual experience rather than to the service of another dream, an idealization of an unborn love.

Rossetti's changed emphasis, from faith to sensation, is revealed in interesting ways in his revisions of "Jenny." The earliest known version of "Jenny" was produced in 1847 or 1848, but it was so substantially revised in 1858 and again in 1869 that the poem printed in 1870 is vastly different from Rossetti's first conception. All versions are dramatic monologues in which the speaker addresses a dozing harlot in her rooms, but unlike "The Portrait," the later version of "Jenny" draws more, not less, attention to the dramatic setting—not surprisingly, since Rossetti feared moral censure of the poem and wanted to make sure that the compromised speaker was not understood to be himself. Nevertheless, as with "The Portrait," the revisions do emphasize the origin of the speaker's thoughts in experience, since the experience itself is more fully developed, with additional details about Jenny's room and about the speaker's character. In fact, the late version consciously calls attention to the disparity between conceptual thought and actual experience. The speaker recognizes his own absurdity as his "thought runs on like this / With wasteful whims more than enough" (*Poems*, 64), characterizes his contemplation as "mere words" and an "empty cloud" (*Poems*, 66), and even, after a particularly fanciful simile comparing lust to a "toad within a stone," rebukes himself for replacing sense with thought:

> Come, come, what use in thoughts like this?
> Poor little Jenny, good to kiss,—
> You'd not believe by what strange roads
> Thought travels, when your beauty goads
> A man to-night to think of toads!
>
> (*Poems*, 70)

The speaker's realization that his thoughts do not well fit his situation, however, does not signify a change in Rossetti's original conception, but a new way of expressing it. Indeed, a main point of the earlier poem had been that nineteenth-century man's attempt to replace sense with thought was ridiculous hypocrisy. One of the two original mottos for "Jenny" had been an ironic quotation from Shelley's translation of Goethe:

> What, still here!
> In this enlightened age too, since you have been
> Proved not to exist![35]

The body of the poem had satirized the nineteenth-century idea of progress, of evolutionary meliorism in which man would shed his gross, earthy nature and "perfect Man" would "be mind through-out."[36] The comparison of lust to a "toad within a stone," a fossil, had been part of this original conception, an assertion that centuries of geological change and human progress had altered much but had left man his atavistic desires. Further, the speaker had fully realized the irony of his situation as he addressed Jenny:

> Thou call'st on Sense,—that's past and o'er,
> Surely, and shall not hold us more;
> Yet to thy call, in earth and air
> Thou find'st an answer everywhere,
> And stickest even to me, thou bur,
> Who'd write myself philosopher.

And he had concluded his reverie with an elaboration on the idea that "Man gropes, but Matter clings to him."[37]

Rossetti's satire was pointed, in both versions, at man's foolishness in attempting to separate thought and sense, but the revised version, nevertheless, reveals a very changed conception. The early poem is a direct satiric attack on a popular philosophic idea and, as satire often does, it seems itself an intellectual, almost schematic, exercise. But in 1870 the irony is less pointed as both the speaker and Jenny emerge as more fully human characters. Jenny, for example, is no longer merely a harlot, but a woman like other women, as the speaker's rather sentimental comparison of her with his Cousin Nell reveals. Her childhood and probable misfortunes are described to enable the reader to feel sympathy for her, and to understand her true nature. Rossetti is no longer attacking an idea so much as examining the psychology of a man who develops such ideas in the chambers of a woman whose dishonor is a result of them. Further, the original version decries the hypocrisy that would deny man's sensual nature, but does not attack the notion that man's sensuality is an unfortunate part of his nature. In the revised poem, however, sensuality is so much a part of the characters and the characters are so sympathetic that the reader accepts it and them without question. When near the end of the poem the speaker compares Jenny to a wise virgin, the irony is obvious but it has no sting, implies no harsh judgment. The new motto for the poem, Mrs. Quickly's "Vengeance of Jenny's case! Fie on her! Never name her, child" (Poems, 63) was used, in fact, to make the point that such judgments are absurdly foolish. Rossetti's reason for acknowledging Mrs. Quickly as the speaker makes his intentions, for the motto and for the poem, very clear: "I want to put Mrs. Q. (instead of Merry Wives etc.) at end of the sentence to remind the virtuous reader strongly whose words they are that his own mind is echoing at the moment."[38] Rossetti's clear intention was to defend the harlot, to defend the senses. And the new acceptance of sensuality, and especially of sexuality as extremely, and possibly dangerously, attractive helps, of course, to make "Jenny" compatible with other poems in the volume.

The revision of "Jenny," however, does not only incorporate ideas about the psychological development of false philosophic ideas and a defense of sensuality. The new emphasis on experience leads to a consideration of how art and faith themselves may evolve. The speaker's most serious and most pained consideration of Jenny's state results from a recognition that desecration of her beauty is no less than sacrilege:

> Fair shines the gilded aureole
> In which our highest painters place
> Some living woman's simple face.
> And the stilled features thus descried
> As Jenny's long throat droops aside, —

> The shadows where the cheeks are thin,
> And pure wide curve from ear to chin,—
> With Raffael's or Da Vinci's hand
> To show them to men's souls, might stand,
> Whole ages long, the whole world through
> For preachings of what God can do.
> What has man done here?
>
> (*Poems*, 68–69)

The speaker's Christian morality is not, of course, Rossetti's, but his realization that the proper response to beauty is akin to worship assuredly reflects Rossetti's own notion. In fact, the description of the painting that an artist might produce from Jenny precisely describes many of Rossetti's own paintings—the stilled features, long throat, thin cheeks and "pure wide curve from ear to chin" are typical of his painted women. The proper response to Jenny's beauty, then, is not a moral sermon, but an artistic appreciation that would speak directly to men's souls. Sensual appreciation becomes the basis for man's highest achievements in art. With the speaker's notion that Jenny's beauty is evidence of God's work, Rossetti is again showing the basis of myth in direct sensual experience. He is not endorsing his character's conclusions, but is showing how such conclusions come about, how faiths are evolved. Again the emphasis is on experience and psychological process. When at the end of the poem the speaker whimsically compares Jenny to two mythic women, the Paphian Venus and then to Danae, his playful irony is evidently an attempt to detach himself from an otherwise painful situation, but once again Rossetti's point is more serious than his speaker's. The myths of the Paphian Venus and of Danae did result, in less self-conscious and ironic ages, Rossetti implies, from an appreciation of the exalted mystery of sensual beauty. The sensuality of human nature, repressed in the nineteenth century, is the basis of myth. The poverty of faith in the modern ages paradoxically results, as Nietzsche argued, from the elevation of faith over sensation.

Perhaps the most startling of Rossetti's late revisions of early poems occurs in the 1870 volume's other major dramatic monologue, "A Last Confession." One of the most memorable moments in the published poem occurs when the speaker, the murderer of a young woman he had raised and then fallen in love with, recalls his earlier gift to her:

> A little image of a flying Love
> Made of our coloured glass-ware, in his hands
> A dart of gilded metal and a torch.
> And him she kissed and me, and fain would know
> Why were his poor eyes blindfold, why the wings
> And why the arrow. What I knew I told
> Of Venus and of Cupid,—strange old tales.
>
> (*Poems*, 37)

The incident is evidently a kind of initiation into love—still more evidently an initiation into sexual love when the girl breaks the Cupid and is cut by its dart: "The dart had entered deeply and drawn blood" (*Poems*, 38). Since "A Last Confession" is dated 1847, these lines have generally been understood as characteristic of Rossetti's precocity in handling psychosexual themes, but in fact the whole passage was added late. His original image was, not surprisingly, far more characteristic of his actual concerns at that time:

> I brought her from the city, one such day,
> The earliest gift I mind my giving her,—
> A little image of great Jesus Christ
> Whom yet she knew but dimly. I had not
> Yet told her all the wondrous things of Faith
> For in our life of deadly haste, the child
> Might ill be taught that God and Truth were sure.[39]

The substitutions of Love for "great Jesus Christ" and of "strange old tales" of Venus and Cupid for "all the wondrous things of Faith" epitomize the ways in which Rossetti revised his early poems. Sexual love replaces religious faith, the somewhat empty rhetoric about "God and Truth" is eliminated, and a previously absent level of psychological penetration is added to the poem.

In one way or another, all of the substantial revisions altered the significance of poems in similar ways. Even such small changes as the alteration of "God's grace" to "Time's Grace" in the 1853 sonnet "A Dark Day" consistently reveal the same intention. In fact, the substitution of Time for God is characteristic of a number of changes that indicate how Rossetti had come to regard all such abstractions as interchangeable. His changes to "Love-Lily," not written until 1869, seem almost whimsical in this respect: he changed "soul" to "mind," "Love" to "Truth," and "God" to "Love" without, I think, changing his conception of the poem.[40] The revised poems consistently show a more pronounced skepticism, an emphasis on sensation rather than thought, and a consequent appreciation of sexual love and of woman as symbol of man's desire. But Rossetti did not attempt to achieve a unified volume only by revising his early poems to bring them into line with his mature views. His concern, frequently expressed in his letters, to arrange the order of his poems reveals that he was as eager to achieve a significant sequence throughout the volume as he was to order the sonnets of *The House of Life* into a coherent pattern. Futher, he carefully reviewed his poems before publication, selecting those which fitted, or could be made to fit, his mature views and rejecting others. The third section of the completed volume, "Sonnets for Pictures, and Other Sonnets," for example, draws heavily on his early work, opening with four sonnets for pictures, much revised, that had originally been published in *The Germ*. The sonnets he reprinted express no religious point of view—one, "For An Allegorical Dance of Women, by Andrea Mantegna," expresses, especially in its revised form, the view that whatever the artist intended, art communicates by sensation rather than by abstract allegorical thought. The sonnets he rejected, on two paintings by Hans Memling, had both been about religious mystery, the first beginning "Mystery: God, Man's Life, born into man / Of woman" and the second "Mystery: Katharine, the bride of Christ."[41] The only early sonnets on religious themes that Rossetti retained, in fact, were sonnets for his own early pictures, "Mary's Girlhood," "The Passover in the Holy Family," and "Mary Magdalene at the Door of Simon the Pharisee." Just as he had included "My Sister's Sleep" because he thought it might do him some good with the reviewers, one of whom had singled it out for praise, so he may have felt that these sonnets might usefully enlist the sympathies of readers who knew his painting, or, on the other hand, might attract the attention of readers not familiar with his painting. The religious sonnets, in other words, may well have been included as a matter of business even though they do not wholly fit the tone of the volume.

Without discussing every poem in the volume in relation to the others, it would be impossible fully to investigate Rossetti's arrangement, but some general comments can be made. The work is divided into three parts, "Poems," "Sonnets and Songs: Towards a Work to be called 'The House of Life' " and "Sonnets for Pictures, and Other Sonnets." Most of the first section consists of revisions of early work. The arrangement of this section seems deliberately designed to undercut the lighter, optimistic and, in the case of "Ave," religious implications that remained in these poems even after revision. The opening poem, "The Blessed Damozel," somewhat optimistically envisages a heaven of lovers as consolation for the death of the beloved, but it is immediately followed by the darkly skeptical "Love's Nocturn," which echoes the situation of the bereaved lover, and in which the only alternative world envisaged is one of dreams and "poets' fancies." The conjunction of poems not only implies that the heaven of "The Blessed Damozel" is an empty dream, but even that dreams dreamed in grief will take their coloring from that emotion: "Reft of her, my dreams are all / Clammy trance that fears the sky" (*Poems*, 8). "Love's Nocturn" is then followed by "Troy Town," a poem about destructive, fatal beauty that further undercuts the idea of the beatific maiden in "The Blessed Damozel," and then by "The Burden of Nineveh," which fully enunciates Rossetti's ironic skepticism. Consistently, doubts about the soul in Rossetti's poetry lead to an affirmation of the flesh, so the next poem, appropriately, is "Eden Bower," a poem about the soulless, inhuman Lilith, the sensuous serpent-woman who was Adam's first wife. Only after the Christian ideal has been well laid to rest, and after Rossetti has established his "inner standing-point" with respect to all myths, does he then print "Ave," which can no longer possibly be regarded as representing the poet's own beliefs. Similarly, the other poem that Rossetti was concerned about, "My Sister's Sleep," is printed immediately after "The Card Dealer," a poem in which death is the province of inscrutable fate. After this, the reader cannot easily believe the possible implication of "My Sister's Sleep" that the death on Christmas Eve was providentially ordained.

Each of the three parts of the volume closes with a poem that specifically enunciates a skeptical point of view. The last original poem in Part One (it is followed by five translations) is "Aspecta Medusa," which Rossetti moved to that position after the volume was already in proofs.[42] The poem, originally intended for a picture that was never completed, describes how Andromeda avoided looking directly at the Gorgon's head, but saw it "mirrored in the wave," and concludes with a moral:

> Let not thine eyes know
> Any forbidden thing itself, although
> It once should save as well as kill: but be
> Its shadow upon life enough for thee.
> *(Poems, 100)*

The lines, reminiscent of Shelley's "Preface" to *Alastor* and of his sonnet "Lift Not the Painted Veil," suggest that any attempt to see beyond the bounds of normal human perception is dangerous. Man must be content with what he can see, the reflection or the painted veil, without attempting to penetrate the mysteries of death.

The last poem of the second section, "The Sea-limits," much more clearly expresses a skepticism that now borders on solipsism. The first two stanzas of "The Sea-limits" are a greatly revised version of a poem first written in 1849, and originally called "At Boulogne. Upon the Cliffs: Noon." The revisions are characteristic—the first version had suggested the limitations of sense, but not of thought. At the horizon "Sense, without Thought, can pass / No stadium further."[43] In the 1870 version the idea that thought may reach where sense cannot has been eliminated:

> Secret continuance sublime
> Is the sea's end: our sight may pass
> No furlong further.
> *(Poems, 136)*

What the eyes cannot see remains secret. But the real point of "The Sea-limits" is expressed in two stanzas added at some later date (William Rossetti dates the revised poem 1849, an error that illustrates the danger of relying on his datings, which characteristically make Rossetti appear more precocious than he was and confuse his earlier thought with his later). The added stanzas exhort the reader to "Listen alone beside the sea":

Gather a shell from the strown beach
   And listen at its lips: they [the sea and woods] sigh
   The same desire and mystery,
The echo of the whole sea's speech.
   And all mankind is thus at heart
   Not anything but what thou art,
And Earth, Sea, Man, are all in each.

                       (*Poems*, 136)

All knowledge is sensual apprehension—everything that man can know is in the sound of the shell. The poem expresses a complete solipsism, of course, since everything that man can know, "Earth, Sea, Man" is not anything but what he is, and his knowledge, gained from the shell, is only the sound of his own blood rushing in his ears. All perception is thus reduced to what man feels upon his pulses.

Finally, "The Monochord," the last poem of Part Three, the last poem of the volume, expresses skepticism in a series of four unanswered and unanswerable questions. The poet cannot identify what is "Life's self" or even distinguish between "Life or Death." A biblical allusion in the sestet draws attention to the pillars of cloud and fire that showed the way to God's chosen people, but only to illustrate that in a skeptical age signs are unreadable and the way remains lost:

Oh! what is this that knows the road I came,
The flame turned cloud, the cloud returned to flame
   The lifted shifted steeps and all the way?—
                     (*Poems*, 148)

The volume ends, then, with a series of questions that imply the inscrutability of life, and with an allusion that acknowledges and denies the old grounds of faith.

All of Rossetti's enormous labors in finally preparing his poems for publication in 1870, then, were aimed at obscuring his own tracks, eradicating immaturities of style and obliterating any traces of his early thought. He included a note on the title page of *Poems* that was obviously intended for the same purpose: "Many poems in this volume were written between 1847 and 1853. Others are of recent date, and a few belong to the intervening period. It has been thought unnecessary to specify the earlier work, as nothing is included which the author believes to be immature" (*Poems*, 1). Of course nothing is immature because, in fact, practically none of the poems as published can be said to belong to the earlier period. His revisions and studied arrangement had rendered the volume entirely a product of 1870. Unfortunately for Rossetti's posthumous reputation, his systematic obliteration of his footsteps has led many critics to condemn him for failure to "develop with the years."[44] Yet his successful efforts to produce a volume unified in style and sensibility is praiseworthy, however much it has muddied the waters of criticism. Rossetti would readily have agreed that what is most important is the finished work of art, not the history of its production. His revisions and careful arrangement made *Poems* a coherent, polished work that beautifully articulates the somber mood of Rossetti's middle years, his skepticism, his recognition that the primary experience of sensation is all he could be certain of, his consequent solipsism and fleshliness.

Notes

1.   William Michael Rossetti, *Rossetti Papers: 1862 to 1870* (New York: Scribner, 1903), p. 408.
2.   See Oswald Doughty, *A Victorian Romantic: Dante Gabriel Rossetti* (London: Frederick Muller, 1949), pp. 369–392.
3.   Ronnalie Roper Howard, *The Dark Glass: Vision and Technique in the Poetry of Dante Gabriel Rossetti* (Athens: Ohio University Press, 1972), pp. 12–18. Howard acknowledges, in a note, that the poem was substantially revised, but nevertheless uses the late version to illustrate Rossetti's early thought and technique. She follows much the same procedure in discussing "My Sister's Sleep," pp. 2–5 (though here her footnote is more specific about the early version), and "The Card Dealer," pp. 8–12. Howard should not be singled out, however, since many others have made similar errors. Robert D. Johnston, for example, in his *Dante Gabriel Rossetti* (New York: Twayne, 1969), quotes a passage from "The Portrait," which he dates 1847, and notes that it anticipates lines written in 1869 and 1871 (p. 57). The passage in question, however, was written in 1870 (see Robert N. Keane, "Rossetti: The Artist and 'The Portrait,' " *English Language Notes*, 12 [1974], 96–102). A more careful study of Rossetti's poetic development is Florence Saunders Boos's *The Poetry of Dante G. Rossetti: A Critical Reading and Source Study* (The Hague: Mouton, 1976).
4.   *Letters*, II:823.
5.   William Bell Scott, *Autobiographical Notes*, ed. W. Minto, 2 vols. (New York: Harper & Brothers, 1892), I:291, 290.
6.   *Letters*, II:582.
7.   Quoted by Robert S. Fraser, "The Rossetti Collection of Janet Camp Troxell: A Survey with Some Sidelights," in *Essays on the Rossettis*, ed. Robert S. Fraser (Princeton: Princeton University Library, 1972), p. 169.
8.   *Letters*, II:714. Swinburne is quoted in a footnote to the letter.
9.   *Works*, p. 661. William Rossetti quotes the aborted footnote as evidence of his brother's agnosticism, and observes that though it would be erroneous to infer from "Ave" that Rossetti was a Roman Catholic, it is "of all Rossetti's poems . . . the one which seems most to indicate definite Christian belief, and of a strongly Roman Catholic kind."
10.   *Letters*, II:722.
11.   *Letters*, II:731.
12.   *The Germ: Thoughts Towards Nature in Poetry, Literature and Art* (rpt., Portland, Maine: Thomas B. Mosher, 1898), pp. 21–22.
13.   Quotations from Rossetti's 1870 volume are all from *Poems by Dante Gabriel Rossetti, 1870*, Section One of *Dante Gabriel Rossetti: Poems*, ed. Oswald Doughty (London: Dent, 1961, rpt., New York: Dutton, 1974). Doughty's text, actually of 1872 rather than of 1870, is taken from the sixth edition.

14. Richard Stein, *The Ritual of Interpretation: The Fine Arts as Literature in Ruskin, Rossetti, and Pater* (Cambridge: Harvard University Press, 1975), p. 204.

15. Jerome McGann, "Rossetti's Significant Details," *Victorian Poetry*, 7 (1969), 42.

16. The earliest known text of "The Blessed Damozel" is the Morgan manuscript, dated 1847, but as J. A. Sanford has argued, the text was almost certainly fabricated by Rossetti at a much later date, perhaps to help advance the idea of his precocity. For the various texts of the poem, see *Dante Gabriel Rossetti: The Blessed Damozel: The Unpublished Manuscript, Texts and Collation*, ed. Paull Franklin Baum (Chapel Hill: University of North Carolina Press, 1937). For the argument against the validity of the 1847 manuscript, see J. A. Sanford, "The Morgan Library Manuscript of Rossetti's 'The Blessed Damozel,' " *Studies in Philology*, 35 (1938), 471–486.

17. *Letters*, I:39.

18. For a fuller discussion, see K. L. Knickerbocker, "Rossetti's 'The Blessed Damozel,' " *Studies in Philology*, 29 (1932), 485–504.

19. *The Germ* text, Baum, p. 15.

20. *The Oxford and Cambridge Magazine for 1856* (London: Bell and Dalby, 1856), p. 773.

21. Ibid., p. 774.

22. Ibid.

23. Rossetti's avowed intention in revising "The Staff and Scrip" was to clarify the structure and story: "In S{taff} and S{crip} there was something added where the damsel gives her the relics to develop this incident and help the transition": *Letters*, II:721.

24. *The Oxford and Cambridge Magazine*, p. 775.

25. Ibid.

26. Ibid., pp. 512–516.

27. The poem is printed in *Dante Gabriel Rossetti: An Analytical List of Manuscripts in the Duke University Library, with Hitherto Unpublished Verse and Prose*, ed. Paull Franklin Baum (Durham: Duke University Press, 1931), pp. 67–71.

28. Keane, p. 97.

29. Baum, *An Analytical List*, p. 68.

30. Ibid.

31. Ibid., p. 70.

32. Keane, p. 102, notes that even after 1869 significant revisions were made: "Where the 1869 poem depicted the arrival of the lady's soul in Heaven where it would know 'the silence there for God,' the 1870 version envisions the artist's own arrival in a Heaven composed of his lady's soul. As in much of Rossetti's work, Paradise is the union of lovers forever."

33. Baum, *An Analytical List*, p. 69.

34. Quoted from a manuscript in the Fitzwilliam Museum, Cambridge University.

35. The early version is printed in Paull F. Baum, "The Bancroft Manuscripts of Dante Gabriel Rossetti," *Modern Philology*, 39 (1941), 48–52.

36. Ibid., p. 50

37. Ibid., p. 51.

38. *Letters*, II:774.

39. Quoted from the manuscript in the Fitzwilliam Museum, Cambridge University.

40. There are manuscripts of "Love-Lily" in both the Janet Camp Troxell collection at Princeton University and the Fitzwilliam Museum, Cambridge University.

41. *The Germ*, p. 199.

42. *Letters*, II:812. Rossetti did not fully explain his reason for moving the poem, but said only that it "seemed best as an inscription which it really was."

43. *Letters*, I:61–62. A revised version of the poem appeared in *The Germ*, with the title "From the Cliffs: Noon."

44. Doughty, *A Victorian Romantic*, p. 475.

Pornography and Art: The Case of "Jenny"

ROBIN SHEETS

In his diary, George Boyce, a minor Pre-Raphaelite painter, casually describes a day when Dante Gabriel Rossetti perused a pornographic novel, attended an art exhibition, and procured a model for his own painting: "Joined Rossetti at Swinburne's rooms, where they were looking over 'Justine,' by the Marquis de Sade, recent acquisition of the latter. We then went on to the International Exhibition. Had some ices at a stall near the Egyptian things where there was a very lovely girl of whom Gabriel obtained a promise to sit to him."[1] This 1862 record of seemingly unrelated events suggests an important question for the study of Victorian culture: how were the conventions of pornography—a genre usually defined by content (the explicit depiction of sexual activity) and intention (to arouse the male reader)—related to the production and interpretation of art? Critics have made surprisingly few attempts to answer this question, perhaps because Steven Marcus made such sharp distinctions between "pornography" and "art" in *The Other Victorians*. For Marcus, pornography was the product of a specific subculture, a fugitive group of anonymous and pseudonymous authors distributing materials through Holywell Street bookshops. Characterizing the genre as "a representation of the fantasies of infantile sexual life, as these fantasies are edited and reorganized in the masturbatory daydreams of adolescence,"[2] Marcus argued that its values were antithetical to those of the great Victorian novels; the view of human sexuality represented in pornography and the view held by the official culture were "reversals, mirror images, negative analogues of one another" (*OV*, p. 283). Noting the inconclusiveness of pornography, its lack of emotion, and its hostility toward language, Marcus also attempted to distinguish pornography from art in formal terms.

However, in subsequent years, it has become more difficult to relegate pornography to the margins of culture. Literary historians continue to discover pornographic works by "great" writers, such as Byron, Mark Twain, and Edith Wharton. Other scholars study the influence of pornography on "great" works of art, such as Edouard Manet's *Olympia*, or trace its effects on such diverse texts as gynecological manuals, children's fiction, and the

Reprinted from *Critical Inquiry* 14 (1988): 315–34. Reprinted with permission of the author and the University of Chicago Press.

propaganda of the antivivisectionist movement.[3] Susan Sontag has used formal principles of analysis to show that some pornographic novels satisfy aesthetic criteria, while Kate Millett has demonstrated "how contemporary literature has absorbed not only the truthful explicitness of pornography, but its anti-social character as well."[4] Exploring the link between pornography and modernism, Susan Rubin Suleiman asks a crucial question: "to what extent are the 'high-cultural' productions of the avant-gardes of our century in a relation of complicity rather than in a relation of rupture vis-à-vis dominant ideologies?" According to Susan Gubar, the distinctions between art and pornography have been blurred by two antithetical views: (1) "that pornography is actually a vanguard form of artistry" and (2) "that all art is (or historically has been) pornographic in its defamation or domination of women." Some critics now situate pornography at the center of culture as the most extreme and explicit manifestation of social value. Pornography "reflects through hyperbolic distortion," says Eva Feder Kittay; it is the "exaggerated image of male-female sexual relations within cultures where men dominate." Rejecting what Irene Diamond calls liberal assumptions— "that the content of pornography is sex and that the genre is essentially a medium for sexual expression"—contemporary feminists such as Andrea Dworkin and Susan Griffin treat pornography "primarily as a medium for expressing norms about male power and domination."[5] Most recently, Susanne Kappeler has urged that the feminist critique of pornography move "from a content orientation to an analysis of representation."[6] Kappeler describes the pornographer bonding with his male spectator/reader to objectify the woman: "once as object of the action in the scenario, and once as object of the representation, the object of viewing" (PR, p. 52). She maintains:

> In terms of representation, and with respect to the objectification of the female gender, the pornographer only reproduces, on a less elevated level and within a less exclusive circulation, what the artist does in the esoteric fields of high culture . . .
>
> What feminist analysis identifies as the pornographic structure of representation—not the presence of a variable quality of "sex," but the systematic objectification of women in the interest of the exclusive subjectification of men—is a common place of art and literature as well as of conventional pornography.
>
> (PR, pp. 102, 103)

If pornography constructs gender, displays men's social, economic, and sexual power, denies women's subjectivity, and orders ways of seeing, then a study of its codes will be useful in interpreting a wide range of materials, including some texts which do not include the graphic representation of sexual experience.

In contrast to Sontag, who used the tools of literary criticism to evaluate sexually explicit fiction, I will use the conventions of pornography to interpret a dramatic monologue in which an expected sexual encounter fails to take place. In analyzing Rossetti's "Jenny," I will employ an interpretive model based on the work of Marcus, Griffin, and Dworkin. Despite different assumptions about sexuality—Marcus is a Freudian, Griffin believes in a mystical eros residing in the psyche and waiting to be rediscovered, Dworkin regards heterosexuality as a construct for subjugating women and masking men's homoerotic drive—they share several ideas applicable to "Jenny." (1) Although pornography features, and indeed perpetuates, various kinds of masculine power, especially the powers of money, class, and culture, it purports to be ahistorical in order to obscure its status as ideology. (2) It depicts male sexuality as fear-laden aggression resulting in very little pleasure; thus it is not liberating on either a political or a personal basis. (3) Pornography does not include "others." Women are present only to be silenced, objectified, treated as screens on which a man projects his fantasies. Marcus, Griffin, and Dworkin are all concerned with what Suleiman calls "the representational or fantasmatic content" of pornography and "the political (in the sense of sexual politics) implications of that content." The risks of emphasizing the representational—most especially, the denigration of language and style that result from Dworkin's approach—can, as Suleiman says, be mitigated by careful attention to a particular text (see P, pp. 122–30).

In Rossetti's poem, a young man attempts to purchase a night's pleasure with a London prostitute named Jenny. After she thwarts his plans by falling asleep, he spends the night meditating about her beauty, speculating about her past, present, and future, and thinking about the causes of prostitution.[7] Although Rossetti's subject matter is consistent with the etymological definition of pornography as "writing about prostitutes," he avoids the explicit depiction of sexual activity which has been the common element in most modern accounts of the genre. Indeed, the only physical contact between the narrator and Jenny occurs at daybreak when he places coins in her hair and gives her a parting kiss.

However, similarities between Rossetti's poem and pornographic fiction become apparent when discussion centers on the narrator. Previous criticism has noted the narrator's sympathy for Jenny, his generosity, his helplessness against the oppressive social system, his awareness of his own complicity.[8] But as Daniel A. Harris observes, the narrator is "the compassionate liberal seeking social justice" and "the reactionary male jealous of his power" ("SM," p. 205). Exerting powers essential to pornography—powers of money, class, and culture—the narrator bears a disturbing resemblance to the libertines in Justine (1791), the influential de Sade novel Rossetti discussed with Swinburne, and to "Walter,"[9] the narrator of My Secret Life, whose life was roughly contemporaneous with Rossetti's (see OV, pp. 82–97).[10]

The first part of this essay analyzes the patron-prostitute relationship, emphasizing the narrator's use of money and his assumptions about the inevitability of sexual oppression. The second concentrates on his role as artist and his responsibility for the making of a woman/text. While the narrator struggles with his fear of female sexuality and his increasing animosity toward Jenny herself, he raises unsettling questions about male art, about its association with lust, its hostility to and dependence on female beauty. The third part explores Rossetti's obsession with the poem by placing its composition, revision, and publication in a biographical context. The essay will undermine the authority of the text, the speaker, and the poet by challenging two kinds of categorization. First, instead of separating "pornography" and "art," the essay places the poem along a continuum of discourse involving shared images, conventions, and values.[11] Second, it questions the distinction between speaker and poet which has been so important in the critical history of the poem. After Robert Buchanan attacked Rossetti for projecting himself into his poetry—"always attitudinizing, posturing, and describing his own exquisite emotions"—Rossetti tried to distance himself from "the speaker put forward in the poem . . . a young and thoughtful man of the world."[12] The distinction was emphasized in the nineteenth century by friends anxious to avoid scandal and in the twentieth by readers committed to the ideology of New Criticism. "In the contemporary conception of art," argues Kappeler, "there is no author behind the work in terms of a social and political being, as there is apparently no process of production behind its publication in terms of social and commercial decisions" (*PR*, p. 110). Without denying the poem's dramatic nature, I am suggesting that Rossetti shared more of the protagonist's anxieties than he and his followers realized. In other words, I am trying to find the author behind the work.

1

The would-be patron in "Jenny" is a scholar or writer well acquainted with classical mythology, the Bible, and Renaissance art. He has already committed himself to a proper young woman, his cousin Nell, "the girl I'm proudest of."[13] More complex than protagonists in typical pornographic novels, who inhabit "a world in which conscience and real conflict do not exist" (*OV*, p. 209), this young man experiences moments of insight guilt, and even despair. Not only does he ruminate about the "careless life" of his past (1. 37), he also attempts to move beyond his personal dilemma to moralize about larger, more abstract issues. D.M.R. Bentley and others argue that the narrator develops moral insight as the night proceeds, attaining "a measure of spiritual regeneration" at the end ("RFW," p. 192). However, it seems to me that the narrator's commentary, like his conduct, is fraught with contradiction. The young man cannot explain how his past is related to his present, and like "Walter," he seems confused about his reasons for coming to the prostitute's apartment. If his speculations about "man's" responsibility for Jenny's situation bring him too close to the knowledge of his own wrongdoing, he breaks the line of thought, changes the mood, or tangles himself in metaphors.

When he turns outward and proposes to generalize about the human condition, his voice becomes "omniscient, imperative, and prophetic in tone," as Jules Paul Seigel says.[14] However, this mode of philosophical analysis is self-serving and consistent with the assumptions that permeate nineteenth-century pornography. While some social critics of the 1840s and 1850s, such as William Tait, Henry Mayhew, W. R. Greg, and William Acton, were describing the social and economic conditions that drove women into prostitution, the young man consistently sets such practicalities aside. By taking a "moral" stance which emphasizes the inevitability of sin and suffering, he avoids the ongoing debates over rescue, repression, and regulation and projects the continued existence of sexual oppression.[15]

Note the narrator's despairing conclusions in lines 250–97. In the first sequence (ll. 250–75), he considers—and then rejects—the possibility that good women might acknowledge the prostitute's plight and begin to alleviate her suffering. Although it was commonplace to insist that wives and daughters of the middle class must be protected from any knowledge of prostitution, women in evangelical circles had been doing rescue work since the 1840s; during the 1860s, Rossetti's sister Christina assisted at the St. Mary Magdalen Home for Fallen Women.[16] In an 1864 lecture, John Ruskin, Rossetti's erstwhile friend and patron, urged ladies to leave the sheltered gardens of their homes and go down into "the darkness of the terrible streets" in order to save the "feeble florets [who] are lying, with all their fresh leaves torn, and their stems broken."[17] Adopting Ruskin's elaborate floral imagery but repudiating his argument, the narrator of "Jenny" insists that love between women "can never be" (ll. 252, 274). The young man, like the pornographer, undercuts bonds between women, either by isolating them or by depicting their cruelty toward one another. The first strategy makes them powerless; the second renders them punishable. Rossetti's final text deletes an earlier description of Jenny's mother, whose strong voice had continued to instruct her daughter even after their separation, and emphasizes the barriers between women: here; in the passage on Nell, who will obviously never know of Jenny's existence (ll. 185–202); in the sketch of the pale working girl who looks at Jenny in resentment (ll. 69–76); and even in the epigraph.

The second sequence (ll. 276–97), which concerns men's responsibility for prostitution, conveys the same sense of futility. Comparing male lust to a toad within a stone, the young man describes his own instincts as ugly and bestial. The allusion to Milton's Satan "Squat like a Toad, close at the ear of Eve," traces the origin of sexuality to the Garden of Eden.[18] According to Bentley, the problem of evil is "firmly placed in the context of Christian eschatology" ("RFW," p. 191). Lust drove man to his first transgression; it will survive "through all centuries" (l. 286), assumes the narrator. Premising a Christianity which equates sexuality with sin, the young man must acknowledge his desire for Jenny as an inescapable sign of man's fallen nature. Yet the description of male lust as inevitable and uncontrollable appears as frequently in Victorian pornography as it does in the writings of the Church Fathers. It expresses the nineteenth-century fear of sexuality, and, as Marcus has shown, it also exonerates men. If male lust is an unrestrainable, ageless, impersonal force which "shall not be driven out" until the end of time (l. 292), then the individual cannot be blamed for his actions, however reprehensible. The narrator's version of Christianity provides a justification for his behavior.

In his commentary, the thoughtful young man presents sexual oppression as an essential part of the human dilemma; through his conduct, he participates in an economically based system of domination. The source of his wealth remains undisclosed—guineas are simply his to give. Like "Walter," he uses money to distance himself from women emotionally and socially. By framing his encounter with Jenny in financial terms, he absolves himself from blame: he is neither seducer nor rapist, only an ordinary consumer willing to pay for services. Like the authors studied by Dworkin, he portrays woman's participation in prostitution as the result of her "greed for money or pleasure or both"[19] as he introduces "Lazy laughing languid Jenny, / Fond of a kiss and fond of a guinea" (ll. 1–2). He implies that Jenny enters freely into the night's activities and that she will not have to work very hard to gain what she wants. The narrator acts as if his money is an appropriate expression of masculinity, a sure sign of substance and authority, but he believes that Jenny's desire for wealth is evidence of vanity, ignorance, and greed. Here, as in explicitly pornographic literature, the meaning of money, like the meaning of time, is "significantly different for men than for women" (MPW, p. 20).

According to the narrator, Jenny's fascination with money causes her to dream about purses (ll. 20–21, 341–43). However, given the association between purses and female genitalia, the young man's account of Jenny's fantasies probably represents a displacement of his own. For Freud, Dora's reticule was "only a substitute for the shell of Venus, for the female genitals."[20] For "Walter," the vagina was also a purse; his eighty-five shillings inserted into Nelly L., a surrogate penis. For the narrator, a night with Jenny initially promises an occasion to possess her person and her "purse." When his plans falter, the daydream of placing coins in her purse must substitute for the sexual act. Locating the "purse" obsession in the mind of the male narrator complicates the meaning of the "grim web . . . clogged with shrivelled flies" (l. 345). The speaker intends for web to denote a network purse. Set in apposition to "the magic purse," the metaphor of the "grim web" conveys the sinister voraciousness of Jenny's greed; the dead insects, her dirty profits. The web also suggests an intricate work of art, like the "magic web with colors gay" woven by the Lady of Shalott.[21] The narrator believes that Jenny's web is "grim" because she cannot create anything beautiful; she can imagine only a series of sordid scenes. When the web becomes a cobweb, the patron reveals his misogyny by associating the "purse," or female genitalia, with a hairy spider's treacherous trap for "shrivelled flies." Jenny's vagina, like her mind, is a receptacle for dirt, animal waste, and death.

After the young man leaves his money in Jenny's hair, he likens himself to a god—the all-powerful but highly promiscuous Zeus who descends to Danae's lap in a shower of gold. While some classical commentators interpret the golden shower as the god's seminal fluid, others see it as coinage to bribe guards for entrance to Danae's tower. Thus the mythographic tradition allows Rossetti to draw upon the associations between money and the male sex organ, with the former once again substituting for the latter. Although Rossetti's man of the world does not have the life-begetting energy of Zeus, he does aspire to celestial authority, assuming a superior, often godlike position in relation to the woman; he does violate her psychologically if not sexually; and he does have something of Zeus' tendency to leave the woman behind.

The young man's decision to leave money with Jenny is not "an act of charity" or "chivalric generosity."[22] He has not received sexual services from Jenny, but he has used her to provoke his thoughts and to stimulate aesthetic self-pleasure. Morever, the coins reveal his desire for sexual dominance.[23] Although the narrator knows economic terms cannot adequately define the moral complexities of his relationship with Jenny, the money left on her pillow demonstrates his autonomy and aloofness. It reminds one of "Walter"'s gift to Lucy, his penchant for paying prostitutes more than they asked for, and similar acts in which "brutality and benevolence" consort without the character's awareness (*OV*, p. 136).

In the end, the narrator's resolutions regarding his future conduct are so vague as to be practically meaningless. His "redemption" demands that he remove himself from Jenny's presence rather than take responsibility for her plight. Linking his intention to reform with the breaking dawn, he claims time as his ally; its passage permits him the possibility of a moral awakening. But while he envisions for himself the beginning of a new life beyond the exigencies of death and desire, he consigns Jenny to the world of nature where time will wreak her destruction. "Tomorrow" Jenny's branches will be bare (l. 16); when winter comes roses die (ll. 111–17). William Acton observed that "prostitution is a transitory state, through which an untold number of British women are ever on their passage" to better work, marriage, and a more or less regular course of life (quoted in *OV*, p. 6), but the young man sees nothing ahead for Jenny except death. Transfixed by the radiant loveliness of her body, why does he hasten to foretell its decay? Several critics assume that his ability to transcend the appeal of her sensuality is evidence of a heightened moral sensitivity, as if he stands beyond time and looks at Jenny with the eyes of God. But Jenny reminds the young man of his own flesh and recalls him to the knowledge of his mortality.[24] In order to deny the corruptibility of body and soul, he must prove that her beauty will ultimately be nothing. Such denigration of female physicality is central to pornography. According to Griffin, "pornography is an expression not of human erotic feeling and desire, and not of a love of the life of the body, but of a fear of bodily knowledge, and a desire to silence eros."[25] Furthermore, this narrator, unlike his counterparts in pornographic novels, has a particular reason to be angry when he gazes upon Jenny's warm breasts, sensuous throat, and loosely flowing golden hair. He may address her as "Fair Jenny *mine*" (l. 7). And "handsome Jenny *mine*" (l. 89, my emphasis), but he does not in fact possess her. Instead of being "excited all the time" like the women in pornographic novels (*OV*, p. 29), Jenny has gone to sleep. In response, the narrator subjects her delicate beauty to the ravages of time and prepares for the coming regeneration of his own soul. Like lyric poets who use the *carpe diem* argument to punish their reluctant ladies, the thoughtful young man does violence to Jenny—not physically but poetically.

2

Jenny might reproduce biologically; indeed, given the strange twists of fate, her "children's children" might someday provide charity for the legitimate descendants of the narrator and Nell (ll. 211–13). But only the thoughtful young man can produce a work of art, a monologue rich in imagery, metaphor, and allusion. During the nineteenth century, when a full intellectual and artistic life was often said to depend on conservation of sperm, the speaker's skillful manipulation of words could be directly connected to his lack of sexual activity. Victorian doctors were attempting to recast the ancient fascination with semen—Pythagoras called it "the flower of the blood"—in scientific terms. In 1815, M. Venel defined semen as "the most ethereal or subtilized portion of the blood, a highly rectified and refined distillation from every part of the system, particularly the brain and spinal marrow"; in 1872, Dr. Augustus Gardner called it "the purest extract of the blood."[26] Whatever the composition, its discharge was held to weaken a man intellectually as well as physically. If, however, a man remained continent, his semen would be reabsorbed and carried through the bloodstream, reinvigorating mind and spirit. Anxiety about sperm loss was usually expressed in warnings against masturbation, but some doctors carried the theory to its logical extreme. One 1897 sex manual said, "The young man who would secure the highest and best development of his physical and intellectual powers will carefully seek to avoid, as far as possible, all loss of sexual fluid, either in the form of emissions or even in the form of lawful sexual intercourse."[27] Other authorities, such as Theophilus Parvin, offered a consolation for abstinence: geniuses like Newton, Kant, Pascal, and Beethoven lived "without sexual intercourse, and some of them had their years wonderfully prolonged, and though they left no children to perpetuate their names, they were prolific in great works" (H, p. 183). Rossetti's narrator has given money to the prostitute, but he has not "spent" his sperm. The woman's roses and lilies are ruined, but the man's "flower" remains intact.

While the young man is prolific in words, perhaps as a result of abstinence, Jenny remains completely silent. When the narrator thinks of her youth, he envisions Jenny listening to stories of city life. Her attentive silence, which he associates with the rural past and sexual innocence, is set in opposition to narration, the city, and sin. Yet when Jenny "knows" the city, she still remains silent; now, in her fallen state she cannot even listen intelligently (ll. 156–62). Since Jenny has no voice the young man purports to speak for her, recalling her memories of the past (ll. 124–34) and expressing her wishes for the future (ll. 347–64). He even presumes to record her dreams and to interpret them with unquestioned authority to his audience: "Ah, Jenny, yes, we know your dreams" (l. 364, my emphasis). Such male control of language is a central feature of pornography: the genre, observes Griffin, "expresses an almost morbid fear of female speech." As Roland Barthes says in his study of de Sade, "The master is he who speaks, who disposes of the entirety of language; the object is he who is silent, who remains separate, by a mutilation more absolute than any erotic torture, from any access to discourse, because he does not even have any right to receive the master's word."[28]

The connection between the prostitute's silence and her subordination is glossed in an early version of The Waste Land, where T. S. Eliot uses Jenny as a point of contrast to Fresca, that smelly abomination of a modern woman poet. Fresca is a harlot dreaming of "love and pleasant rapes," "a doorslip dunged by every dog in town." Unlike Jenny, she awakens, reads, corresponds with friends, and composes poetry. Her success intensifies the persona's anxieties: how can he be a twentieth-century bard when the bawd has so much to say? Waxing nostalgic for her Victorian predecessor, he cries:

> Fresca! In other time or place had been
> A meek and lowly weeping Magdalene;
> More sinned against than sinning, bruised and marred,
> The lazy laughing Jenny of the bard.[29]

Eliot's speaker would prefer to keep Jenny as a literary type, rendered passive in a prior text. A mutely suffering prostitute, "bruised and marred," is much less threatening than one who reads and writes.

In Rossetti's poem, title and epigraph call attention to the act of naming, which, as Dworkin observes, "enables men to define experience, . . . to control perception itself" (*MPW*, p. 17). "Jenny" 's epigraph comes from the grammar lesson in *The Merry Wives of Windsor*. When Will is asked to decline the genitive case plural of the demonstrative pronoun, he responds, "Genitivo, horum, harum, horum." Mrs. Quickly's interruption—"Vengeance of Jenny's case! Fie on her! Never name her, child, if she be a whore"[30]—emphasizes women's hostility toward women. According to G. L. Hersey, Quickly denounces a "horum" not when she takes money for sex, but when she engages in "plural genitive acts" ("RA," p. 19). "Jenny's case" results from Mrs. Quickly's revulsion against the female capacity to give birth. When narrator and author disregard Quickly's injunction against speaking the prostitute's name, they seem to be defying the widespread hypocrisy of Victorian England. But if naming Jenny is intended as an act of honesty, it is also an act of power. The truncation of Quickly's line forces the reader to finish her sentence, thereby emphasizing the omitted words. Jenny is named "whore" while the narrator remains anonymous, perhaps as an example of the way men have historically used the "cloak of namelessness" for pornography.[31] As the night proceeds and the metaphors become more intricate, the narrator also names the woman hole, cipher, and sewer. Even a schoolboy can describe "what thing" she is to a classmate, while the young girl who sees Jenny can only respond with a "*dumb* rebuke" (ll. 79, 73, my emphasis).

The book metaphor also indicates that the narrator regards culture as a form of male privilege. His initial use of the metaphor—"You know not what a book you seem, / Half-read by lightning in a dream!" (ll. 51–52)—which comes after a sensuous account of Jenny's flowing hair and ungirdled silks, seems designed to flatter Jenny and to distance him from the lure of her body. Following conventions of Elizabethan love poetry, the narrator described her as a book written by nature for the poet's study and admiration. However, in a nineteenth-century context, the narrator may also be identifying Jenny as one of those "bad books" denounced by preachers for inflaming the male imagination and inducing masturbation (see *H*, pp. 169–74). Such books are dangerous, but they are also susceptible to defloration. "To deflower," according to the *Oxford English Dictionary*, means to deprive a woman of her virginity, to strip a plant of its flowers, or "to cull or excerpt from (a book, etc.) its choice or most valuable parts."[32] The narrator is owner, reader, interpreter; Jenny, an object to be opened in pursuit of textual pleasures. Having left his library, exasperated by his inability to work, the thoughtful young man was relieved to find Jenny's room free of books. When he reverts so quickly to the book metaphor, he may be assuming that she is the one text he will be able to master. Nevertheless, the metaphor carries unconscious hostility and it suggests to the reader that Jenny will be as impenetrable as his other books.

The book metaphor takes on different connotations when the speaker tries to imagine what it would be like to talk to Jenny. Instead of referring to her body, the image is now associated with her mind, a "volume seldom read" (l. 158). Perhaps her mind is less interesting than her body; perhaps the narrator is beginning to suspect he cannot open the Jenny-text. The image becomes sexual as he anticipates his words pushing against the book's taut binding and penetrating her brain. (Rossetti deleted worries of "wretched impotence" before publishing the poem.[33]) The sewer image, like the "grim web," absorbs and renders indistinguishable brain and vagina: to enter either is to sink within the sewer "of the middle street" (l. 166). The young man believes that Jenny discharges disease-carrying urine—the "contagious currents" of line 165—and sluggish excremental sediment. Like "Walter" and the male characters in conventional pornographic novels, he fears that women will contaminate him. He now intends for the book to contain the surging female filth.[34] Jenny is the antithesis of art: matter without hue or shape, motion without sound. She cannot even serve as mirror, for she does not possess what Virginia Woolf called "the magic and delicious power of reflecting the figure of a man at twice its natural size."[35] Jenny will neither reflect nor remember the young man's face.

In its last appearance, the book is not associated with Jenny, but with the forces that suppress her: Jenny becomes a dead rose smashed between its "base pages." Her "sanguine stain" marks the book like the rubrication of medieval manuscripts, its redness signifying the spilled blood of saints.[36] Yet in making "Jenny" into a modern book of martyrs, Rossetti has rejected the more optimistic strategy of Rogier Van der Weyden: the Magdalen reading her Bible offered an iconographical tradition of an erring woman restored to grace, reconciled to culture, and rejuvenated intellectually as well as spiritually.[37] While "Jenny"'s bleeding rose recalls the sacrificial blood of saintly victims, it also suggests the vaginal blood of sexually mature women. What Louis Montrose says of the love-juice in A Midsummer Night's Dream is true of Jenny's "sanguine stain" (l. 270). It is "a conflation of menstrual blood—which is the sign of women's generative power and of their pollution, their dangerousness to men—with the blood of defloration— which is the sign of men's mastery of women's bodies, of their generative powers and of their dangerousness."[38] According to the young man, the "life-blood" flowing from Jenny's body is "Puddled with shameful knowledge" (ll. 264–65). Denying the woman's generative power, he reduces her to an oozing substance which must be contained by male form. The "vile text" (l. 259) represents social structures that crush the individual prostitute while preserving the institution, the vile texts of laws invoked to arrest prostitutes, the vile texts of Scripture cited in the campaign for the Contagious Diseases Acts, and the vile text of the speaker's discourse. The poem does to Jenny what the book does to the rose: in preserving the image of her loveliness, it renders her lifeless.[39] Failing to open the Jenny-book, the young man utilizes flower imagery to situate the woman in the realm of nature, claims culture as his own, and wields its power to destroy.[40] At the same time, he insists that the book remain closed to "pure women" (l. 254). Women readers would be moved by the Jenny-text, but they would also be shamed and corrupted. The narrator's prohibitions would keep women apart from one another and isolate them from female experience. If the "chaste hand" is forbidden to unclose the "leaves" of the book *and* the leaves of the female flower, then women are being denied knowledge not only of the prostitute's existence but also of their own bodies (l. 266).

At this point, the artist all but annihilates his model simply by taking a long look at her. As the woman "almost fades from view" (l. 277), a cipher remains, fusing the text and the female figure. A cipher is secret writing, a code that defies interpretation to the uninitiated. In another sense, the cipher is nothing, O, the hole, the receptacle for man's lust. Thus Rossetti reaffirms the implications of the water imagery in the first stanza. There Jenny is the "handful of bright spring-water" (l. 16), but as Hersey observes, she is also "what the drops so quickly become part of—the dark engulfing hole of death" ("RA," p. 21). The woman is reduced from text to cipher, from Jenny to O.

The speaker's involvement in the destruction of the female is apparent in the three passages dealing with artists and their artifacts. In the first, the narrator idealizes female beauty—its creation by a benevolent god and its representation by earlier artists, such as Raphael and Leonardo, whose works were not intended to arouse male desire but rather to touch "men's souls" (ll. 230–40).[41] For these painters, woman's body became the Word of God; in her features, they found "preachings of what God can do" (l. 240). The narrator regrets that he cannot portray Jenny in such saintly form, partly because hordes of dance-hall patrons have spoiled her beauty, partly because he lacks the spirit and skill. However, as Harris says, the narrator's nostalgic view of Renaissance painting is exceedingly problematic. Reading the "gilded aureole" as a "gold coin that monetizes the female model and the spiritual life alike," Harris argues that religious art is being depicted as "an unregenerate quest for material wealth" and as a form of male domination that negates women "while pretending to idealize them" ("SM," pp. 207–8).

The second passage, which draws upon the biblical metaphor of the potter and his clay, raises disturbing questions about artistic intention. The narrator resorts to the parable from Paul's epistle to the Romans (9:21) when he discovers the resemblances between Jenny and his cousin Nell. Since both women are made of the same material, the "same lump" of clay (l. 182), how did they develop so differently—one for "honour," the other for "dishonour"? Paul asserts the absolute sovereignty of God—the "awful secret sway" (l. 180) to shape the inert mass of clay into any form. As artist, the thoughtful young man must separate himself from the shapeless materiality of the female. The association of art with feminine values which Barbara Gelpi has discovered in Rossetti's other poetry does not operate in "Jenny."[42] Here artistic creation is a male act, and a morally suspect one. If God—or any other artist—makes a vessel knowing its purpose is to be dishonored, then the action is capricious and arbitrary. Twice the stunned narrator describes the dreadful dilemma: "Of the same lump . . . / For honour and dishonour made, / Two sister vessels" (ll. 182–84, 203–5). But he cannot directly confront the issue of artistic responsibility: he cannot name the agent. He comes closest to articulating despair in a line located near the poem's center: "It makes a goblin of the sun" (l. 206). The created world is blighted by the monstrous intentions of its creator. The sun/Son, Apollo and Christ, god of poetry and Word of God have all become demonic. By this point, the narrator has undermined his own status as artist, for he has made Jenny— the character and the poem—into a vessel for dishonoring the fallen and fleshly woman.

In the third passage (ll. 282–97), a judgmental God waits until the end of time to strike down his creation. Smashing the toad within the stone in what Hersey calls "a kind of anti-Pygmalionic vision" ("RA," p. 31), the divine sculptor releases Lust, but he also annihilates the human race and returns the earth to dust. To eradicate male desire would not only terminate the cycle of human reproduction; it would also mean the end of art. The narrator assumes that the making of art, like the begetting of life, is located in "the seed of Man" (l. 296). Unfortunately, the man who possesses that generative capability continues to participate in the cycle of desire and destruction. The woman's beauty, which stimulates him aesthetically and sexually, leaves him wracked with the conflicting emotions of attraction and revulsion, a fear of dependency and the will to dominate. Despite the moral quandary that results from his relationship with the prostitute, the young man acknowledges that she does goad him into formulating complex metaphors (ll. 298–302). Her silence is essential to provoke his soliloquy, just as Dora's recalcitrance is necessary to generate Freud's discourse.

The model's function is clear; the man's responsibilities are not. At no point does the narrator define himself as artist, poet, or author of a text. This lack of artistic self-consciousness is characteristic of the pornography Marcus analyzes: it "typically undertakes to represent itself not as a story or fantasy but as something that 'really' happened" (OV, p. 46). It is also consistent with the thematics of the poem. With language indicted as a corrupt system of communication, reading reserved for those with "hard eyes" (l. 263), and the production of artifacts associated with greed, frustration, and anger, the narrator has no way to defend the morality of art. Like the potter, he can assert his power in an arbitrary act of creation which debases the female form; or, like a righteous god he can anticipate the annihilation of art and life. He must be willing to construct discourse which reduces the woman to nothing, or to deny—and eventually destroy—his own creation. The questions raised by lines 182–84 and 203–5 are central to the meaning of the poem and the status of the narrator. *Who* has said? *Who* has made? The narrator occasionally senses that he himself has made Jenny into what she is in social terms, a prostitute; in verbal terms, the subject of his monologue. But the general inability to name himself as agent reflects profound guilt and confusion, not only about his participation in prostitution but also about his objectification of women in art.[43]

3

Like the narrator of "Jenny," Rossetti needed beautiful women as subjects for aesthetic contemplation. He sought models everywhere and sometimes found them by standing at his window. "If a lovely creature passed, I used to rush out and say, 'I'm a painter and I want to paint you. Sometimes they would scream, then I would rush in and slam the front door."[44] The women he brought in from the streets to model often became his mistresses, too (see *VR*, pp. 343–44). However, at some level, Rossetti seems to have feared that women could be destroyed by the artist's endeavors. In "Saint Agnes of the Intercession," an unfinished story begun in the late 1840s and partially revised in 1870, and in "Bonifazio's Mistress," a watercolor which occupied Rossetti during the late 1850s, the woman dies while her artist-lover finishes her portrait.[45]

"Jenny" holds a significant place in Rossetti's poetic development and in the history of his relationships with women. He began the poem when he was nineteen but was unable to complete it. "I felt it was quite beyond me then—a world I was then happy enough to be a stranger to" (*VR*, p. 122). The 1847–48 version relies on simple characterizations—the sensuous woman is a "stumbling stone" for the narrator, a philosopher who aspires to become pure "mind," and the image patterns are undeveloped. Completion of the poem, with its complex insights into sexual, economic, and artistic transactions and its sophisticated metaphoric structures, seemed to require the author's sorrowful entrance into the realm of sexual experience. He returned to the poem in the late 1850s when he and other members of his coterie became interested in fallen women—as a social problem, a subject for art, and a source of pleasure. During this time, Rossetti visited the notorious Argyll Rooms at Picadilly, flirted with prostitute Annie Miller, and began his relationship with Fanny Cornforth, a prostitute who modeled for some of his most sensuous paintings and later became his companion at Cheyne Walk.[46] Rossetti's plans to publish "Jenny" were disrupted in 1862 by the death of his wife, artist and model Elizabeth Siddall. The grieving poet did not express much guilt for his extramarital affairs; instead he blamed himself for spending too much time with art. Burying his poems with Elizabeth's body would be an act of atonement. He told Ford Madox Brown,

"I have often been writing at those poems when Lizzie was ill and suffering, and I might have been attending to her, and now they shall go" (*VR*, p. 303). The poems remained in Siddall's coffin until 1869 when Rossetti's friends convinced him to attempt publication. After the "ghastly business" of the exhumation, Rossetti described the recovered manuscript in a letter to his brother William: "The poem of 'Jenny' which is the one I most wanted, has got a great worm-hole right through every page of it. . . . I could not examine it much, as the greater part still sticks together. I shall not have it here for some days yet. It has a dreadful smell,—partly no doubt the disinfectants,—but the doctor says there is nothing dangerous."[47] Sticky, smelly, potentially disease-ridden, and marked by a great hole at its center, the manuscript of "Jenny" bore a strong resemblance to its female subject. Rossetti was determined "to re-establish the whole in a perfect state" (*L*, 2:753). In a letter to Swinburne, Rossetti insisted that the opening of the coffin was not a forced entry but rather a way of fulfilling his wife's deepest unspoken desires: "Had it been possible to her, I should have found the book on my pillow the night she was buried; and could she have opened the grave no other hand would have been needed" (*L*, 2:761). Nonetheless, the manuscript's retrieval caused considerable suffering. According to Hall Caine, when Rossetti collapsed in 1872, he was having delusions "that related to the exhumation of his wife's body, and the curse that was supposed to have followed him for that desecration" (*VR*, p. 531).

In anticipating responses, Rossetti did not worry about "coarseness," "indelicacy," or "impropriety," the standard terms of disapprobation. Instead, he feared that readers would think he had produced the poem in an "aggressive" spirit (*L*, 2:837). Determined to see art and aggression as antithetical forces, he told C. E. Norton that his poems "have been written neither recklessly nor aggressively (moods which I think are sure to result in the ruin of Art), but from a true impulse to deal with subjects which seem to me capable of being brought rightly within Art's province" (*L*, 2:838). In fact, the speaker of "Jenny" harbors a number of aggressive impulses, some of which the poet shared. Like the narrator, Rossetti is drawn to a woman when she arouses him sexually and aesthetically. But he is also frightened by the erotic lure of her body, repelled by the mortality of her flesh, and bewildered by his dependency on her beauty.[48] Whether the narrator/author speaks as a "compassionate liberal seeking social justice" or as a "reactionary male jealous of his power," he still inhabits a culture permeated by pornography. Nothing in the circumstances of Rossetti's life would prove that he stood far enough outside that culture to fully understand the connection between a social system which subjugates women in prostitution and an aesthetic system which objectifies them in art.[49] Yet in establishing analogies between the patron/prostitute relationship and the artist/model relationship, Rossetti must have sensed that he was involved in a process of self-reflection. Perhaps that is why he called "Jenny," which continued to obsess him even after its publication, "the most serious thing I have written" (*L*, 1:384).

Notes

I would like to thank Linda Dowling, Sally Kamholtz, Ellen Messer-Davidow, and Jill Rubenstein for their many helpful comments and suggestions. I would also like to express my appreciation to the Taft Foundation for a grant that helped support the research for this essay.

1. Virginia Surtees, ed., *The Diaries of George Price Boyce* (Norwich, 1980), p. 35.
2. Steven Marcus, *The Other Victorians: A Study of Sexuality and Pornography in Mid-Nineteenth-Century England* (1964; New York, 1977), p. 286; all further references to this work, abbreviated *OV*, will be included in the text.
3. For example, in studying women's participation in the antivivisectionist movement, Coral Lansbury finds "an extraordinary degree of identification between women and animals," especially in "an unconsious or semi-conscious" fusion of imagery from gynecological, pornographic, and literary sources ("Gynaecology, Pornography, and the Antivivisectionist Movement," *Victorian Studies* 28 [Spring 1985]: 414, 415).
4. See Susan Sontag, "The Pornographic Imagination," *Partisan Review* 34 (Spring 1967): 181–212; Kate Millett, *Sexual Politics* (New York, 1970), p. 46.
5. Susan Rubin Suleiman, "Pornography, Transgression, and the Avant-Garde: Bataille's *Story of the Eye*," in *The Poetics of Gender*, ed. Nancy K. Miller (New York, 1986), p. 128; Susan Gubar, "Representing Pornography: Feminism, Criticism, and Depictions of Female Violation," *Critical Inquiry* 13 (Summer 1987): 724; Eva Feder Kittay, "Pornography and the Erotics of Domination," in *Beyond Domination: New Perspectives on Women and Philosophy*, ed. Carol C. Gould (Totowa, N.J., 1984), p. 167; Irene Diamond, "Pornography and Repression: A Reconsideration," *Signs* 5 (Summer 1980): 687, 686.
6. Susanne Kappeler, *The Pornography of Representation* (Minneapolis, 1986), p. 3; all further references to this work, abbreviated *PR*, will be included in the text.
7. Whether the narrator actually speaks aloud has been a matter of critical conjecture. Jules Paul Seigel describes the poem as a spoken "dialogue of the mind with itself" ("*Jenny*: The Divided Sensibility of a Young and Thoughtful Man of the World," *Studies in English Literature* 9 [Autumn 1969]: 685); Lise Rodgers and G. L. Hersey, as a dramatic monologue (see Rodgers, "The Book and the Flower: Rationality and Sensuality in Dante Gabriel Rossetti's *Jenny*," *Journal of Narrative Technique* 10 [Fall 1980]: 159–69; Hersey, "Rossetti's *Jenny*: A Realist Altarpiece," *Yale Review* 69 [Autumn 1979]: 17–32; all further references to this article, abbreviated "RA," will be included in the text). Daniel A. Harris defines the poem as an interior monologue, arguing that the protagonist's silence represents his alienation from communal relationships and a despairing acknowledgment that his "thoroughly monetized" language makes authentic speech impossible (see Harris, "D. G. Rossetti's *Jenny*: Sex, Money, and the Interior Monologue," *Victorian Poetry* 22 [Summer 1984]: 197–215; all further references to this article, abbreviated "SM," will be included in the text). For the purposes of this paper, it does not matter if the young man is speaking or thinking; he is organizing language for his own ends.
8. There is no reason to doubt the narrator's word on descriptive details—the golden color of Jenny's hair, for example—but everything else is entirely subjective. Although this would seem to be an obvious point in any first-person narrative, it is surprising to see how many critics have accepted the speaker's authority. Florence Saunders Boos argues that "Jenny

is a weak, trivial person, attracted solely to money, personal finery, and gaudy luxuries" (*The Poetry of Dante G. Rossetti: A Critical Reading and Source Study*, Studies in English Literature, vol. 104 [The Hague, 1976], p. 156); Nicholas Shrimpton finds ll. 341–64 necessary to reassert Jenny's "trivial, vain and mercenary *reality*" ("Rossetti's Pornography," *Essays in Criticism* 29 [Oct. 1979]: 337); insisting on the speaker's moral redemption, D.M.R. Bentley concludes that the young man is at last able to see Jenny "as she *really* is—a prostitute with the dreams of a prostitute" (" 'Ah, Poor Jenny's Case': Rossetti and the Fallen Woman/ Flower," *University of Toronto Quarterly* 50 [Winter 1980–81]: 192; all further references to this article, abbreviated "RFW," will be included in the text) (my emphasis). In contrast, art historian Linda Nochlin observes that the poem is "so subjective, even egocentric" that "at the critical moment the actual Jenny fades from view" ("Lost and *Found*: Once More the Fallen Woman," in *Feminism and Art History: Questioning the Litany*, ed. Norma Broude and Mary D. Garrad [New York, 1982], p. 235).

9.   In his letters, Swinburne linked Rossetti's poem to de Sade's novel. During the 1869–70 revisions, Swinburne warned Rossetti that canceling two passages from the poem would be an act of mutilation: the poet would be doing to the text of "Jenny" what de Sade's libertines had done to Justine—"curtailing her natural members"—but he wouldn't even gain "any fleshly sense of enjoyment therefrom" (*The Swinburne Letters*, ed. Cecil Y. Lang, 6 vols. [New Haven, Conn., 1959–62]: 2:88, 73).

10.   It is not my intention to establish specific sources for Rossetti's art. Whatever interest Rossetti had in pornography would not have been documented by family and friends committed to protecting his reputation. One finds glancing references in private sources, such as Boyce's diary entry for 16 Aug. 1862, which is quoted at the beginning of this essay. Another entry for 19 July 1862 depicts Rossetti and cohorts heading off to see *Judge and Jury*, which was, according to Surtees, an entertainment "abounding in obscenities" (see Boyce, *Diaries*, p. 34). According to Alastair Grieve, the imagery in Rossetti's watercolor, "Writing on the Sand," was probably derived from a scatological journal (see Grieve, "Writing on the Sand," in Alan Bowness et al., *The Pre-Raphaelites* [exhibition catalog, London, The Tate Gallery, 1984], p. 287). Several of Rossetti's friends, including Swinburne, Richard Monckton Milnes, and Charles Augustus Howell, were avid readers of pornography.

11.   Jan Marsh is proceeding along these lines when she describes a great deal of nineteenth-century art as "high-class pornography, based on the visual and sexual exploitation of women by producers and consumers" (*The Pre-Raphaelite Sisterhood* [New York, 1985], p. 56).

12.   Thomas Maitland [Robert Buchanan], "The Fleshly School of Poetry: Mr. D. G. Rossetti," *Contemporary Review* 18 (Oct. 1871): 339; Dante Gabriel Rossetti, "The Stealthy School of Criticism," *Athenaeum*, 16 Dec. 1871, p. 793.

13.   Rossetti, "Jenny" in *The Pre-Raphaelites and Their Circle*, ed. Cecil Y. Lang (Chicago, 1975), l. 191. The 1847–48 version of "Jenny" is printed in Paull F. Baum, "The Bancroft Manuscripts of Dante Gabriel Rossetti," *Modern Philology* 39 (Aug. 1941): 47–68. The Fitzwilliam Museum at Cambridge owns a copy of the 1865 version and manuscripts of the 1869 revisions.

14.   Seigel, "The Divided Sensibility," p. 687.

15.   *Found*, Rossetti's painting of the fallen woman which occupied him between 1853 and 1859, is based on similar assumptions. As Nochlin says, "falling in the feminine is considered a metaphysical absolute rather than a social and ethical issue that might be dealt with and changed by means of human effort and action" ("Lost and *Found*," p. 241).

16.   This is not to suggest that rescue work undertaken by middle-class women offered easy or appropriate remedies for the problems associated with prostitution; indeed, historian Judith Walkowitz has argued that the purity crusaders were limited by class bias and by adherence to an ideology that demanded the repression of female sexuality (see "The Politics of Prostitution," *Signs* 6 [Autumn 1980]: 123–35). With reference to the poem, I want to

emphasize the extent to which the narrator, like the pornographer, insists upon separating women from one another.

17.   John Ruskin, "Of Queen's Gardens," *The Works of John Ruskin*, ed. E. T. Cook and Alexander Wedderburn, 39 vols. (London, 1903–12), 18:142–43.

18.   *Paradise Lost* 4:800.

19.   Andrea Dworkin, *Pornography: Men Possessing Women* (New York, 1981), p. 206; further references to this work, abbreviated *MPW*, will be included in the text.

20.   Sigmund Freud, *The Case of Dora and Other Papers*, trans. Joan Riviere et al. (1905; New York, 1952), p. 95.

21.   *The Lady of Shalott* was a popular figure among Pre-Raphaelite artists, drawn and painted by William Holman Hunt, John Everett Millais, Elizabeth Siddall, and Rossetti.

22.   Shrimpton, "Rossetti's Pornography," p. 325; David Sonstroem, *Rossetti and the Fair Lady* (Middletown, Conn., 1970), p. 58.

23.   See Elisabeth G. Gitter, "The Power of Women's Hair in the Victorian Era," *PMLA* 99 (Oct. 1984): 936–54, and Harris, "SM."

24.   See Rodgers, "The Book and the Flower."

25.   Susan Griffin, *Pornography and Silence: Culture's Revenge against Nature* (New York, 1981), p. 1.

26.   Quoted in John S. Haller, Jr., and Robin M. Haller, *The Physician and Sexuality in Victorian America* (1974; New York, 1977), p. 196; quoted in G. J. Barker-Benfield, *The Horrors of the Half-Known Life: Male Attitudes Toward Women and Sexuality in Nineteenth-Century America* (New York, 1976), p. 181; further references to this work, abbreviated *H*, will be included in the text.

27.   Quoted in Haller and Haller, *The Physician and Sexuality*, p. 219.

28.   Griffin, *Pornography and Silence*, p. 89; Roland Barthes, *Sade, Fourier, Loyola*, trans Richard Miller (London, 1976). Of course silence was characteristic not only of the woman represented in pornography but also of the successful artist's model. See Frances Borzello, *The Artist's Model* (London, 1982), pp. 7, 104, 148.

29.   T. S. Eliot, *The Waste Land: A Facsimile and Transcript of the Original Drafts Including the Annotations of Ezra Pound*, ed. Valerie Eliot (New York, 1971), pp. 39, 41. Aldous Huxley and Ezra Pound have also alluded to "Jenny." In *Point Counter Point* (Garden City, N. Y., 1928), the description of Jenny Smith, John Bidlake's "loveliest model," seems to derive from Rossetti's poem. The narrator says that Jenny is a "goddess as long as she was naked, kept her mouth shut, or had it kept shut for her with kisses." However, when she talks the angry painter declares, "You ought to be muzzled, Jenny" (p. 44). Pound refers to "Jenny" in "Yeux Glauques" (1915), his poem about Rossetti's model and wife, Elizabeth Siddall. With her faun's beauty, her "vacant gaze," her "half-ruin'd face," and her bewilderment at men's betrayal, Siddall reminds the speaker of "poor Jenny's case" (see *Personae: The Collected Poems of Ezra Pound* [New York, 1926], p. 192).

30.   *The Merry Wives of Windsor*, act 4, sc.1, ll. 64–65.

31.   Lawrence Lipking, "Aristotle's Sister: A Poetics of Abandonment," *Critical Inquiry* 10 (Sept. 1983): 72.

32.   *Oxford English Dictionary*, s.v. "deflower."

33.   See Baum, "The Bancroft Manuscripts," p. 50.

34.   In accepting the speaker's judgment here, Kris Lackey completely misreads the passage: "So disordered has her life been and so infected has her moral sense become that only some kind of imaginative order imposed upon her experience by a healthier, more objective mind can give her experience meaning" ("A Scholar-John: The Speaker in 'Jenny,' " *Victorian Poetry* 21 [Winter 1983]: 429).

35.   Virginia Woolf, *A Room of One's Own* (1929; New York, 1957), p. 35.

36.   See Ernst Robert Curtius, *European Literature and the Latin Middle Ages*, trans. Willard Trask (1953; New York, 1963), p. 316.

37.   The figure of the "contemplative Magdalen" is discussed in Marjorie M. Malvern, *Venus in Sackcloth: The Magdalen's Origins and Metamorphoses* (Carbondale, Ill., 1975), pp. 126–29 and 172–73. It seems likely that Rossetti would have seen Rogier van der Weyden's *The Magdalen Reading* at the National Gallery because it was acquired under the directorship of Sir Charles Eastlake.

38.   Louis Adrian Montrose, " 'Shaping Fantasies': Figurations of Gender and Power in Elizabeth Culture," *Representations* 1 (Spring 1983): 193.

39.   John P. McGowan makes the same point when he asks, "Has the poet not taken the 'rose,' Jenny, and shut her into his own book?" Although McGowan sees that the artistic act may destroy the "actual Jenny," he regards the sexual act as normative. Assuming that the poem presents physical love as "an analogue of spiritual love," McGowan implies that it would have been beneficial to the speaker if he had "penetrated this incomprehensible being" (" 'The Bitterness of Things Occult'. D. G. Rossetti's Search for the Real," *Victorian Poetry* 20 [Autumn/Winter 1982]: 52, 49, 48).

40.   Rossetti often incorporated books into sketches and paintings of women he admired: "Elizabeth Siddall" (n.d.; no. 511 in Surtees, *The Paintings and Drawings of Dante Gabriel Rossetti [1828–1882]*, 2 vols. [Oxford, 1971]); "Elizabeth Siddall" (1854; no. 465); "Christina Rossetti" (1866; no. 429). Although the book is a source of erotic temptation in "Paolo and Francesca da Rimini" (1855; no. 75), in other works drawn from Dante the woman has an aura of piety as well as untouchable beauty: "The Salutation of Beatrice" (1880–81; no. 260) and "La Pia de' Tolomei" (1868–80; no. 207). In two somewhat idealized portraits, Jane Burden Morris is shown holding an open book with a flower lying across it: "Mrs. William Morris" (1868; no. 372) and "The Day-Dream" (1880, no. 259). Thus when the speaker of "Jenny" uses the book to destroy the rose, he is reversing the associations of imagery which Rossetti normally uses to praise female beauty.

41.   Compare Rossetti's treatment of the artist-model relationship in "A Painter at Work" (ca. 1850–52; no. 677 in Surtees, ibid.); "Giorgione Painting" (ca. 1853; no. 695); "Fra Angelico Painting" (ca. 1853; no. 694); and "St. Catherine" (1857; no. 89).

42.   See Barbara Charlesworth Gelpi, "The Feminization of D. G. Rossetti," in *The Victorian Experience: The Poets*, ed. Richard A. Levine (Athens, Ohio, 1982), pp. 94–114.

43.   Borzello describes the link between modeling and prostitution during the nineteenth century in *The Artist's Model*, pp. 65–80.

44.   Oswald Doughty, *A Victorian Romantic: Dante Gabriel Rossetti*, 2d ed. (London, 1960), p. 424; see also Boyce, *Diaries*, pp. 34, 35, 44.

45.   See "Saint Agnes of the Intercession," *The Collected Works of Dante Gabriel Rossetti*, ed. William M. Rossetti, 2 vols. (London, 1886), 1:399–426. See also Surtees, *The Paintings and Drawings*, no. 121 A–B. Surtees writes, "It is permissible to reflect whether the artist was himself haunted by a possible parallel situation in his own life" (1:76).

46.   See Marsh, *The Pre-Raphaelite Sisterhood*, pp. 142–46.

47.   *The Letters of Dante Gabriel Rossetti*, ed. Doughty and John Robert Wahl, 4 vols. (Oxford, 1965), 2:685; all further references to this work, abbreviated *L*, will be included in the text. For Rossetti's remarkable letter to his brother, see William E. Fredeman, "Prelude to the Last Decade: Dante Gabriel Rossetti in the Summer of 1872," pt. 1, *Bulletin of the John Rylands Library* 53 (Autumn 1970): 108. Fredeman notes that William Michael Rossetti "severely edited" this letter for publication, and that Doughty and Wahl have only published a fragment of it.

48.   Although Harris' analysis of the narrator's anxieties regarding sex, money, and language is often brilliant, his assumptions about Rossetti's life are askew. Harris believes that the poet consciously undertook a radical critique of male attitudes toward prostitution and that his own "reformist interest" in the subject is reflected in his friendship with Josephine Butler, leader in the campaign to repeal the Contagious Diseases Acts ("SM," p. 198). According to Glen Petrie, whose biography Harris cites, Butler admired Rossetti's painting,

but she "could not regard his private life and heavy flirtatiousness with amused detachment" (*A Singular Iniquity: The Campaigns of Josephine Butler* [New York, 1971], p. 35). There is no indication that Butler believed Rossetti to have a "reformist interest" in her cause.

49. In "The Feminization of D. G. Rossetti," Gelpi attributes Rossetti's ambivalence about women to his relationship with his mother. She writes, "Rossetti's dependence on the feminine, stemming from his strong attachment to his mother, moved him imaginatively into the feminine sphere and made it possible for him to identify with women's feelings. That same dependence, however, in its creation of ambivalence caused him to fear and resent women's power" (p. 111).

Dante Gabriel Rossetti and
the Betrayal of Truth

Jerome J. McGann

Rossetti has a notebook entry dating from the early 1870s in which he speaks of certain "Days when the characters of men came out as strongly as secret writing exposed to fire."[1] What is illuminating and complex in this figure centers in the pun on the word "characters," where both people and writing are imagined as encrypted forms—indeed, as encrypted transforms of each other. Their respective truths appear only when the false innocence of the surface is removed.

As with Blake, when he spoke of a similar process in *The Marriage of Heaven and Hell*, the agent of revelation here is fire, and a fire associated, as in Blake, with hell. But in Blake there is nothing sinister in such fire, which is seen as a "divine" agency (that is to say, as part of the human process of engraving). In Rossetti, however, the fire threatens because the "characters" are sinister and threatening. Lurking below Rossetti's metaphor are suggestions of torture and even damnation, of a world in which "the characters of men" practice concealment and deceit.

This is not an image which Rossetti would have produced when he began to test his imaginative resources in the 1840s. But it has arrived at the heart of his work, and it can help to guide us should we choose to approach him from more customary angles—for example, down the avenues of his early prose works like "Hand and Soul" or the fragmentary "St. Agnes of Intercession." These tales seem typically Rossettian in their treatment of the relation between love and art; but their extreme deceptiveness, their preoccupation with false appearances, is equally central to what they are doing, and equally a Rossettian trademark.

Like its companion tale "Hand and Soul," "St. Agnes of Intercession" anatomizes the character and situation of a young painter whose "impulse towards art" was "a vital passion" (1:400).[2] When he falls in love with a young woman of comfortable means—as he puts it, "of more ease than my own" (1:402)—he is driven to seek "such a position as would secure me from reproaching myself with any sacrifice made for her sake." That is the young man's painfully delicate way of saying that he set about trying to become a

Reprinted from *Victorian Poetry* 26 (1988): 339–61, by permission of the journal.

commercially successful painter, which meant, in practical terms, submitting his work for exhibition. To this end he "laboured constantly and unweariedly" for many days and nights on a work whose "principal female figure" was his betrothed, Miss Mary Arden.

In these initial details we glimpse the characteristic tension which will dominate Rossetti's story: between an exalted ideal of art, on one hand, and certain quotidian practical exigencies on the other. The young man's reflections on the opening day of the exhibition make these contradictions very explicit:

> My picture, I knew, had been accepted, but I was ignorant of a matter perhaps still more important,—its situation on the walls. On that now depended its success. . . . That is not the least curious feature of life as evolved in society,— . . . When a man, having endured labour, gives its fruits into the hands of other men, that they may do their work between him and mankind: confiding it to them, unknown, without seeking knowledge of them . . . without appeal to the sympathy of kindred experience: submitting to them his naked soul, himself, blind and unseen.
>
> (1:403)

Centrally at issue here is the public and commercial "success" of the work, as opposed to its "artistic achievement" or "intrinsic value." Or rather, the passage shows how the sensibility of a man who is committed to the "intrinsic values" of art suffers a crucifixion of the imagination when he feels compelled to operate in and through the mediations "evolved in society." His initial anxiety about whether his picture will even be accepted for exhibition succeeds to a whole train of others which crystallize in one immediate concern: whether the painting will be prominently displayed—in the jargon of the day, whether it will be "on the line"—or whether it will be relegated to some less prestigious, or even less visible, position.

These misgivings surface as soon as he begins to make a tour of the exhibition with another man, also unnamed in the story, whom the painter accidentally encounters. This man, a poet and an art critic, gives a further turn of the screw to the young painter's anxieties. Rossetti's painter fears and respects his companion's power in the culture-industry of their world, but he has only contempt for the man's artistic taste and poetic skills. He is able to conceal his actual views and feelings until the poet-critic pauses in their tour of the exhibition, pulls out a sheaf of his poems, and asks the painter for his opinion. After reading them hurriedly the young man manages an answer. It is a nice moment:

> "I think," I coolly replied, "that when a poet strikes out for himself a new path in style, he should first be quite convinced that it possesses sufficient advantages to counterbalance the contempt which the swarm of his imitators will bring upon poetry."

My ambiguity was successful. I could see him take the compliment to himself, and inhale it like a scent, while a slow broad smile covered his face. It was much as if, at some meeting, on a speech being made complimentary to the chairman, one of the waiters should elbow that personage aside, plant his knuckles on the table, and proceed to return thanks.

(1:407)

This passage dramatizes the deep connections joining the painter's artistic fastidiousness and "idealism" to his tortured duplicity and servile cowardice. "Successful" is just the right word, in this context, to describe his wary but contemptuous reply to the other man's fatuous request for praise. If he wants to be "successful" as an artist, he cannot afford to offend this man. Indeed, he even has to cultivate him to some extent. So the young painter stays with him throughout the exhibition, suffering his absurd displays of self-importance. Through it all, however, the young painter keeps his distance from the man—inwardly, spiritually, in secret. He practices a fraud on his companion when he equivocates about the man's bad verse. That false representation is his way of preserving his sense of integrity and his commitment to true art. The moment is troubled and troubling, however, because it sets those key Rossettian values quite literally on a false ground.

The entire scene from "St. Agnes of Intercession," written in 1848–50 (but revised in 1870),[3] is thus an emblem of Rossetti's career as an artist and poet. Later I will return to deal with the matter of Miss Mary Arden—that is to say, with Rossetti's habit of linking his artistic ideals and imaginative practices to the women whose images dominated his life. For now I wish to concentrate on the problem of the material conditions of artistic production as Rossetti experienced them in his age. Unlike Blake's and Byron's, Rossetti's work does not foreground the artistic opportunities which are offered when an artist seeks to utilize the physical and institutional structures within which all such work is necessarily carried out. Rossetti is as self-conscious as they are about those media, but to him the structures more often rose up as obstacles to be overcome rather than adventures to be risked. "St. Agnes of Intercession," in the scene I have been recapitulating, pays greatest attention to the difficulties raised by the institutions of imagination: most particularly, those means of production which establish the possibility, or the terms, on which a painter or a poet is able to encounter an audience.

If Rossetti's feeling for those difficulties makes him a less innocent poet than either Blake or Byron, it also set him in a position where he could explore, far more profoundly than any English poet had previously done, the significance of imaginative work in an age of mechanical reproduction, in an age where "the best that has been known and thought in the world" is seen to be quite literally a *product*, the output of what we now call the "culture" or the "consciousness industries." Like Baudelaire in France, Rossetti was the first poet in England to see this very clearly; and, again like Baudelaire, he recoiled from it, and tried to imagine ways for evading those institutional powers, and for recovering an ideal of artistic and poetic transcendence. But like Baudelaire once again, what he accomplished was far otherwise and far more important. What he accomplished was a critical definition of the symbolistic imagination when its work has been forced by circumstance to be carried out within a marketing and commercial frame of reference.

II

In that context, Rossetti is constantly driven to work by indirection. This happens because he operates in the belief—the ideology—that life is one thing, art another. Art for Rossetti appeared to him—as in Chiaro's vision in "Hand and Soul"—as life in its finer tone, the one certain means by which human beings can soar beyond the confusions of a mortal and veiled existence. His ideology of the sacred character of the poetic life made him an acute observer of the illusions of the quotidian world—in this he is like his sister Christina. But whereas, for her, sacramentalism—the ritually practiced religious life—was the one fundamental necessity, for Dante Gabriel that necessity was located in the practice of art.

This point of view established the basic contradiction within which Rossetti's work was to develop. The practical dimension of the contradiction can be expressed as follows: how does one paint or write poetry when the world of getting and spending constantly impinges, transforming the fair illusion of a pure pursuit of Beauty into other, darker forms—at worst unworthy, at best distracting, but in any case equally illusionistic? This is the great contradiction raised by poetry in the age of Victorian commercial imperialism, and first given profound expression in Tennyson's 1832 *Poems*. Rossetti would not find a solution to that problem, any more than anyone else would. In fact the problem has no solution, because its importance as a problem lies not in any realities it consciously questions but in the illusions it unwittingly exposes. It is a problem without a solution because it is a problem framed within its own rooted misunderstanding about the nature of art and imagination: that these are transcendental forms standing free of the sublunary orders of human things.

One face of the illusion appears as the idea that "effort and expectation and desire," or striving seeking and finding, will eventually produce a solution. Rossetti is the first Victorian poet to show clearly the falseness of such convictions. The important secondary illusion is that the sublunary world and the world of art differ from each other in every important respect—as the material world is thought to differ in all important respects from the world of spirit. This illusion Rossetti will also discredit, at first with excitement and confidence, in his explorations of erotic experience, but finally in fear and trembling, as the full import of his erotic explorations slowly dawns upon him. In the end Rossetti's poetry (and his art as well, though I shall not be concentrating on that aspect of his work)[4] will repeat Dante's journey in the opposite direction, descending from various illusory heavens through a purgatory of unveilings to the nightmares and hells of his greatest work, the unwilled revelations arrived at in *The House of Life*.

It is important to realize that Rossetti did not set out to discredit that ideology. "Hand and Soul," for example, tells a story of the triumph of art and the artistic life over base circumstances. The problem is that the story doubts the truth of its own apparent theme. It is a hoaxing tale in more ways than one. It is a hoax, formally speaking, in that it consciously imitates the hoaxes of Edgar Allan Poe—those tales like "Von Kempelen and his Discovery" which present themselves to the reader as nonfictions. Rossetti's work is written to secure a real belief in its fictional representations. Written in the form of a personal essay, it deceived "more than one admirer . . . who made enquiry in Florence and Dresden after the pictures of Chiaro" (2:524).

Like Poe and Baudelaire, Rossetti catches the reader out by feeding him the illusions he wants to believe. The ultimate effect of such a story is to expose the structure of those illusions. But, unlike Poe and Baudelaire, Rossetti himself more than half believed in the illusions he was calling out. For Rossetti, then, the story is not initially conceived as a hoax at all but as a serious conjuring trick. R. L. Megroz was acute to see that "in his imaginative adventures, Rossetti was always casting the horoscope of his life."[5] "Hand and Soul" is in this respect, at least initially, a serious act of magic, an effort to put into writing a story that might prove to be the actual plot of Rossetti's own life. If the story could be imagined to be true, in the second half of the nineteenth century in England (either as a piece of "past" history or as the sketch of the true "future"), then art could be said to transcend circumstance. And Rossetti was not the only one who sought to turn the fictions of that story into truths.

The greatness, as well as the horror, of Rossetti's career can be traced to his insistence upon interrogating that cherished belief in the mission of art to unveil, or achieve, transcendence. To discover the truth of that belief Rossetti made an experiment of his life and his life's work, where his deepest convictions were put to a series of empirical tests. Rossetti's work is an effort to confirm empirically those narrative imaginings he had initially set forth in "St. Agnes of Intercession" and "Hand and Soul."

The experiment led Rossetti to complete the curve of the demonic imagination outlined half a century before by Blake when he showed that "he who will not defend Truth may be compelled to / Defend a Lie, that he may be snared & caught & taken" (*Milton* 8:47). For the truths Rossetti discovered did not confirm the story he was committed to. In the first place, the artist's life Rossetti came to know in those years had none of the mythic purity of Chiaro's tale. Rossetti had to scramble for success, seek out commissions, constantly resupply himself with the money he loved to call "tin" (thereby dismissing it from the serious concerns he kept imagining for himself). The more he made his way as an artist, the more difficult he found the demands that such a life placed upon him. These were not the grandiose spiritual difficulties laid upon the high-minded Chiaro; they were crass and quotidian demands, nightmarishly worse even than those glimpsed in "St. Agnes of Intercession."

Rossetti had various tricks by which he held off the enormity of this experimental life that he was pursuing. He paraded his refusals to exhibit in the ordinary professional ways, and nurtured the myth, both for himself and for others, of bohemian genius. But while Millais, Brown, and Edward Jones were making their way by more conventional means, Rossetti was nonetheless making his way—in certain respects, not least of all monetary, even more successfully. But it was a way that left only ashes in his mouth.

Nothing shows his situation so well as his relations with the people whose commissions he was seeking. It began with the earliest of them, Francis McCracken for instance, in the early fifties. Perceiving McCracken as "an absolute Guy—worse than Patmore" (L 1:185),[6] Rossetti manipulated him into buying things at grossly inflated prices, and then ridiculed him to his friends—for example in his contemptuous parody of Tennyson's "The Kraken" which Rossetti called "MacCraken."[7] Throughout the fifties and sixties Rossetti cosseted and condescended to his buyers. They seemed, most of them, altogether too easy marks: eager, relatively ignorant, contemptible in the end. To Ford Madox Brown, for example, he remarked, "I'll forebear from springing at the unaccustomed throat of Trist, if possible; but really a man shouldn't buy pictures without nerving himself beforehand against commercial garotte" (L 2:520). This sort of thing is a refrain in his letters. Yet his own idealization of the practice of art turned his behavior into a kind of self-immolation. If Trist and the other buyers were suffering executions in their pocketbooks, Rossetti's "commercial garotte" was strangling his own soul.

By 1865–66 Rossetti had become a very successful painter indeed, measured both in terms of his celebrity and his income. At the same time it had become apparent to himself, in any case, that his experiment with his life and his ideals had not gone well. The course of his commercial career had its parallel in the course of his devotional life—by which I mean his love life. Elizabeth's suicide in 1862 was no more than the exponent and capstone of his disastrous quests for the Beatrice which his experiment required. Their life together had not been an "ideal" in any sense, either before or after the marriage, though his initial imagination of her meaning for him was—just that, that she was to be deeply meaningful. Then too there were his infidelities, we do not know exactly how many. In a sense they were not infidelities to Elizabeth at all, since his attachment to her was never personal. What he worshiped was her image, and that he had himself created, first in his imagination, and then later, in the series of incredible drawings and paintings which he devoted to that image. His were infidelities, therefore, to his own soul, to his idea of himself, to the vision which had come to Chiaro in the late 1840s.

The extent of those infidelities was defined for him in the death of his wife and unborn child. The most celebrated act of his life—burying his volume of largely unpublished poems in the coffin with Elizabeth—was a form of expiation, of course, but its full significance has to be understood in the context of his artistic and poetic careers. His steady success as a painter became for Rossetti an index of how he was betraying his mission as an artist. The greater his success in securing commissions, the more erratic his output as a painter became. His cynical attitude toward his various patrons was matched only by his scandalous failure to meet obligations even after he had been paid. Through it all, however, he began to imagine that what he was betraying as a painter he was preserving as a poet. His paintings were hopelessly entangled with commercial affairs, but his poetry, it seemed to him, had been nurtured apart from worldly concerns. When in the fall of 1860 he sent a manuscript book of his original poetry to William Allingham for comments and criticism, his accompanying remarks are revealing: "When I think how old most of these things are, it seems like a sort of mania to keep thinking of them still, but I suppose one's leaning still to them depends mainly on their having no trade associations, and being still a sort of thing of one's own. I have no definite ideas as to doing anything with them, but should like, even if they lie at rest, to make them as good as I can" (L 1:377). After he published, successfully, his 1861 The Early Italian Poets, a volume of his original work, Dante at Verona and other Poems, was advertised. But Elizabeth's death intervened, along with the accompanying sense that his unfaithfulness was not simply, or even fundamentally, marital. The gift of his book of poems to Elizabeth's corpse was a gesture asserting that his artistic soul was still alive, and that he still had the integrity to preserve its life. He sent his poems out of the world.

But this left him more painfully in the world than ever, and the years 1862–68 are a record of what Oswald Doughty once labelled "Disillusion" and "Success."[8] For Rossetti these were two faces of the same reality. Doughty's terms apply to Rossetti's artistic career, but they carry ironical overtones because, so far as Rossetti was concerned, his very success as a painter only multiplied his sense of moral disillusion. In this connection, though we must be very clear about the commercialism of the paintings, we are precisely not to judge the significance of those paintings through Rossetti's contradicted Victorian ideology. He despised the commercial face he saw in his work, but we must read and judge that work in another light.

If the paintings were commercial to a degree—and they were—they triumph in and through that commercialism. Like the poems, they are deceptions, sometimes even self-deceptions. Formally considered, they often appear to us as genre paintings; but the appearance is fraudulent. Rossetti's paintings come forth showing different kinds of representational faces. In every case the representational surface is distorted or disfigured, however, and those disruptions signal the truth about his work which Rossetti was concealing, partly from himself, and wholly from his contemporary audience. For his oils are not at all representational, they are abstract experiments in the use of color and (most importantly) the conventions of painterly space. Critics have never seriously faulted Rossetti's composition and his use of color, of course, but many have complained about his draughtsmanship. It is the drawing, however, which most graphically reveals the experimental character of his work, for it is the drawing which tilts his pictures out of their conventional structures. These paintings seduce and then abandon the corrupted eye of the conventional viewer, and in the process they contrive to deliver a secret meaning through the surface of betrayed appearances.

In this way Rossetti experienced an overthrow of certain traditional ideas about success and failure in art, illusion and disillusion in life. His success and disillusion are both real. But in his work we observe success being measured by disillusion, and disillusion being founded on success.

This pattern is recurrent and graphically displayed in the case of his poetical work as well. In 1868–69, finding it impossible to paint at all, he began writing poetry again. After much urging by relatives and friends, he published sixteen of these new sonnets in the *Fortnightly Review* (March 1869), and in the succeeding months he continued to write. Eventually he began to articulate the possibility of exhuming the book he had buried with Elizabeth, as part of a project to print "some old and new poems . . . for private circulation" (L 2:716). Rossetti's tentative moves toward returning his poetry to the world were given a crucial impetus when he read an anonymous article on his verse in *Tinsley's Magazine* in August 1869, at the very time he was working on the proofs for his "Trial Book" of poems. Once again he clearly describes the dialectic which is driving his new writing: "So after twenty years one stranger does seem to have discovered one's existence. However I have no cause to complain, since I have all I need of an essential kind, and have taken little trouble about it,—except always in the nature of my work,—the poetry especially in which I have done no pot-boiling at any rate. So I am grateful to that art, and nourish against the other that base grudge which we bear those whom we have treated shabbily" (L 2:729). It is an astonishing passage for a man who, in 1869, had the kind of celebrity and success which Rossetti enjoyed. That H. Buxton Forman—the young author of the *Tinsley's* piece—would write an essay on Rossetti's poetry, when so little had appeared in print, and most of that in relatively inaccessible places, testifies to the kind of attention which his name commanded. Yet to Rossetti it seemed that his very existence had only just then been discovered, after twenty years of—what, invisibility? Yes, this was the way he saw it:

the blankness which his commercial work as a painter had left where the image of his soul had once appeared.

III

Late in 1869, therefore, Rossetti began putting together a book of poetry which was to recoup those losses and betrayals he had been accumulating since the early fifties. He was full of anxiety about every detail of this project. Between mid-August 1869 and March 1, 1870, he received for correction and revision at least three sets of initial proofs (August 20–September 21), two so-called Trial Books (October 3–November 25), and a final complete proof of the first edition. The changes made in these proofs and Trial Books were massive: many poems were added and some were removed; large additions were written into the proof materials at all six major stages; titles were changed, and numerous local corrections and alterations were made; and finally, not least significant, the ordering of the poems underwent important and radical transformations. In the next two months, April and May, Rossetti continued to harass his publishers with extensive revisions and large-scale alterations of every kind. Nor was the physical appearance of the book a matter of small moment: the paper, the binding, the cloth, the color, the kind of dies to be struck for the embossed cover designs, and so forth—all these matters engrossed his attention. Rossetti's *Poems* of 1870 were bringing the whole soul of the man into activity.[9]

To Rossetti's imagination, that soul was the one he had almost lost through his life of betrayal—through his worldliness. But in objective truth it was another, more demonic soul to which his life's work had been devoted, and entirely faithful. Rossetti's concern that his book make a good appearance, in every sense, reflects his desire that it be a perfect image of beauty, of finishedness, of his commitment to perfection. His notorious efforts to control as completely as possible the immediate critical reception of the book must be understood as part of this obsession with the appearance of his work, the impression it would create. By 1870 he had a large network of friends and friendly acquaintances who were well-connected in the periodical press. All were enlisted to launch the book into the world—in pre-publication reviews wherever possible—not simply to a chorus of praise, but in terms that were to represent Rossetti's *Poems* as a work of the greatest artistic moment—indeed, as the very exponent and symbol of what "a work of art" means.[10]

In this sense, Rossetti's *Poems* (1870)—even more than Swinburne's *Poems and Ballads* (1866), which had created such a sensation four years earlier—is a manifesto for what Pater would call "Aesthetic Poetry." Comprised in that event, however, as Walter Benjamin so acutely observed in his great work on Baudelaire, is the understanding that the "work of art" has now identified itself with, and as, the commodity.[11] The work was to be so carefully prepared, so thoroughly worked and polished, so packaged and promoted that it would ravish its audience and establish Rossetti's fame. The book was meant to "succeed" in the same way, only far more absolutely, that the painter, in "St. Agnes of Intercession," set out to succeed. Consumed for months with his corrections and revisions, Rossetti was perhaps able to blink the commercial forms and "trade associations" that were concealed in this attention to his craft, but the commodity-status of his work emerges very clearly in those other investments: his obsession with the physical appearance of his book, on one hand, and—crucially—his campaign to manage the reviews, on the other.

But if Rossetti's *Poems* (1870) return and re-establish the contradictions he had begun to explore in the late forties and early fifties, the intervening years had made an enormous difference in his work. In those years a happy liberal view might look for, and might even discover, signs of a "growing artistic maturity," of a "development" toward some "greater self-conscious-ness" in his work which could suggest that he had "transcended" in some measure the network of initial contradictions.[12] But in fact Rossetti's "devel-opment," if one can call it that, is in the opposite direction—toward a more complete immersion within the contradictions, indeed, toward an enslavement to them. In twenty years Rossetti had moved from the margin to the very heart of his culture: as Blake would have said, "he became what he beheld." In tracing that movement, *Poems* (1870) achieved its greatness. The analogy to *Les Fleurs du Mal* is quite exact, so that what Benjamin said of the latter can be applied, pari passu, to Rossetti: "Baudelaire was a secret agent—an agent of the secret discontent of his class with its own rule."[13] In Rossetti's case as well, therefore, "the point of departure is the object riddled with error" (Benjamin, p. 103). And in the nineteenth century there are few English books of poetry more secretly discontented, more riddled with error, than this book of Rossetti's.

We may begin to unriddle that error by a critical retracing of the history of the book. In his reply to Buchanan's "The Fleshly School of Poetry," Rossetti defended his dramatic monologue "Jenny" by a general argument about the nature of art. When he first wrote the poem "some thirteen years ago," he says, he understood that the subject-matter—a young man's visit to a prostitute—might have called for "a treatment from without." Such an objective treatment would have set a critical distance between the poem and its problematic subject. Rossetti rejected the option because "the motive powers of art reverse the requirement of science, and demand first of all an *inner* standing-point such as the speaker put forward in the poem,—that is, of a young and thoughtful man of the world" (2:484–485). This is more than the classic defense, that poems are not to be read as "personal expres-sions." Rossetti is rather speaking as a student of Browning, whose work with the dramatic monologue Rossetti so much admired. In that form an effort is made to confine subjectivity to the core of what Coleridge once called the "dramatic truth of such . . . situations, supposing them real."[14] The dramatic monologue moves to take the "lyrical" out of the "ballad." Rossetti's "*inner* standing-point" is thus a Victorian explanation of what Keats called "negative capability," or the process by which the author's conscious separation from his subject—the typical structure of a poem by, say, Rochester or Pope—is canceled in a process of deep sympathetic engagement. In Rossetti's case, however, as in Browning's, the chameleonic turn involves a transfer of sympathy from the poet to some figure or character who is concretely imagined in the poem. The so-called "poetry of experience" becomes, in Victorian hands, a form for introducing modes of subjectivity into historically removed materials, or into contemporary materials which might be, for various reasons, problematic.

In the Victorian dramatic monologue, this transfer of sympathy cancels the traditional structure on which the identity of the poet, formally speaking, depends. Browning was not especially interested in, or perhaps even aware of, the crisis (and therefore the opportunity) which was emerging for poetry in this dismantling of the conventions of sincerity. But Rossetti was. Browning's spy will succeed to the absent gods of Flaubert and later Joyce, who stand apart from their creations, paring their fingernails. This is the theory, or rather the ideology, in which Rossetti too has taken his stand.

But as with Baudelaire's *flaneur*, Rossetti's disengagement becomes an exponent of social alienation, as is quite clear in "Jenny" itself. The sympathy of Rossetti's "young and thoughtful man of the world" is for a sleeping figure, a prostitute who never responds and who in the poem cannot respond. Her condition merely replicates the incompetent thought and limited sympathies of the young man, however. He does not understand her, or her "case," because she exists for him in an aesthetic condition alone, that state where sympathy appears as the indifference of appreciation. In the end, both prostitute and young man are figures of the latent structures of alienation of poetry itself as these structures have descended into Rossetti's hands. In fact, he here reveals the image of that "thoughtful" young man's soul as self-contradicted, an image with the face of a prostitute superimposed on the face of his sister.

In "Jenny," the frame erected by the dramatic monologue works to reveal alienation rather than establish sympathy, and to suggest—ultimately—that the dramatic monologue is a construction of chinese boxes. More than recording a failed quest for sympathetic engagement, the poem judges this to be the failure of poetry (or art) itself. This judgment is an extremely critical one, in the nineteenth century, because poetry and art were then generally regarded as the ultimate depositories, and even the creators, of spiritual and human values. In calling that ideology into question, Rossetti's work has contrived to imagine the experience of being distanced altogether from experience. It is to have fashioned a vehicle for conveying, quite literally, the feeling of the absence of feeling.[15]

Nowhere is this experience more clearly visible than in *The House of Life*, which must be the most alienated, and probably the most horrifying, major poem in the language. This culminant achievement is so integrated with his whole life's work, and in particular with the project that became *Poems* (1870), that the connections have to be sketched. *Poems* (1870), we may recall, is separated into three parts. The initial section is composed principally of a series of longer pieces—dramatic monologues, stories, ballads, and a few translations. Here the deployment of Rossetti's *"inner* standing-point" is most clearly shown—not simply in monologues like "A Last Confession" and "Jenny," but in all the literary ballads ("Troy Town," "Stratton Water," "Sister Helen," and so forth), where the use of the ballad convention historicizes the style and voicing as well as the narrative materials. The point of view in "Dante at Verona," similarly antiqued, is much closer to Dante's age than to Rossetti's. Likewise, Rossetti employs translation, here and elsewhere, as yet another depersonalizing convention. The third section of *Poems* (1870), which follows *The House of Life*, is largely devoted to a variant type of Rossettian translation: "Sonnets for Pictures," so-called.

Paradoxically, Rossetti's use of these nonsubjective verse forms intensifies the aura of poetic self-consciousness. He turns away from his own age and self, but in doing so the contemporaneous relevance of his acts of historical displacement is only heightened. "Dante at Verona" is in this respect a clear allegory, but an allegory which deconstructs itself. Dante's alienation has its contemporary (Rossettian) analogy in the speaker of the poem, who celebrates Dante's critique of luxurious society. But whereas the Dante of Rossetti's poem speaks out openly and plainly against the world of Can Grande, there is no plain speaking at the contemporary level, merely gestures and vague allusions.

Yet "Dante at Verona" does not exemplify what is best and most innovative in Rossetti's poetry. To see that, in the nonpersonal and antiqued material, we have to look at some other things—for example, the excellent "An Old Song Ended," which begins by quoting the last stanza of an antique ballad and then "ends" it with four more stanzas. The story, rendered in the convention of a dialogue between a dying lady—a Mariana figure—and an unnamed interlocutor, lets us know that she will die before her lover returns. The poem finishes with the lady's last reply to the final question put to her:

> "Can you say to me some word
>   I shall say to him?"
> "Say I'm looking in his eyes
>   Though my eyes are dim."

This is quintessential Rossetti, an ambiguous icon constructed from a play on the phrase "looking in." Henceforth the lady will be haunting her absent lover, in the same way that Rossetti is haunted by the old song. (That connection between lady and old song, in fact, makes the absent lover an obvious figura of Rossetti and the contemporary poet.) Henceforth an "external" presence who will be looking into his eyes as he observes the external world, she becomes as well an internal ghost who, though dead, is destined to live on in the way he looks at his world.

This haunted and self-conscious figure is at the heart of all Rossetti's poems and paintings. We rightly see a poem like "The Blessed Damozel" as typical work for just that reason. Of all the verse printed in the first section of *Poems* (1870), "The Stream's Secret" is closest to *The House of Life*. But "The Blessed Damozel" is more relevant for understanding the sonnet sequence because its antiqued character highlights how the "*inner* standing-point" works in those sonnets. Rossetti disjoins himself from the first-person speaker in "The Blessed Damozel" by invoking the formalities of the ballad convention; but because he does not historicize his materials as clearly and resolutely as he does, for example, in "Stratton Water" or his other old tales, the scenes in the poem appear to float in a kind of abstraction, outside space and time. That ambiguous condition, where one feels unmoored and alienated even as one seems to live a determinate and eventual existence, defines what we know as *The House of Life*.

IV

The House of Life is more than a mere presentation, or case history, of personality dismemberment. It is that, of course, but it is also part of a project—an execution—of such dismemberment, an active agent in the destructive project it is unfolding. This complicity is what makes the work, and the whole volume which it epitomizes, so fearful and so magnificent. The sonnets record a history by which "changes" associated with a period of "Youth"—these are figured principally as the changing experiences of love—are finally transfixed in (and as) the immobilized forms of "Fate." The history unfolds through a set of losses and disintegrations which culminate as the loss of identity.[16]

At the outset of the sequence, the notorious "Nuptial Sleep" appears far removed from the terrible images which emerge in the concluding six sonnets:

> At length their long kiss severed with sweet smart:
>   And as the last slow sudden drops are shed
>   From sparkling eaves when all the storm has fled,

So singly flagged the pulses of each heart.
Their bosoms sundered, with the opening start
    Of married flowers to either side outspread
    From the knit stem; yet still their mouths, burnt red,
Fawned on each other where they lay apart.

Sleep sank them lower than the tide of dreams
    And their dreams watched them sink, and slid away.
Slowly their souls swam up again, through gleams
    Of watered light and dull drowned waifs of day;
Till from some wonder of new woods and streams
    He woke, and wondered more: for there she lay.

$$(6a/5)^{17}$$

Here is the supreme imagination of triumph in the work. One might not appreciate this fact because the previous sonnet, "The Kiss," represents an actual experience of erotic consummation. It is, moreover, an experience recorded for us in the first person:

I was a child beneath her touch,—a man
    When breast to breast we clung, even I and she,—
    A spirit when her spirit looked through me,—
A god when all our life-breath met to fan
Our life-blood, till love's emulous ardours ran,
    Fire within fire, desire in deity.

(6/4, ll. 9–14)

After those lines, the movement to the third person in "Nuptial Sleep," a modulation from major to minor, comes as a shock, since it conveys the impression of incredible detachment on the part of the speaker, whom we associate with the lover. That shock is the rhetorical equivalent of the "wonder" recorded at the end of the sonnet, where—following an experience of ecstatic physical union—the beloved appears to the eyes of the lover as a unique identity, wholly individuated despite the previous moments of mutual absorption. The lover's (actual) "wonder" is thus reduplicated, or realized, in the rhetoric of the speaker, who is spellbound before his imagination of the separate lovers. "Nuptial Sleep" argues, in other words, that the heart of the "poignant thirst / And exquisite hunger" ("Bridal Birth," 2/1) of this work is an ecstasy which culminates not in the extinction but in the establishment of individual identities through love. This argument is clinched by the tense shift executed between the sonnets, which transfers to identity and self-consciousness the values associated, both traditionally and in the previous sonnet(s), with intense feeling: immediateness, and spontaneity.

But the achievement in the sonnet is tenuous and fragile, and finally self-conflicted. Lover observes beloved much as the young man in "Jenny" observes, lovingly, the sleeping prostitute; and the perspective is here explicitly revealed as the perspective of art and poetry. This "wonder" matches passivities to passivities, and thus contradicts the developing energetic impulses of the poem itself. Furthermore, although the watery medium of sleep and dreams does not here directly threaten the ideal of self-identity in the sonnet, those forms prefigure the conditions of loss later realized in "Willowwood."

As in "Hand and Soul," then, the apparitions here are images of the artist's "soul," or that to which he is ultimately committed. That is to say, the sonnet raises up an imagining of self-identity achieved through artistic practice. As *The House of Life* gradually delineates the features of that soul, however, a hollowed-out figure emerges from the expectant shadows of Beauty. For the story told by the sequence is that the images are insubstantial: literally, that the supreme moment of "Nuptial Sleep" was a supreme fiction only. In this respect *The House of Life* is the story of betrayed hopes; and if that were all it had to tell us, it would scarcely deserve to hold more than our minimal interest. As we shall see, however, what Rossetti's work ultimately reveals are not its betrayals but its self-betrayals.

The instabilities we glimpse in "Nuptial Sleep" initiate the sequence of illusions that forms the ground of the conclusive nightmares of the work. These will culminate in the terror of "He and I" (98/47), the definitive representation of identity-loss in the sequence. The sonnet operates through the simple contradiction of first-and third-person pronouns, both of which are "identified with" the poet. They are the residua of the first-and-third-person narrators whose careers in *The House of Life* we initially traced in "The Kiss" and "Nuptial Sleep." Here they emerge as the obverse and reverse of a single self-conflicted figure, the schizoid form of a disintegrated identity which has lost itself in a house of mirrors.[18]

Pronouns, those ultimate shifters, figure largely in Rossetti's sonnet sequence. The inconographical status of "He and I," however, contrasts with the more fluid pronominal ambiguities which play themselves out in most of the earlier sonnets. This happens because Rossetti depicts first the process and then the achievement, first "Change" and then "Fate." "He and I" is the "Fate" that awaits Rossettian "Change," an entropic nightmare immortalized in one dead deathless sonnet.

"Life-in-Love" is very different, a not untypical instance of Rossettian deconstruction observed in a "changing" phase.

> Not in thy body is thy life at all,
>> But in this lady's lips and hands and eyes;
>> Through these she yields thee life that vivifies
> What else were sorrow's servant and death's thrall.
> Look on thyself without her, and recall

> The waste remembrance and forlorn surmise
> That lived but in a dead-drawn breath of sighs
> O'er vanished hours and hours eventual.
>
> Even so much life hath the poor tress of hair
>   Which, stored apart, is all love hath to show
>   For heart-beats and for fire-heats long ago;
> Even so much life endures unknown, even where,
>   'Mid change the changeless night environeth,
>   Lies all that golden hair undimmed in death.
>
> (36/16)

The second person pronoun here slides from ambiguity to ambiguity. Isolated thus, in solitary quotation, we register the simple alternative that it may be taken to refer either to "the poet" (a.k.a. D. G. Rossetti) or to the "old love" (a.k.a. Elizabeth Siddal Rossetti), with "this lady" standing as the "new love" (a.k.a. Jane Morris).[19] The "meaning" in each case is that both "poet" and "old love" are resurrected in the experience of "new love," which revivifies and redeems what would otherwise be encorpsed forever.

Were we to restore the sonnet to its larger (1881) context in the sequence, we would observe a further fall into ambiguity; for it is impossible to read "Life-in-Love" after the preceding sonnet, "The Lamp's Shrine," and not respond to the inertia of the latter's second person pronouns, which all refer to the allegorical figure "Lord Love." Finally, because Rossetti rhymes this sonnet with the soon to follow "Death-in-Love," yet another nominal presence comes to fill the shifting pronoun, and even names itself: "I am Death."

In this case, the fact that "The Lamp's Shrine" was only added to *The House of Life* in 1881 reduces by one the number of substantive options in the 1870 sequence, but its addition also calls attention to the unstable and shifting form of the work as a whole. In Rossetti's lifetime *The House of Life* appeared in no less than four relatively coherent forms: as a sequence of 16 sonnets; as a sequence of 50 sonnets and 11 songs; as a sequence of 25 sonnets and 5 songs; and as a sequence of 101 sonnets. Rossetti treated that last as the finished sequence even though it lacked the crucial sonnet "Nuptial Sleep."[20] Today, as for many years, most readers enter the work through the 102 sonnet version, where "Nuptial Sleep," sequenced with the appropriately unstable number 6a/5, is restored.

And indeed this ambiguous presence of "Nuptial Sleep" in *The House of Life* is singularly appropriate, for only in that sonnet is the ultimate ideal of the work, self-identify through love, defined. That Rossetti repeatedly unsettled the forms of the sequence emphasizes the overall lack of resolution of the work, but that he should have removed "Nuptial Sleep" from his last imagination of the work is a truly remarkable revelation of his loss of faith in the identity he set out to fashion and represent. Needless to say, this surrender of faith, this betrayal, is the ambiguous sign under which the work will triumph.

V

Poems (1870) is the first chapter in Rossetti's history of ultimate dissolution/ disillusion. But the book is more than the record of a personal and psychic catastrophe, it is the portrait of an age. We glimpse this most clearly, if also most simply, when we recall that the book is full of various social and political poems with distinct, if obliquely presented, points of contemporary reference. "The Burden of Nineveh," an unusually direct work, involves an ironic meditation on England's imperial imagination. This fact is glossed in the multiple pun of the title. At the proof stage Rossetti set an explanatory headnote under that title to emphasize his word play: "BURDEN. Heavy calamity; the chorus of a song.—*Dictionary.*"[21] Rossetti directs us to read the poem as a "burden" in the Old Testament prophetic sense, with a relevance for England emphasized by the storied names (Thebes, Rome, Babylon, Greece, Egypt) called in the roll of the poem. Finally, that Nineveh is also "a burden to" England, an example of the self-destructive imperialism under which she currently labors, is made all but explicit at the conclusion of the poem. It is particularly apt, in Rossetti's book, that the focus in the poem on decadence should be the British Museum, the repository of the nation's cultural treasures. Rossetti's poem reflects the excitement of cultural imperialism with a special force because the British Museum, at that time, was relatively small, so that recent acquisitions of Near Eastern treasure were peculiarly visible and celebrated occurrences. "The Burden of Nineveh" draws out the implications of what Byron, sixty years earlier, had already sketched in *The Curse of Minerva*.

But this is a unique poem in a book which generally proceeds by careful, not to stay stealthy, indirection. "Troy Town" generates an entire network of references to that fabled history of a civilization which, according to the myth, found destruction through indulgence and illicit love. This Troy theme plays a key role in linking *The House of Life* poems to the less personal material, as Rossetti must have realized: through all the proof stages "Troy Town" was the opening poem. In that position it would have emphasized more strongly the social dimensions of the book. But at the last minute Rossetti replaced it with "The Blessed Damozel."

Changes of that and other kinds are the hallmark of Rossetti's discontented book. This is why, from a social point of view, the steps that Rossetti takes to marginalize his "social themes" are in the end more important, more significant, than the themes themselves. They remind us that works like "Troy Town" are in themselves even more obliquely mediated, as pieces of social commentary, than *The Idylls of the King*. What we should attend to, here and throughout *Poems* (1870), are not any of the "ideas" but what the book is doing and being made to do, how carefully its materials are managed, packaged, and polished. Unlike Swinburne in his deliberately outrageous *Poems and Ballads*, Rossetti does everything in his power to make sure his book will behave.

This manic sense of decorum makes the book not more "crafted" but more "crafty." It is a monument to its own shame, a kind of whited sepulchre. We can see how this comes about if we trace the structure of change in Rossetti's book. We begin by reflecting once again on those disintegrative mechanisms we observed earlier. One notes for instance that they are heavily "languaged," so to speak, and that the extreme level of the verbal artifice is a mode that holds off, brackets out, "reality." All is arranged so that what occurs seems to occur at the level of the signs alone, as a play of signifiers and signifieds. No names are given, no definite events are alluded to, no places, no times, no "referential" concretions of any kind—other than the (1870) book in which *The House of Life* is printed. Many of the works in that book have points of reference, as we have seen, but not *The House of Life* poems, which occupy the abstract space first clearly delineated in "The Blessed Damozel." Yet, paradoxically, these sonnets and songs constitute the most "personal" work in the entire volume.

The book itself, in other words, provides the key referential point which alone really clarifies what is happening in *The House of Life*. Critics have often observed the claustrophobia and abstraction of the sonnets, but if we consider the sequence wholly in itself, we would have to see it simply as an event in language. By printing and publishing the work when and how he did, Rossetti provided the local habitation which could give social and ethical names—rather than merely technical ones—to the sonnets.

In simplest terms—they are critical for Rossetti—the act of printing and publishing establishes the "trade associations" of his work. These associations are, however, what he wants to avoid or cancel out, in order to "prove" that art occupies a transcendental order. Rossetti wants to establish what the Romantics called "the truth of imagination," but *Poems* (1870) ends by showing instead how that "truth" is rather "an imagination" of imagination—and an imagining which, when carried out in the world, can have disastrous consequences. The most prominent sign of disaster in the book is psychic disintegration, but the social significances of that sign are never far to seek. Perhaps the greatest "moral" of Rossetti's book, for instance, could be expressed as follows: that active moves to escape "trade associations"—to evade or avoid them rather than to oppose, in concrete and positive ways, the compromised "world" they represent—inevitably involve a complicity with that world. It was a truth Rossetti glimpsed early in "St. Agnes," but in *Poems* (1870) it is fully exposed. Indeed, it is executed. In the horrors of this book Rossetti carried out the (concealed) truth of imagination for his age: that it has a truth, that it serves the world even in fleeing the world, that the truth is both a dream and a nightmare, and that it destroys the individual.

The marvel of Rossetti's work is that he chose to follow his own *"inner standing-point"* in declaring those contradictory truths, that he submitted to their "execution." We therefore trace the choices made by his work even in what must seem (for Rossetti) the least likely of places, the early reviews. One observes initially that they mirror the contradictions exposed in Rossetti's book. Whether written by friends or enemies, accomplices or neutral observers, two lines of understanding are repeated. *Poems* (1870) is a celebration of art, on one hand, or of love on the other; and to the degree that a mediation of the two is carried out, the book is said to be devoted to Beauty. But the mediating concept of Beauty merely resituates the contradictory registrations elsewhere. Thus, we can alternately see the book as a manifesto of "fleshliness" and eroticism, or of "mysticism" and spirituality. The contradictions are multiplied: what many find labored and obscure others see as crafted and sharply defined; and so the descriptive terms proliferate: abstract, ornate, pictorial, self-conscious, impersonal, and so forth.

These varied responses are the integrals of Rossetti's differential achievements. So much finish at the surface, so much apparent control—in a work that is also, plainly, nervous and highly unstable. Rossetti's perpetual acts of revision at every level, in the months immediately preceding publication, are but a dramatic instance of the consummate lack of resolution in the book. The book shifts and changes as it seeks its ideal of articulation, that monochord of which audience approval is the tonic, reciprocity the dominant. It is a mad, an inhuman ideal—what Marx ironically called "the soul of the commodity": a form crafted so as to be universally irresistible. It is the nineteenth-century's revenant of Dante's summum bonum, the encorpsed form of what was once alive.

Rossetti was more deeply complicit with his immediate institutions of reception than appears even from his attempt to manage the reviews. This became most obvious when the voices of negation began to be heard, the critical notices which culminate in Buchanan's famous review. Its date of publication—well over a year after the initial appearance of *Poems* (1870)—is quite important, because it tells us how far Rossetti identified himself with Buchanan. "The Stealthy School of Criticism" shouts back at the champion of late Victorian moral and poetic order, but it does not challenge that order, or argue that Rossetti's book challenged it. Furthermore, the poem particularly singled out by Buchanan for denunciation, "Nuptial Sleep," which was also the key sonnet of *The House of Life*, was removed from the sequence by Rossetti when he published his new and (otherwise augmented) version of the work in 1881. Like the young painter in "St. Agnes," Rossetti despised and sneered at the "poet-critic" who attacked his work, but Rossetti too, in the end, deferred.

It is an illuminating act of bad faith and betrayal, reminding us of the fear and trembling in which Rossetti worked out his damnation. We might wish that he would have done otherwise, that he would have braved it and defied his critics. But in fact he took the better part, for the shame of that betrayal is an eloquent sign of the ambiguous situation Rossetti's book has exposed. Buchanan is what Shelley would have called "The Phantasm of Rossetti" in a play where Prometheus does not appear as a character. What is Promethean in *Poems* (1870) is not "Rossetti" but what Rossetti has done. Assuming the inner standing point throughout, the book dramatizes Rossetti's enslavement to the commercial culture he despises. That culture thereby grows again in Rossetti's book, like some terrible virus in a laboratory dish. *Poems* (1870) is a coin "whose face reveals / The soul—its converse, to what Power 'tis due."

Rossetti's work set out to prove the Victorian theory of cultural touchstones which Arnold was developing elsewhere in his ideological prose: to prove that Ideal Beauty was transcendent. His achievement was to have shown that the theory was a confidence trick which Victorian society played on itself. Thus, the clear path to fulfillment sketched in "Hand and Soul" becomes, in the empirical testing of that prediction which Rossetti's work carried out, a field of endless wandering—in Rossetti's recurrent figuration, a maze.[22] Similarly, the Beatricean vision which was to mediate the quest for perfection continually shifted out of focus, or turned into nightmare forms.

The characteristic experience here is to be found in various pictures which Rossetti, obsessively overpainting, turned into palimpsests and cryptic surfaces. Somewhere beneath the face of Alexa Wilding hovered the unseen head of Fanny Cornforth, or Elizabeth Siddal would float about the canvas occupied by the face of Jane Morris. Rossetti fled his haunted and haunting canvasses and sought relief in poetry, which for a brief time seemed open to pure forms, transparent expressions. But the hope turned to illusion as his poetry delivered up its secret and invisible texts to the fire of his art. In the 1870s, as he plunged deeper into that abyss of Beauty, neither poetry nor painting offered any sustaining fantasies of escape.

"An untruth was never yet the husk of a truth," Rossetti argues at the conclusion to "The Stealthy School of Criticism" (1.488) as he makes a final dismissal of the various deceits of Robert Buchanan. Perhaps that relation of truth to untruth never held before, but the observation—the metaphor—is wonderfully apt for Rossetti's work, which tells the truth of false appearances, the truth that is in the husks of beauty and truth. Rossetti's poetry crucifies itself on its own infernal machineries. These always want to appear otherwise, as benevolences, but for the sake of truth Rossetti chose an unusual and lonely path: to will a suspension of disbelief in those inherited lies of art. Thence the nightmares of paradise appear in his work in their many forms, the most critical being called, commonly, Love and Art. They are dangerous and deceitful names, like the realities they denote, and in Rossetti's work none—neither names nor realities—are ever just what they seem.

This is an art difficult to practice, the index of a world not easy to survive. Rossetti allegorized both in a dramatic figure which became familiar to us only much later. It appears in another of Rossetti's notebooks, an entry of uncertain date, though it was clearly written a few years later than the passage I quoted at the outset. This time Rossetti copies a passage from Petronius and then translates it to his own verse.

> I saw the Sibyl at Cumae
> (One said) with my own eye
> She hung in a cage to read her runes
> To all the passers-by
> Said the boys "What wouldst thou Sibyl?"
> She answered "I would die"![23]

That scene of cultural desperation Eliot later made famous as the epigraph to a poem about another wasted world. To find it written almost fifty years before in a Rossetti notebook will surprise us only if we read as twentieth-century literary historians, that is to say, if we continue to misunderstand what Rossetti's poetry is actually about.

Notes

1. This is from one of the notebooks in the British Library (Ashley 1410; Notebook I, 4r), much of whose material remains unpublished, though W. M. Rossetti reproduced large portions of it in his 1911 edition of the works of his brother; see below n.2.

2. My texts for Rossetti's work will be taken from *The Collected Works of Dante Gabriel Rossetti* (London, 1886), 2 vols. For texts not available in this edition I have used *The Works of Dante Gabriel Rossetti* (London, 1911). Both collected editions were edited by W. M. Rossetti. Where necessary, page numbers are given in the text.

3. According to W. M. Rossetti (*Works* 1:525–526).

4. See David Riede, *Dante Gabriel Rossetti and the Limits of Victorian Vision* (Ithaca, 1983) for an excellent handling of the parallel forms of Rossetti's imaginative work.

5. Rodolphe L. Megroz, *Dante Gabriel Rossetti, Painter Poet of Heaven and Earth* (London, 1928), p. 185.

6. References to Rossetti's letters are from *Letters of Dante Gabriel Rossetti*, ed. Oswald Doughty and John Robert Wahl, 4 vols. (Oxford, 1965), cited in the text as *L* followed by volume and page number.

7. The poem is printed in *L* 1:164.

8. These are the titles of Chapters I and II in Book III in Doughty's biography *Dante Gabriel Rossetti: A Victorian Romantic* (London, 1949).

9. The best account of the Trial Books and the publication history of the 1870 volume is Janet Camp Troxell's "The 'Trial Books' of Dante Gabriel Rossetti," reprinted from *The Colophon*, New Series III, no. 2 (1938) in *The Princeton University Library Chronicle* 33 (1972):

177–192; but see also Robert N. Keane, "D. G. Rossetti's *Poems*, 1870: A Study in Craftsmanship," *Princeton University Library Chronicle* 33:193–209.

10. See Doughty, *Dante Gabriel Rossetti*, pp. 439–453 for a good account of Rossetti's campaign to control the reviews.

11. See Walter Benjamin, *Charles Baudelaire: A Lyric Poet in the Era of High Capitalism*, trans. Harry Zohn (London, 1973).

12. In a sense, of course, Rossetti's work does make an advance from the relative unselfconscious and even innocent work of the early years. What I mean to indicate here is the inadequacy of the commonplace idea that Rossetti's poetry, as it develops, gains some kind of wisdom or imitable moral depth. Indeed, it seems to me that the climax of his career was "penultimate" in the sense that, after completing the work for the 1870 volume and the associated *House of Life* poetry, Rossetti's poetry experienced a sharp falling-off, a collapse that parallels the curve of his last years.

13. Benjamin, p. 104n. The quotation immediately following is from p. 103.

14. See *Biographia Literaria*, ed. James Engell and W. J. Bate (Princeton, 1983) 2:6.

15. Rossetti's paintings—and Burne-Jones's, for that matter—are similarly charged.

16. Joan Rees has an excellent general comment on Rossetti's significance as a poet: "A slight shift of position, and what has been taken as an emblem of salvation becomes a mark of damnation. This is the central moral insight of Rossetti's work" (Joan Rees, *The Poetry of Dante Gabriel Rossetti: Modes of Self-Expression* [Cambridge, 1981], p. 101).

17. In identifying the sonnets I always give two numbers: the second being the number in the 1870 volume, the first the number in 1881. The one exception is for this sonnet, the so-called 6a (a number which indicates that Rossetti removed it from the sequence printed in 1881, though later editors, perceiving its centrality, have always restored it).

18. See Henry Treffry Dunn, *Recollections of Dante Gabriel Rossetti and His Circle, or Cheyne Walk Life*, ed. Rosalie Mander (Westerham, 1984), p. 14: "Mirrors and looking-glasses of all shapes, sizes and design lined the walls. Whichever way I looked I saw myself gazing at myself."

19. I refer here to the traditional "biographical" level of exegesis, which plots the poem as a story of Rossetti's relations with Elizabeth Siddal (the Old Love) and Jane Morris (the New Love). The fullest treatment of this subject is in Doughty, but the best discussion of the subject in terms of the formal structure of the sonnet sequence is William E. Fredeman's "Rossetti's 'In Memoriam': An Elegiac Reading of *The House of Life*," *Bulletin of the John Rylands Library* 47 (1965): 298–341.

20. The twenty-five sonnet, five-song version is the MS Rossetti made of the poems he wrote in 1870–71. He made a gift of it to Jane Morris, the person who had inspired most of the work. The MS (Bodleian Library) was printed (most of it) in *The Kelmscott Love Sonnets of Dante Gabriel Rossetti*, ed. John Robert Wahl (Capetown, 1954).

21. The following discussion depends heavily upon a study of the MS and proof material in the Ashley Library (British Museum) and the Fitzwilliam Museum.

22. The central "maze" poem by Rossetti is "Troy Town," whose title means (at one level) a labyrinth (see OED).

23. W. M. Rossetti printed these lines in 1911; his text differs slightly from the Notebook's (II. 12v).

Dante Rossetti: Parody and Ideology

ANTONY H. HARRISON

In a recent essay, Claus Uhlig comes to the problematic conclusion that many literary works, because of their deliberate intertextuality, concern themselves preeminently with their own histories or genealogies. "It is doubtlessly true, and all the more so since the Romantic era," he insists, "that the aging of poetic forms and genres constantly increases their self-consciousness as knowledge of their own historicity. Through this progressive self-reflection, whose sphere is intertextuality, literature is in the end transformed into metaliterature, mere references to its own history."[1] For Uhlig views of history and of the self in relation to history—especially our creations or works in relation to past works—are deeply ideological.[2] As has often been observed, it was during the nineteenth century that "the modern discipline of history first came fully into its own as a truly rigorous inquiry into the past."[3] Ultimately, however, because of "the very success of scientific history at reconstituting the past," the powerful awareness of the past itself became "burdensome and intimidating . . . revealing—in Tennyson's metaphor—all the models that could not be remodeled." In fact, the apocalyptic aims of the Romantic poets early in the century begin to reflect "the idea that history, simply by existing, exhausts possibilities, leaving its readers with a despairing sense of their own belatedness and impotence. And this despair in turn leads to anxious quests for novelty, to a hectic avant-gardism, and in the end to an inescapable fin de siècle ennui."[4]

As self-appointed heirs of the Romantics, the Pre-Raphaelite poets—Dante Rossetti foremost among them—display in their works an extraordinary degree of historical self-consciousness, as would seem appropriate to their concept of themselves as a transitional, literary avant-garde.[5] Once observed, the powerful effects of Rossetti's own historical self-consciousness upon his poetry compel us to look at his work in new ways. Many of his poems are deliberate intertexts, works that manipulate palimpsests parodically in order both to resist the social actuality which obsessed his contemporaries and to open up new tracks for future writers. This is a fundamentally Romantic, specifically Wordsworthian project.[6] There is a crucial difference,

Reprinted from Antony H. Harrison, *Victorian Poets and Romantic Poems: Intertextuality and Ideology* (Charlottesville: University Press of Virginia, 1990), 90–107. Reprinted by permission of the University Press of Virginia.

191

however, between Rossetti's project and that of Wordsworth—or Blake, Shelley, and Keats, for that matter. Whereas these historically hyperconscious Romantics were visibly dedicated to supplanting the ideologies of their literary precursors with their own literary and political ideologies, Rossetti attempts uniquely to employ the intertextual dimensions of his work to create the illusion of altogether eliding and superseding ideology, as it is commonly conceived. Moving beyond even Uhlig's formulation of the metaliterary implications of intertextuality, Rossetti appears virtually to embrace intertextuality *as* a coherent and self-sufficient ideology. The intertextual dimensions of his poetry enable him seemingly to marginalize "those modes of feeling, valuing, perceiving and believing which have some kind of relation to the maintenance and reproduction of social power,"[7] by refocusing all such modes of experience on the structure, history, and intrinsic qualities of literary textuality itself, propounding as a supreme value the creation and deciphering of texts that are highly ornamental, artistically complex, and layered. Since no text is autonomous, all texts being derivative (as are all creators of texts), this dialectical activity becomes for Rossetti the preeminent mode of self-definition, intellectual inquiry, social understanding, and spiritual self-generation.

In a brief preface to his translations of the early Italian poets (1861), Rossetti laments the deteriorating form in which thirteenth-century Italian poems have become available to nineteenth-century readers because of "clumsy transcription and pedantic superstructure." He insists that, "At this stage the task of talking much more about them in any language is hardly to be entered upon; and a translation . . . remains perhaps the most direct form of commentary."[8] Here Rossetti quite properly implies that a translation *is* an interpretation, but one which most closely echoes or contains an originary text. These remarks may, in fact, be seen as Rossetti's first comments in print to broach matters of literary appropriation, transvaluation, and intertextuality. That his first published volume consists entirely of translations suggests a useful starting place for any study of Rossetti's own poetic works, whose sources in the poetry of Dante, Petrarch, Milton, Poe, Keats, Shelley, and even the Gothic novelists have been thoroughly discussed by critics, but without helping us to grapple in genuinely productive ways with the unique difficulties presented by Rossetti's verse.

The more often we read certain poems by Rossetti, the more puzzling, uncertain, and ambiguous their tone, their purpose, and of course, therefore, their meaning seems to become. Such is the case with works that we sense are to some extent derivative, referring to earlier texts formally, imagistically, or ideologically. Some of Rossetti's most important poems, these works are often pervasively self-reflexive, and their original versions date from the late 1840s and early 1850s when, as David Riede has made clear, Rossetti was still intensively searching for "an idea of the world." During this period, "gradually, Rossetti was beginning to distill a personal style and voice from the multitudinous mass of literary and artistic precedents and from his own mixed ethnic heritage, but despite his uneasy balancing of traditions, he remained uncertain about his artistic direction and purpose. For this reason, in both his writing and his painting, his best works of the late 1840s and early 1850s are all attempts to explore or expound the relation of the artist to his art, to nature, to society."[9] A short list of these works would include the "Old and New Art" sonnets, "The Portrait," "Ave," "The Staff and the Scrip," "Sister Helen," "The Bride's Prelude," numerous other sonnets from *The House of Life*, "Jenny," "The Burden of Nineveh," and "The Blessed Damozel." In these poems, as in the bulk of Rossetti's paintings, stylistic mannerisms, tonal ambiguities, and echoes of form and conventions from certain of his literary precursors—Keats, Browning, Milton, and Dante especially—so obtrude that the intertextual effects upon the reader are disorienting and for some readers distracting. That is to say that the poem's ostensible subject matter and purpose seem to be subsumed and overpowered by such an extreme degree of artistic self-consciousness that the poetic project itself is surrounded by uncertainty.

We finish the last stanza of *The Portrait*, for instance, trying to unravel a constellation of interactive images and elaborate conceits that invite symbolic or even allegorical interpretation and that vaguely echo Poe, Browning, and Petrarchan tradition. By the poem's conclusion the speaker has fully demonstrated the depth of his passion for his dead beloved. He has done so while contemplating the portrait he had painted of her when alive and remembering the circumstances that led to its creation:

> Here with her face doth memory sit
> Meanwhile, and wait the day's decline,
> Till other eyes shall look from it,
>   Eyes of the spirit's Palestine,
> Even than the old gaze tenderer:
> While hopes and aims long lost with her
>   Stand round her image side by side
>   Like tombs of pilgrims that have died
> About the Holy Sepulchre.[10]

Once we have deciphered this stanza and the poem that it concludes, attention has shifted altogether from the ostensible subject of the poem (the prospect of salvation through the haunting memories of a dead beloved)—to the hermeneutic project itself. The problems of reading, interpreting, making sense of the elaborate ornamental surfaces of the poem have thrust themselves so far forward and required such "fundamental brainwork" of us, that we become finally more interested in surfaces, in techniques and their employment, than in the subject matter being presented. Issues of aesthetics—

symbolism, form, style, tone, etc.—fully displace and supersede matters of substance—theme or philosophy or ideology. Rather than a "willing suspension of disbelief," Rossetti seems bent at every turn on enforcing disbelief and distraction upon the reader in ways that remind us of the new generation of radically self-conscious parodic novelists—Fowles, Barth, Borges, or Eco, for instance.

One simple explanation of the purpose and effect of Rossetti's deliberate destabilization and subversion of his own texts might fall properly into line with Jerome McGann's insistence (some twenty years ago) that Rossetti's procedures serve to reinforce his central aestheticism: literature's last gift, like love's, is merely literature itself.[11] Art and artistry must, therefore, like a beautiful woman, draw attention to themselves—their elaborate, complex, ornamental surfaces—in order to enthrall or seduce us. This explanation, however, does not finally do justice to the complex of responses that Rossetti's best poems evoke. The frequent reader of these texts finds them not only ornate and beautiful but also rich and deep in their allusiveness to other texts and to the entire literary enterprise. He finds them simultaneously sincere and parodic; derivative yet original; fraught with ineffable philosophic weight yet somehow hollow; ambiguous; ironic—and finally, elusive.

A general approach to Rossetti's poems that proves more adequate in explaining their complex operations than those of the past—biographical, new critical, or aestheticist—derives from recent expansions of our modes of critical thinking that have emerged from the concern among semioticians, deconstructionists, and new historical critics with all matters related to intertextuality and self-reflexiveness in literature. Rossetti's best known poem, "The Blessed Damozel," serves as an illuminating exemplary text.

As all readers of this inverted elegy know, it dramatizes the craving for reunion felt by two lovers separated by death. The central dialogue is between the full-bosomed Damozel—lamenting her separation while leaning earthward from the gold bar of heaven—and her distant beloved who thinks about her from below. The poem's pathos derives, for some readers, from the fact that for the Damozel the distance between the two is finally insuperable; however, her lover, whose voice and perspective gradually merge with that of the narrator, ironically claims to hear her voice, her words, her tears, but their communication is one-sided, and the Damozel remains a victim of Heaven's exquisite torture of separation, as her languorous suffering is exacerbated by witnessing the pairs of joyous lovers reuniting around her. As all readers of the poem also know, the lovers' dialogue is embedded in an elaborate setting and is at various levels fantastical: the narrator's cosmic vision seems so portentous, and at once detailed yet ambiguous, as to be fantastic; each lover fantasizes about the present circumstances of the other; and the Damozel fantasizes about the pair's future together after reunion in heaven.[12]

The reader of this poem is likely to scrutinize it with special attention, because a number of its features strike us as curious—hyperconscious, oddly derivative, even self-mocking. The more we contemplate the poem's possible purpose and meaning, the more unsettling and disorienting we find the work. As almost every commentator on the poem has noted, we are puzzled, for instance, from the very first stanzas by the unorthodox combination of the spiritual and the sensual or erotic. The former elements include an array of traditional religious symbols and an insistence upon medieval numerology, while the latter elements are introduced into the poem with images of the Damozel's gown "ungirt from clasp to hem," her hair "yellow like ripe corn," and her "bosom" pressing against the bar of heaven (*Poetical Works*, p. 1). Further, the attempt at cosmological mapping early in the poem is accomplished in such deliberately vague terms that it seems disorienting rather than helpful. That the "rampart of God's house" looks downward over absolute Space toward the solar system is clear enough from stanza 5. That Rossetti insistently refines upon this scheme in stanza 6, using redefinitions even more abstract than their originals (Space becomes a "flood of ether"), along with mixed metaphors, seems altogether to undercut the project of mapping the cosmos, however. We are no wiser afterwards than we were before. The language of stanza 7 is so trite and hyperbolic—invoking such phrases as "deathless love" and "heart-remembered names"—that it verges on the ironic, especially as the associations of spirituality that such terminology elicits are abruptly truncated in the next stanza's notorious description of the Damozel's palpably "warm" bosom. Such startling pseudoeroticism, seemingly determined to explode all former theological concepts of heaven, culminates in mid poem when the Damozel describes the rebaptism of their love at the anticipated moment of reunion: "As unto a stream we will step down, / And bathe there in God's sight."

Unsettling descriptions and events punctuate the last third of the poem as well. How are we to respond to the moment at which the earth-bound lover, for the first time with certainty, perceives the sound of the Damozel's voice in a continuation of what is presumably "that bird's song" of stanza II: "We two, we two, thou says't?" he says. Somehow the source of this light chirrup seems incommensurate with the lover's insistence (in an allusion to II Corinthians 6:14) upon the eternal union of his and the Damozel's souls. The presentation of the heavenly court in the next stanza also seems overly literal. Indeed, the depiction of Mary and her five handmaidens sitting round to pass judgment on the cases of lovers is deflated by the scene's evocation of the historical courts of love presided over by Eleanor of Acquitaine in late twelfth-century France. This association is reinforced by the image of an audience of angels playing citherns and citholes, as well as the poem's pervasive archaisms, including its title. The penultimate demystification of the poem's issues comes with the damozel's plea "Only to live as once on earth / With Love"—surely a radical literalization of Keats's antitraditional notion of enjoying "ourselves here after by having what we call happiness on Earth repeated in a finer tone."[13] And the poem's final perplexing move—drawing our attention away from its substance to the problem of narrative form—is the last stanza's perspectival sleight of hand, in which the identity of the omniscient narrator merges with that of the aggrieved lover. This formal trick for some readers makes the conclusion seem as equivocal or hollow or contrived as it is full of pathos.

How then does the reader deal with this curious poem whose tone seems to exist in some unexplored grey area—some void of linguistic ether—between sincerity on the one hand and parody, as it is traditionally understood, on the other? He may go so far as to conclude that "The Blessed Damozel" is, in some rare and complex fashion, a hoax; that it was written with tongue partially in cheek; or that it awkwardly presents itself as at once serious and mocking and thus a novel kind of parody for the mid-nineteenth century, a work that is self-reflexive and self-parodic while densely allusive—echoing, imitating, or parodying a number of originary or enabling texts and traditions. That is to say, it is pervasively, complexly intertextual and dialogic. Given the extent to which tonal ambiguities, dialogism, and intertextuality are striking features of other major poems by Rossetti as well as "The Blessed Damozel," it is worth investigating, in theoretical as well as practical terms, the full implications of the parodic horizons in Rossetti's verse.

Some especially useful theoretical discussion of parody has appeared in recent years in the writing of Barthes, Genette, Riffaterre, and Bakhtin. But these theorists have done work that serves, finally, to marginalize, bracket, or in other ways delimit and deflate parody both as a literary genre (or subgenre) and as a medium for self-conscious ideological discourse. Linda Hutcheon's recent book, *A Theory of Parody*, however, largely succeeds in rehabilitating parody by cogently redefining it as a specific mode of discourse and by enlarging our notions of what constitutes parody and what literary parody can accomplish.[14] In doing so, she forcefully demonstrates the interrelations between parody and some central issues that emerge in recent semiotic, formalist, and new historical approaches to literature and literary theory.

According to Hutcheon, in her own appropriation and reification of recent theorists, "a parodic text [is] defined as a formal synthesis, an incorporation of a backgrounded text into itself. But the textual doubling of parody (unlike pastiche, allusion, quotation, and so on) functions to mark difference. . . . on a pragmatic level parody [is] not limited to producing a ridiculous effect (*para* as 'counter' or 'against'), but . . . the equally strong suggestion of complicity and accord (*para* as 'beside') allow[s] for an opening up of the range of parody."[15] Thus, there exist "both comic and serious types of parody." Indeed, as Hutcheon points out, "even in the nineteenth century, when the ridiculing definition of parody was most current . . . reverence was often perceived as underlying the intention of parody."[16] Further, parody "is never a mode of parasitic symbiosis. On the formal level, it is always a paradoxical structure of contrasting synthesis, a kind of differential dependence of one text upon another." Parody, moreover, can involve a whole ethos or set of conventions rather than a single text: paradoxically, "parody's trangressions [or transvaluations of a text or a set of conventions] ultimately [are] authorized by the very norm it seeks to subvert. . . . In formal terms, it inscribes the mocked conventions onto itself thereby guaranteeing their continued existence." But, of course, "this paradox of legalized though unofficial subversion . . . posits, as a prerequisite to its very existence, a certain aesthetic institutionalization which entails the acknowledgment of recognizable, stable forms and conventions."[17] But the texts, conventions, traditions, or institutions encoded by an author in a parodic text require a sophisticated reader to recognize them and to decode the text, that is, to perceive the work at hand as parodic and dialogic, as transcontextual and transvaluative. Most works thus understood are also perceived finally as avant-garde. They engage in a form of what Barthes termed "double-directed" discourse, often "rework[ing] those discourses whose weight has become tyrannical." (For Rossetti, these would include the traditions of Dante and Milton.)

I would argue that these descriptions of parody powerfully illuminate the operations of many poems by Rossetti that clearly present themselves *as* avant-garde works. The dominant traditions with which they are in dialogue and which they attempt to transvalue are those of Petrarchism, Christianity, and Romanticism—especially in its exotic or supernatural and its medievalist guises.

In the case of "The Blessed Damozel" a unique equilibrium between preservation and subversion of originary texts, their conventions and values, is achieved. As I have already suggested, formally Rossetti's poem inverts the traditional conventions of the pastoral elegy; here it is primarily the dead beloved who grieves volubly for her lover who remains alive. The expected natural details of the genre's setting are also displaced: that is, they are either thoroughly etherealized or replaced with deliberately artificial props, such as the gold bar of heaven and its fountains of light. Symbolism full of potentially Christian meaning—such as the seven stars in the Damozel's hair and the three lilies in her hand—are drained of all such meaning and become merely ornamental.[18] Courtly and Petrarchan conventions, like the poem's pseudo-Dantean cosmology with its heavenly vistas, are thrust upon us with such literalness that they become at best disorienting and at worst absurd. The bizarre deployment of the supernatural here, too, displaces our usual conceptions of God, Heaven, angels, and the rituals conventionally associated with them. This heaven of lovers is a nontraditional fantasy, a bricolage of previous religious and literary conventions, images, values, and beliefs here appropriated and reformulated to authorize a new romantic ideology. This ideology is entirely aesthetic and insists that internalized sensory responses to experience alone constitute the spiritual. But such responses require a sense of loss or separation as a catalyst for their generation and thus seem to become wholly solipsistic and self-reflexive, as does the art which undertakes to represent them. In the world(s) of this poem, fantasy finally subsumes experience, and the most powerful fantasies emerge as much from previous art and literature as from experience itself. "The Blessed Damozel" read in this way must be seen finally as *seriously* parodic of its pretexts. The poem presents various dialogues—with medieval, Miltonic, Romantic, and Gothic precursors; with the traditional elegy; with the lovers who are themselves in dialogue. Finally, however, the poem appears to be in inconclusive dialogue with its own tentative values, images, and aspirations which emerge from its self-conscious reworkings of past artworks and their ideologies. Rather than asserting explicit positions on the amatory, religious, and philosophical questions it raises, the poem elides such questions in favor of emphasizing through its self-reflexivity the purely literary and aesthetic ones which emerge from its complexly dialogical operations.

Such inconclusiveness, equivocation, and ambiguity are common qualities of Rossetti's poems drafted early in his career, as might be seen from analysis of other important works. "The Burden of Nineveh," for instance, is an interior monologue triggered by archaeological events. The speaker contemplates their meaning upon leaving the British Museum, where he has just viewed the Elgin Marbles, "the prize / Dead Greece vouchsafes to living eyes." As he makes "the swing-door spin" and issues from the building, workers are "hoisting in / A winged beast from Nineveh." By the end of the poem the speaker's thoughts have led him to an epiphanic historical vision:

> . . . on my sight . . . burst
> That future of the best or worst
> When some may question which was first,
>   Of London or Nineveh.
>
> (p. 28)

In the course of the poem other questions of historicity and ideology are contemplated explicitly, alongside implicit questions about parody and self-referentiality as qualities that inevitably inhere in every religious artifact and, indeed, every work of art. Ultimately, according to this poem that invokes and argues against Ruskin, art is only an illusory index of the culture which produced it. Art defiantly rejects its originary historical contexts and transgresses—by transcending and eliding—the ideological values of the culture from which it emerges.

Paradoxically, this activity can take place only by means of parodic procedures, which precisely define the texts—as well as their historical positions and their ideologies—that Rossetti's poem presents itself as supplanting. This set of simultaneous moves within the poem draws attention to the phenomenology of the text itself as layered artifact. Just as the "meaning" of the Assyrian Bull-god (and every artwork) depends upon the contexts, the historical and ideological vantage points from which it is read or observed, so the sequence of parodic strategies within the poem draws attention to the phenomenology of *this* text as an accretive fabrication: its "meaning" can be construed only by deciphering the text as palimpsest. The speaker concludes that,

> . . . it may chance indeed that when
> Man's age is hoary among men,—
> His centuries threescore and ten,—
> His furthest childhood shall seem then
>   More clear than later times may be:
> Who, finding in this desert place
> This form, shall hold us for some race
> That walked not in Christ's lowly ways,
> But bowed its pride and vowed its praise
>   Unto the god of Nineveh.
>
> The smile rose first,—anon drew nigh
> The thought: . . . Those heavy wings spread high,
> So sure of flight, which do not fly;
> That set gaze never on the sky;
>   Those scriptured flanks it cannot see;
> Its crown, a brow-contracting load;
> Its planted feet which trust the sod: . . .
> (So grew the image as I trod:)
> O Nineveh, was this thy God,—
>   Thine also, mighty Nineveh?
>
>   (pp. 29–30)

Like the phenomenon of the Bull-god, Rossetti's poem reconstitutes hermeneutics as a branch of archaeology. But also like the Assyrian artifact, this poem, which subsumes all of its pre-texts, appears self-sufficient and elusive: "From their dead Past thou livs't alone; / And still thy shadow is thine own." The Bull-god as text provides a commentary not only upon its progenitors and successors along with their respective contexts but also upon itself as an accommodation of all possible historical and ideological contexts. It is a "dead disbowelled mystery" with "human face," with "hoofs behind and hoofs before," and "flanks with dark runes fretted o'er."

The parodied texts that Rossetti appropriates—the "fretted runes" Rossetti frets over—in his speaker's questions to the Bull-god include works by Shelley and Keats, who are echoed here, but also (and more generally) works by Ruskin and biblical books. By the time Rossetti began reshaping "The Burden of Nineveh" in 1856, Ruskin's absolutist and evangelical view that art is a clear embodiment of the historically specific spiritual and moral values of the culture which produced it had been fully elaborated in *The Stones of Venice*. Against that general position, Rossetti here argues a historically relativistic case. Similarly, references to the book of Jonah and Christ's temptations by Satan (p. 27) serve—especially in light of the poem's conclusion—as an ironic commentary on the myopic absolutism and the ahistoricism of Christian "orthodoxy." They also serve, however, to insist on the much greater longevity of Christian texts (its art) than the historically limited spiritual beliefs that inspired them. These texts, again in a general way, are parodied here in the mock-prophetic tone and substance of the last three stanzas.

Rossetti's appropriations of Shelley's "Ozymandias" and Keats's "Ode on a Grecian Urn" are more direct and specific. His procedure with respect to these texts is deliberately self-parodic, as well: the author in his relation to these pre-texts behaves as the English have behaved in appropriating and assimilating into their own gigantic cultural monument (the British Museum) the works of art from many great civilizations that preceded the British Empire:

> And now,—they and their gods and thou
> All relics here together,—now
> Whose profit? whether bull or cow,
> Isis or Ibis, who or how,
>   Whether of Thebes or Nineveh?
>
> (p. 26)

At the same time Rossetti's use of Shelley and Keats is parodic in the sense of working with and extending the conventions as well as the apparent insights of their poems.

Near the end of "The Burden of Nineveh" Rossetti invokes the central image of "Ozymandias": the half-buried monument to the pharaoh, around which "the lone and level sands stretch far away." Rossetti's speaker retrospectively envisions "the burial-clouds of sand" which, centuries past, "Rose o'er" the Bull-god's eyes "And blinded him with destiny" (p. 29). Rossetti is in a position, however, to update Shelley's historically limited view of the "collossal Wreck" that is Ozymandias's monument. This artifact, too, or portions of it, might well be plundered and given new life as a historical "fact / Connected with [a] zealous tract" in the British collection, as Rossetti gives new life to Shelley's poem and enriches its central irony.

In stanza 3 of "The Burden of Nineveh" Rossetti similarly parodies Keats's "Ode on a Grecian Urn," appropriating a Romantic text that also concerns itself with the transcontextualization of an artifact from an ancient civilization and the hermeneutical problems that result. Rossetti borrows Keats's strategy of asking questions of the artifact and answering them in a way that only proliferates questions. At the same time Rossetti heightens the historical self-consciousness of this project by introducing into his stanzas parodic echoes of Keats's "Ode to Psyche" as well. Rossetti's historical questions—

> What song did the brown maidens sing,
> From purple mouths alternating,
>   When that [rush-wrapping] was woven languidly?
> What vows, what rites, what prayers preferr'd,
> What songs has the strange image heard?
>
>   (p. 22)

—echo not only the concluding questions of stanza I in "Ode on a Grecian Urn," but also Keats's catalogue of rituals and service belatedly needed for the proper worship of Psyche, who has no temple,

> Nor altar heap'd with flowers;
> Nor virgin-choir to make delicious moan
>   Upon the midnight hours;
> No voice, no lute, no pipe, no incense sweet
>   From chain-swung censer teeming;
> No shrine, no grove, no oracle, no heat
> Of pale-mouth'd prophet dreaming.[19]

The questions both poets ask can be answered only with precise and extensive historical knowledge which both poets refuse to supply, insisting that the present artifact supersedes such concerns, as well as all cultural works and rituals that have enabled its production. This text annuls and supplants such absences (to which it paradoxically draws attention) by its exclusive presence.

With its parodies of the Bible, Shelley, and Keats, the "burden" of Rossetti's "Nineveh" thus becomes a weight of critical and self-critical meaning that elides traditional ideologies; it is also a refrain, as an inevitable and recontextualized reenactment of historically layered creative moments and *their* patterns of meaning. This poem tells us not only of the burdens of the past as they are appropriated by the present but of the fact that all parodies as artistic reenactments are burdensome: weighted with critical commentary on all historical eras, all relevant works of art, all ideologies of all writers and readers, including the present ones.

In such poems as "The Blessed Damozel" and "The Burden of Nineveh," begun early in his career, Rossetti was searching not only for an "idea of the world," as David Riede has argued, and a coherent system of aesthetic values; he was also searching with extreme caution for a secure idea of a discrete self, as well as an idea of the self in relation to others.[20] The latter part of this quest, in the early versions of his poems, focuses almost exclusively upon explorations of the amatory self and the artistic self, that is, the self in its highest or quintessential synchronic relations with society individualized in the form of a lover; and the self in its supreme, because creative, diachronic relations with the great creative selves of the past. While the quest for love reveals psychological compulsion, the quest for position displays a willed ambition to demonstrate unique talent.

In the 1848 sonnets included among the three "Old and New Art" poems of the *House of Life*, "Not as These" grapples with the young artist's yearning to distinguish himself from contemporaries and precursors alike. It insists in the end, however, that artistic greatness in the future can be achieved, not by looking to one's contemporaries, but by confronting the "great Past":

> Unto the lights of the great Past, new-lit
>   Fair for the Future's track, look thou instead,—
>   Say thou instead, "I am not as *these* are."
>   (p. 193)

The implication here is unmistakable: the track to the future is in every sense *over* that of the past. In order to *become* the future the prospective artist must reillumine the works of his great precursors; that is, he must appropriate, transvalue, and transcontextualize them. The same point is made, albeit abstractly, in the final sonnet of this subsequence, "The Husbandman." Here the possibility is raised of regenerating in oneself those whom God "Called . . . to labour in his vineyard first." For,

> Which of ye knoweth *he* is not that last
> Who may be first by faith and will?—yea, his
>   The hand which after the appointed days
>   And hours shall give a Future to their Past?
>   (p. 194)

These poems suggest what Rossetti's translations in 1861 and other early works such as "The Blessed Damozel" and "The Burden of Nineveh" confirm: that as early as 1848 Rossetti had formulated at least the outlines of an avant-garde program to achieve success and importance as an artist. And that program was deeply intertextual and dialogic, requiring parodic reworkings of those earlier poets and poetic ethos he reverenced most. This program is visible even in a poem as ostensibly self-referential, ahistorical, and nonideological as "The Portrait."

In this poem Browning's "My Last Duchess" is the pre-text being simultaneously displaced and admired. On a grander scale, however, Rossetti's work sets out obliquely to destabilize and subvert the entire Dantean ethos, especially the orthodox Christian conventions of belief associated with Dante, Petrarch, and their imitators. In form, theme, and characterization, Rossetti's poem presents itself as a sequel to Browning's, which it deliberately echoes from the first stanza. A monologic meditation rather than a dramatic monologue, "The Portrait" presents a speaker whose character is the obverse of the duke of Ferrara's: rather than merely an admirer of art, he is an artist for whom the portrait serves as a potential mode of communion with his dead beloved, not her replacement and a controllable improvement upon the original. Before her death the artist's beloved herself constituted the ideal, while her portrait is "Less than her shadow on the grass / Or than her image in the stream." This speaker is, moreover, a genuine lover rather than one concerned with wives as "objects," symbols of wealth, power, and social station. While Browning's duke is a thoroughgoing materialist, Rossetti's artist-lover is obsessed with the ephemeral and spiritual dimensions of his relationship: having "shrined" his beloved's face "Mid mystic trees," he anticipates the day when his soul shall

> . . . stand rapt and awed,
> When, by the new birth borne abroad
> Throughout the music of the suns,
> It enters in her soul at once
> And knows the silence there for God!
> (p. 132)

Ultimately, Browning's duke is concerned with marriage vows as a means to increased wealth and power, while for Rossetti's painter the twice-spoken words of love—"whose silence wastes and kills"—though "disavowed" by fate, are merely precursors to permanent, visually communicated vows.

In these ways, then, Rossetti's poem responds directly to Browning's presenting the positive amatory *and* aesthetic values absent from "My Last Duchess." Like all true parodies, Rossetti's is thus authorized by and dependent upon its pre-text, but it also supersedes it. At the same time, "The Portrait" appropriates and supersedes the Petrarchan and Dantean conventions of love's spiritualizing influence which inform the value system of the poem and to which it adheres. That is, after unquestionably accepting both the Dantean language and situation that serve to apotheosize a dead beloved as an agent of salvation, Rossetti displaces them from their originary Christian contexts by presenting the moment of the speaker's own apotheosis and reunion with her in a parodic sexual image of penetration. The "knowledge" of God that he hopes to attain in uniting with his beloved's soul is *transcendently* carnal. Yet, such parodic qualities upon which the full "meaning" of Rossetti's poem depends are ambiguously encoded and require decoding by a sophisticated reader. They are embedded in variously vague, abstract, or merely generalized language and metaphors that allow "innocent" readings of the text, thus appearing to elide ideological commitment.

From such a perspective the parodic qualities of Rossetti's early poems, including "The Portrait," "The Blessed Damozel," and "The Burden of Nineveh," seem to be largely self-protective. Through their reliance upon great and familiar literary precursors, his poems accrue authority. Through their self-reflexivity and circularity they preempt any judgment that might easily be passed on matters of ideology. Moreover, through their transvaluation and transcontextualization of the forms, conventions, imagery, and typological structures of originary texts, Rossetti's poems locate their existence at the boundaries of the avant-garde and of ideological commitment. They simultaneously assert and elide values which might, presented differently, be seen to confront and displace the fundamental values embodied in the historically specific texts and traditions Rossetti parodies. Such a visible subversion of the ideological dispositions of his pre-texts, however, would make Rossetti's poem, like those of his precursors, subject to imprisonment by history. To elude such a fate Rossetti employs intertextual strategies to generate poems that present themselves as avant-garde intertexts, whose deep consciousness of historicity itself is deployed to defuse any delimiting ideological or historical critique.

But despite initial appearances, Rossetti's poems do embody a historically specific ideology. As I have suggested, the tentative and oblique repudiation, subversion, and devaluation of conventional ideological statement in Rossetti's work lead to a reconstitution of ideology in exclusively aesthetic terms. Through the processes of allusion, parody, and self-parody by which "new art" is generated, Rossetti's poems individually exalt purely aesthetic valuation above political or social or religious valuation. Art is represented as the unique source of fulfillment, permanence, and transcendence in life. Thus, as a unified body of work, Rossetti's productions do bear a definable "relation to the maintenance and reproduction of social power." They actively participate in the competitive, historically localized phenomenon of poetic supersessions. In doing so they reinforce the aesthetic ideology they inscribe and (revising Shelley and Wordsworth) relocate the structures of immutable worldly and spiritual power in the exclusive habitations of the artist's studio and the poet's study.

Notes

1. Claus Uhlig, "Literature as Textual Palingenesis: On Some Principles of Literary History," *New Literary History* 16 (1985): 503.

2. On this topic see, for instance, the recent work of Jerome J. McGann and Hayden White, as well as that of Marilyn Butler, Terry Eagleton, Frederick Jameson, and Jane Tompkins.

3. Elliot Gilbert, "The Female King: Tennyson's Arthurian Apocalypse," *PMLA* 48 (1983): 866. Also see A. Dwight Culler, *The Victorian Mirror of History* (New Haven: Yale Univ. Press, 1985), and Peter Allen Dale, *The Victorian Critic and the Idea of History: Carlyle, Arnold, Pater* (Cambridge, Mass.: Harvard Univ. Press, 1977).

4. Gilbert, "The Female King," p. 866.

5. See Herbert Sussman, "The Pre-Raphaelite Brotherhood and Their Circle: The Formation of the Victorian Avant-Garde," *The Victorian Newsletter* 57 (1980): 7–9, and, by the same author, *Fact into Figure: Typology in Carlyle, Ruskin, and the Pre-Raphaelite Brotherhood* (Columbus: Ohio State University Press, 1979), pp. 44–45, 55.

6. In *Michael*, for instance, Wordsworth dedicates his work expressly to "youthful Poets, who . . . / Will be my second self when I am gone." *Wordsworth: Poetical Works*, ed. Thomas Hutchinson, rev. Ernest de Selincourt (Oxford: Oxford Univ. Press, 1969), p. 104.

7. Terry Eagleton, *Literary Theory: An Introduction* (Minneapolis: Univ. of Minnesota Press, 1983), p. 15.

8. Dante G. Rossetti, *The Early Italian Poets*, ed. Sally Purcell (Berkeley: Univ. of California Press, 1981), p. 1.

9. David Riede, *Dante Gabriel Rossetti and the Limits of Victorian Vision* (Ithaca, N.Y.: Cornell Univ. Press, 1983), pp. 34–35.

10. *The Complete Poetical Works of Dante Gabriel Rossetti,* ed. William Michael Rossetti (Boston: Roberts Brothers, 1887), pp. 132–33. Hereafter all poems by Rossetti will be cited parenthetically in the text to page numbers from this edition.

11. Jerome J. McGann, "Rossetti's Significant Details," *Victorian Poetry* 7 (1969): 41–54; reprinted in *Pre-Raphaelitism: A Collection of Critical Essays*, ed. David Sambrook (Chicago: Univ. of Chicago Press, 1974).

12. An essay which also concerns itself with matters of fantasy and one which takes a view of "The Blessed Damozel" opposed to my own is D. M. R. Bentley's " 'The Blessed Damozel': A Young Man's Fantasy," *Victorian Poetry* 20 (1982): 31–43.

13. Keats to Benjamin Bailey, Nov. 17, 1817, in *The Letters of John Keats*, ed. Hyder E. Rollins, 2 vols. (Cambridge: Harvard Univ. Press, 1958), 1:185.

14. Linda Hutcheon, *A Theory of Parody* (London: Methuen, 1985).

15. Ibid., p. 54.

16. Ibid., p. 57.

17. Ibid., p. 75.

18. See McGann, "Rossetti's Significant Details."

19. *The Poems of John Keats*, ed. Jack Stillinger (Cambridge: Harvard Univ. Press, 1978), p. 365.

20. See Riede, *Dante Gabriel Rossetti,* p. 273.

Index

◆

Acton, William, 153, 155
Addison, Joseph, 61
Aeschylus, 4
Alighieri, Dante, 4, 6, 17, 31, 36, 45,
50, 59, 61, 68, 69, 72, 73, 74, 77,
99, 115, 173, 180, 187, 192, 193,
197, 203

WORKS
Divine Comedy, The, 37, 72
Vita Nuova, La, 18, 31, 50

Allingham, William, 175
Arnold, Matthew, 1, 22, 24, 67, 73, 74,
188

WORKS
"Harp-Player, The," 22
"Thyrsis," 22

Bakhtin, Mikhail, 196
Barth, John, 194
Barthes, Roland, 157, 196, 197
Baudelaire, Charles, 20, 50, 171–73, 177,
178, 179; *Les Fleurs du Mal*, 178
Baum, Paul Franklin, 8, 69–71, 105, 107
Beaumont, Francis, 36
Beddoes, Thomas, 38
Beethoven, von, Ludwig, 157
Benjamin, Walter, 177, 178
Benson, A. C., 7
Bentley, D.M.R., 152, 153–54
Blake, William, 61, 169, 171, 173, 178,
192

WORKS
"Marriage of Heaven and Hell, The,"
169
Milton, 173

Boas, F. S., 5–6
Borges, Jorge Luis, 194
Bowra, C. M., 9
Boyce, George, 149
Brown, Ford Madox, 94, 162, 174
Brown, Oliver, 94
Browning, Elizabeth Barrett: *Sonnets from
the Portuguese*, 31
Browning, Robert, 1, 4, 5, 8, 19, 22, 23,
24, 31, 33, 37, 67, 73, 178, 179,
193, 202–3

WORKS
Christmas Eve and Easter Day, 19
"Death in the Desert, A," 19
"Epistle of Karshish," 37
"My Last Duchess," 202–3
Ring and the Book, The, 22, 37

Buchanan, Robert, 4–5, 6, 8, 9, 24, 32,
152, 178, 187, 188

WORKS
"Artist and Model," 32
"The Fleshly School: Mr. D. G.
Rossetti," 4–5, *24–39*, 178

Buckley, Jerome Hamilton, 9
Bunyan, John, 46
Burne-Jones, Edward, 1, 128, 174